# INTIMACY
## WITH STRANGERS

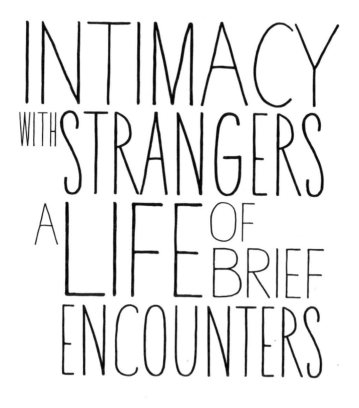

# INTIMACY WITH STRANGERS
## A LIFE OF BRIEF ENCOUNTERS

CIARAN CARTY

THE LILLIPUT PRESS
DUBLIN

Published in 2013 by
THE LILLIPUT PRESS
62–63 Sitric Road, Arbour Hill
Dublin 7, Ireland
www.lilliputpress.ie

Copyright © Ciaran Carty, 2013

ISBN 978 1 84351 275 2

10 9 8 7 6 5 4 3 2 1

A CIP record for this title is available
from The British Library.

Set in 11 pt on 14.8 pt Caslon by Marsha Swan
Printed in Spain by GraphyCems

*For Francis, Estefania, Antonio and Jack, and grand-daughters Ana, Emma and Rachel Cassidy*

# Contents

## SUMMER

## AUTUMN

# Acknowledgments

The interviews that shape the narrative of *Intimacy with Strangers* are based on material originally published in various forms in the *Sunday Independent* and later the *Sunday Tribune*. The quotations haven't changed but the context has in that it brings together in the present tense chance encounters sometimes separated by decades in real time.

I am indebted to all those who gave up their time to talk with me. Sadly some are no longer with us – Antonio Buero Vallejo, Anthony Burgess, Carmen Diez de Rivera, Kieran Hickey, C.R.L. James, Donald Judd, Ellsworth Kelly, Hugh Leonard, John McGahern, Julius Nyerere, Harold Pinter and Natasha Richardson – but they live in their words and in the immediacy of each shared moment.

Many people have helped over the years in arranging introductions and setting up interviews, in particular Christine Aimé, Harry Band, Kate Bowe, Danielle Byrne, Michael Colgan, Geraldine Cooke, Ginger Corbett, Margaret Daly, Gerry Duffy, Gerry Dukes, Louise Fargette, Siobhan Farrell, Mick Hannigan, Fausta Hardy, Maud Haverty, Grainne Humphries, Janice Kearney, Cormac Kinsella, Anna Laverty, Trish Long, Gerry Lundberg, Brendan McCaul, Niamh McCaul, Charles McDonald, Sharon McGarry, Eilish MacPhillips, Joanna Mackle, Caroline Michel, John Miller, Liz Miller, Christine Monk, Barbara Murphy, Patrick Murphy, Rose Parkinson, Garth Pearce, Marie Rooney, Jonathan Rutter, Antonio Sierra, Graham Smith, Manlin Sterner, Lucie Taurines, Debbie Turner and Sarah Wilby.

I am also grateful to photographers Paolo Ardizzoni, Antonio Carty, Charles Collins, Mark Condren, Ann Egan, Francesco Guidicini, Geoff Langan, Trevor McBride, Aengus McMahon, Joanne O'Brien, Guido Ohlenbostel, Dick Scott Steward and Chris Sanders, and to Anna Bogutskaya, Pascal Edelmann, Olivia Guest, Madeleine McGahern, Louise Ryan and Lucki Stipetic for their generosity in providing illustrations.

I have been lucky throughout a career in journalism to work for editors who left me free to interview whoever interested me, wherever and whenever I wanted, and who published whatever I wrote without interference – Vincent Browne, Matt Cooper, Aengus Fanning, Michael Hand, Noirin Hegarty, Hector Legge, Peter Murtagh, Conor O'Brien and Frank Staniforth. Other colleagues who gave invaluable advice and support were Ros Dee, Diarmuid Doyle, Olivia Doyle, Nick Kelly and Brian Trench.

*Intimacy with Strangers* was written on impulse and accepted by the first publisher who read it, a publisher who believes passionately in the importance of each book as an object in its own right. I am grateful to Antony Farrell of The Lilliput Press and his colleagues, Kathy Gilfillan, Sarah Davis-Goff and Djinn von Noorden, and especially my editor Fiona Dunne and designer Marsha Swan, for the enthusiasm and care with which they've guided *Intimacy with Strangers* into print.

Acknowledgments

# Image Credits

Photographs of John McGahern by Madeleine McGahern; Kieran Hickey by Charles Collins; Darren Aronofsky by Ciaran Carty; John Updike by Geoff Langan; Doris Lessing by Chris Saunders; Mia Farrow by Ann Egan; Hugh Leonard by Eamon Gallagher; Julie Christie by Trevor McBride; Liam Neeson by Press Eye Belfast; Pedro Almodovar by Paola Ardizzoni and Emilio Pereda © El Deseo DA SLU; Harold Pinter by Joanne O'Brien; Jonathan Miller by Gerry Sandford/De Facto; Amos Oz by Aengus McMahon; Ken Loach by EFA/Action Press/Guido Ohlenbostel; Wim Wenders and Danny Boyle by EFA/www.jens-braune.de and William Boyd by Dick Scott Stewart.

Images of André Brink, Kieran Hickey, John Updike, Mia Farrow, Julie Christie, Harold Pinter, Jonathan Miller, Amos Oz, William Boyd, Brian Friel, Hugh Leonard, C.R.L. James and William Trevor are courtesy of Independent Newspapers/*The Sunday Tribune*. The photo of Michael Caine in *The Actors*, which was produced by Company of Wolves, is © Bord Scannán na hÉireann/the Irish Film Board.

Drawing of Mickey Rourke by Antonio Carty.

Ciaran Carty and The Lilliput Press express their appreciation to all copyright holders.

# Introduction

While set in 2009, *Intimacy with Strangers* in a sense begins in March 1914 at a kitchen table in a house in Wexford town. My father Francis Carty is editing an issue of *The Examiner*, a journal he brings out at irregular intervals. It is handwritten in a school copybook and provides a commentary on the daily life of his family. He is fourteen, the eldest of five children. His mother, daughter of a sailing-ship captain, is a former teacher – the law required that she give up her job on marriage – and his father has a business on Main Street.

'The railway bridge over the Crescent on Wexford Quay is composed of wooden planks,' he reports in his editorial:

> The storm on Saturday night washed away many of these planks, leaving holes for the unwary to fall into. On Sunday night a commercial traveller was walking over the bridge. He came to one of these holes and trod on the plank that wasn't there. He went under, of course, but was fished out some time afterwards.

A younger brother, James, aged eleven, later to become a historian – his *Class Book of Irish History* was for years a standard text on the Irish school curriculum – reflects on a lecture about earthquakes delivered in the town hall by Father William O'Leary from Mungret Observatory College. 'The science of seismology now only in its infancy is growing and the time is not far distant when not only will it record earthquakes but foretell those that will come,' he predicts.

There is a photograph 'taken by the editor' of his grandparents sitting by the fireplace in the kitchen. He notes that they will be celebrating their golden wedding anniversary on 25 April 1918.

This seems to have been the last issue of *The Examiner*. The Great War broke out later that year. In 1916, Republicans led by Patrick Pearse and James Connolly seized the General Post Office in Dublin, issued a Proclamation of Independence and held out for a week against British forces before surrendering. My father took a train to Dublin hoping to join the revolution, but got off at the wrong station.

His father, a hairdresser who opened a salon in 1896 offering 'the latest London styles', was by then a town alderman. He proposed an amendment to a motion condemning the Easter Rising in which he urged that 'leniency be shown to the rank and file'. It had no effect, of course. The British army rounded up the leaders, summarily executed most of them by firing squad, and deported many others to jails in England.

The amendment was regarded as a stab in the back of John Redmond, the local MP and leader of the Irish Party in Westminster, who had obtained a promise from the British government at the outbreak of the war that if he encouraged large numbers of young Irish men to join up – which they did – Home Rule would be granted when hostilities ceased. Redmond's supporters boycotted the Carty business on Main Street but their custom was soon replaced by supporters of Sinn Féin, the Ourselves Alone party that declared a *de facto* Republic in 1919 following countrywide election successes.

My father as a member of its local publicity committee was appointed registrar of a Republican Arbitration Court, used by the town's mayor, Richard Corish, as a tactic to bypass the British-run local petty sessions court. Law-breakers were arrested by Irish Volunteers and brought to trial, fines were imposed and my father supplied reports to newspapers.

On one occasion the entire court including my father was seized and brought under arrest to the military barracks, but released the following day without charge.

By the summer of 1920 my father had risen to battalion adjutant of the Volunteers in south Wexford, organizing raids on Royal Irish Constabulary barracks, smuggling arms from abroad, raiding the mail trains and blocking roads. He used his home on Main Street as a headquarters. Because he was so openly identified with the civilian side of the campaign for independence, his military activity was not suspected by the Black and Tans, a mercenary force brought in by the British to use terror tactics to subdue the population.

He was an improbable revolutionary, a small quiet man of five-foot-five and not yet twenty-one, an ordinary citizen caught up in a popular resistance movement against occupation forces.

He fictionalized his experiences in a novel, *The Irish Volunteer*, published in 1934 by Dent in London and favourably reviewed by Graham Greene. A second novel, *Legion of the Rearguard*, dealt with the civil war that split the IRA in 1922 when the British, under pressure of international opinion, called a truce and then negotiated a treaty with Michael Collins – bitterly opposed

**Grandfather Francis Carty at the family business of North Main Street, Wexford, 1896.**

by Eamonn de Valera – which established an Irish Free State, but partitioned the country: a familiar imperial strategy of divide and rule.

My father was lucky not to be shot by the Black and Tans or by Free State troops who captured him during the Civil War and imprisoned him in Portlaoise, where he attempted to burn down the gaol. He then took part in a 23-day hunger strike in protest at being forced in punishment to sleep out in the yard in the middle of a winter snowstorm. He survived the ordeal and helped campaign in the election that swept de Valera to power in 1932. Instead of entering politics he became a journalist on *The Irish Press*, a newspaper set up by de Valera because all the existing newspapers opposed him.

After the war my father moved into publishing as manager of The Parkside Press and editor of *The Irish Digest* and *The English Digest*. Going through papers in his study one day I came across a copy of his boyhood magazine, *The Examiner*, and had the idea of resurrecting it as *The Carty Digest*. He allowed me to use the upright Remington typewriter on which he wrote his novels and radio plays. I was fourteen, the same age he had been in 1914.

My young brother Francis Xavier contributed a brief autobiography: 'My life, to the present day, has been a simple one. Part of my school time has been dull, but the rest has been cheerful and happy. I hope my future will be as happy as my past.'

**Alice Carty honeymooning in Belgium, 1934.**

Our mother Alice, a pianist and editor of two English reading books for schools, submitted a short skit about a Fianna Fáil election poster she spotted on the wall of a cemetery urging voters to 'Put Them In'. Her father had worked with Dublin Corporation and was involved in planning Fairview Park in the 1890s. The family sided with Michael Collins in the Civil War – her elder sister married one of his henchmen – and she was an admirer of Dr Noel Browne who, as Minister for Health in the Fine Gael-led coalition government, sought to introduce a 'socialist' Mother and Child scheme against opposition from the

Archbishop of Dublin, John Charles McQuaid. She met my father when she accidentally hit him with her racket at a tennis club. She was obliged to give up her job in the civil service to become his wife: nothing had changed for women in the Free State, they were still not allowed work after marriage.

'The Constitution says a woman's place is in the kitchen,' she told me. 'Get a voice. Speak out against injustice. Don't let that continue.'

· · ·

*Intimacy with Strangers: A Life of Brief Encounters* journeys over time through interviews with writers, actors and artists, living and dead. It maps out the shifting landscape of a world of seemingly unconnected lives and experiences that trigger surprising associations, all against the backdrop of a century of war and violent change.

The cast, playing themselves in this wider narrative of which they are unaware, includes Woody Allen, Kim Basinger, Chuck Berry, Beyoncé, William Boyd, Danny Boyle, Michael Caine, Julie Christie, Leonardo DiCaprio, Brian Friel, Werner Herzog, Angelina Jolie, Hans Küng, Hugh Leonard, Doris Lessing, John McGahern, Liam Neeson, Jack Nicholson, Harold Pinter, Mickey Rourke and John Updike. The book is framed by echoes of past encounters that resurface over the course of a single year in my job as an interviewer, working to newspaper deadlines. The chronology strays beyond the initial journalistic challenge as thoughts and moments from earlier interviews as well as personal memories insist on intruding to form patterns and reflections on the nature of art and time and chance, like a ribbon of dreams, which is how Orson Welles described film. A parallel career as a film critic, it seems, has fed into the experience of interviewing, one conditioning the other.

Four years before his death in 1986, Jorge Luis Borges attended a reception in his honour in Dublin Castle. He sat in a straight-backed chair by the wall, his hand on a polished ebony walking stick, a blind man listening. Although he was fluent in English since childhood, it seemed appropriate to talk to him in Spanish. It was the day Port Stanley was captured in the Falklands/Malvinas war. 'A lost cause,' he said, sadly. The bloodshed appalled him. 'So futile. And the older you get the more futile it seems.'

To know me, all he had to go on was what he heard me say. If it had been an interview all I would have had to go on afterwards would have been what was on the tape. You relive an interview like a blind man, listening without seeing. You are a detective putting together evidence of a life briefly encountered. You bear witness.

All we can ever do, as renowned Australian clinical psychologist Dorothy Rowe argues, is create theories or guesses about what another person is thinking or feeling: 'Our guesses come from our experience and, since no two people ever have exactly the same experience, no two people ever see anything in exactly the same way. Thus we each live in our own individual world of meaning. Empathy is always a leap of the imagination.'

Even those who are closest to us cannot be more than imagined selves. Maybe this is what makes love so compelling, the mystery of longing to know someone intimately but never fully knowing.

When an interview goes well there can be a meeting of minds, an empathy with someone other than our self, which, through the process of writing, communicates some deeper sense of who that other is. But it is ultimately no more than a sketch for a portrait that readers must complete for themselves. There is never a definitive portrait because something of the subject will always remain unknown, an imagined other.

We are our memories and the memories of others. In the beginning was the past and the past is present. Take the experience of Thomas Kinsella when he was putting together *The Oxford Book of Irish Verse*. He unearthed lines of poetry probably written by a monk in the eighth century as he finished his day's more tedious job of transcribing sacred scripts. He was interrupted by a bird singing outside his cell and was moved to jot down some lines in a margin of his manuscript:

> My hand is tired,
> I've had an awful day.
> Isn't that a terrific blackbird.

The freshness of the moment lives on hundreds of years later through the immediacy of a verse. 'You have access to a mind that really is alive and responding to sensual artistic detail in a way you never would from any other source,' says Kinsella.

This was in 1981 at the time of the publication of *An Duanaire*, which he had translated with Seán Ó Tuama, a groundbreaking anthology in Irish and English of 'poems of the dispossessed' from the period between the collapse of the old Gaelic order and the emergence of English as the dominant vernacular.

**Thomas Kinsella, Percy Lane, Dublin, 1981.**

Kinsella is a poet who, like the old Gaelic scribes, had a day job. As private secretary to T.K. Whitaker in the Department of Finance he worked on the Programme for Economic Expansion that brought industrial and social transformation to Ireland in the 1960s. *An Duanaire* is something of a departure from the main body of his poetry, which is written in free form with few concessions to popular appeal. Each of his poems, whether in *Fifteen Dead* or *One and Other Poems*, has a shape of its own, like an uncharted territory without maps to guide the reader.

'You have to make your own maps, especially in these times,' he says. 'You have to find your paper and your pencil and pare it. We're out in the woods as those early scribes were. The whole thing has to be done all over again.'

While he was in the mews of his house in Percy Lane translating the lines about the blackbird, it came back to him how in Philadelphia in the 1960s, when he was translating the Irish prose epic *An Táin*, he had been interrupted by a mockingbird:

There it was, exactly the same. So I jotted down that memory. And then all these years later before I knew what was happening, there was a thrush hopping out and eating an ivy berry off the opposite wall in the garden outside this window. So I had three dimensions of the same thing. The birds are doing what they always did. So are we. To be able to make that sensual contact is a marvellous thing.

• • •

It's early March, ten years later. Paul Auster is sitting on a leather couch beside an open fire in the foyer of the old Shelbourne Hotel in Dublin. Through the glass revolving door people hurry past along windswept St Stephen's Green, huddled under umbrellas. He lights a cigarette, a ritual that will later provide the motif for his film *Smoke*.

He is a tall man with strong sculpted features, vaguely Byronic: long nose, full lips, deep dark eyes and wavy black hair; accidents of birth, no doubt. 'Everything is born out of chance,' he says. 'Just think of the chance that brought your parents or mine together. We are children of chance. Things happen to us at random. So why should fiction not be able to include these kinds of incidents, which seem to me the very stuff of life.'

He recalls being a little boy of four in Newark. 'I had a trick record my mother bought for me. It skipped a groove, and a different story would be told. It was chance whatever story you heard.'

Fiction traditionally imposes order on life, trying to make sense of it. Allowing things to happen out of the blue is frowned on. Plot demands that there should be a reason for everything. By defying this taboo, Auster opened up contemporary fiction to a vast but little-explored area of experience. The more outrageous the coincidence in *New York Trilogy*, *Moon Palace* or *In the Country of Last Things*, the more likely it is to happen. 'You can take any subject or character and start spinning associations,' he says.

In *The Music of Chance* a fireman who has unexpectedly inherited $200,000 from a father he never knew drives aimlessly across America in a red two-door Saab 900, eventually picking up a card shark whom he bankrolls in a bizarre poker game with a couple of elderly eccentrics who won $27 million in the Pennsylvanian State Lottery. 'Never underestimate the flukiness of our existence,' Auster says.

A lot of people don't see coincidences. They walk along a straight path. They have an idea of where they want to be the next day, the next year. But if you're never really going anywhere, which is the feeling I've had all my life, you tend to wander a bit more, you keep more open to the unexpected.

He started wandering as soon as he left high school, heading for Dublin with money he'd saved up.

I stayed in a bed and breakfast in Donnybrook and walked every day, all day, just combing the streets. I was so shy I never spoke to anyone. I didn't dare go into a pub. I didn't do anything. I just walked. And for years afterwards, whenever I closed my eyes and was about to go asleep, I'd be walking through Dublin.

But he did go into a shop to buy a suit. 'And I literally wore it every day for my entire freshman year at Columbia University, until it fell apart.'

It's the coat the eccentric Marco Polo Fogg wears in *Moon Palace* on his search for his lost father, just as Uncle Victor, who goes away leaving him crates of books, is based on one of Auster's uncles:

He was a translator of Dante and went off to Italy for twelve years. My parents had no education. They didn't have any books in the house. So they put his books in the attic. But when I was ten my mother went up and said all the books were going to rot if we kept them in boxes. Let's take them downstairs and put them on shelves. And that's how I started reading. It was completely arbitrary reading, whichever books happened to come out of the boxes.

After graduation, Auster worked as a merchant seaman and lived in France for two years, writing poetry. Samuel Beckett befriended him. 'He was very gracious. But it was terrifying. Tell me about yourself, he said. This was the last thing I wanted to talk about.'

• • •

Now it's autumn, another hotel, same year. Blakes in South Kensington is a haunt for celebrities who don't want to be bothered. The fashionable designer Anouska Hempel combined two Victorian houses into one on a quiet residential street off Brompton Road. The décor has oriental associations.

Robertson Davies is staying here. Tall and imposing in a quaintly old-fashioned three-piece tweed suit with silk handkerchief in top pocket, his bushy white hair and beard give him the aura of a Shavian Methuselah. The youngest of his family, but now seventy-seven, the Canadian novelist and one-time journalist has memories that reach back beyond the last century as if it were yesterday.

As a child he heard talk about how his great-grandmother fled up the Hudson River in a canoe with her family after the defeat of the English in the American War of Independence. 'They had to get out because they were loyal to the crown. They were impoverished and victimized, arriving in Canada with enormous numbers of other refugees. This is what the United States does not like to remember.'

His mother, who gave birth to him when she was forty-four, was born in 1869 and her mother in 1824. 'I remember them both very well, so there is a stretch of memory that goes way back. You get a sense of the absolute reality and actuality of history, hearing it from someone who really has been there or talked to somebody who was.'

Davies injects this sense of a living past into the characters that recur in his novels, like real people accumulating memories. His novels tend to group into trilogies – *The Deptford Trilogy*, *The Saterton Trilogy* and *The Cornish Trilogy* (which includes his 1989 Booker Prize-nominated *What's Bred in the Bone*).

His latest, *Murther and Walking Spirits*, might seem an exception: at his age it would be perhaps presumptuous to contemplate another trilogy. 'It's complete in itself,' he says. But in fact it's really four novels in one. Murdered in the first paragraph, the hero becomes a ghost, time-tripping back and forth through the lives of his various ancestors:

> I wanted to suggest that he might, like any of us, have thought he was alone and self-sufficient, purely an individual. But nobody is that. We are all a combination of what we've been made by people in the past. And we are contributing to what people will be in the future. We're really beads on a string rather than single beautiful gems.

Which gives an ingenious new twist to the autobiographical fiction genre: Davies through his protagonist Gil, a journalist, as he was for much of his life, in effect becomes a witness to his own distant origins. Stories his great-grandparents told their children, who then passed them on to his parents, are woven into the narrative. Chance events and coincidences lead inexorably to his present self through the misadventures of his mother's Loyalist ancestors, driven north to Canada, and through the poverty that forced his Welsh father to emigrate during the great depression of 1894, a printer who used his Celtic feel for words to become publisher of *The Peterborough Examiner*, the paper that Davies himself would edit for nearly twenty years.

Davies was brought up to be curious not only about the past but about everything around him:

We moved a good deal around Canada as my father acquired larger and larger papers. I saw quite a lot of different people and different places when I was very young. I knew all the news that was fit to print and, more interesting still, all the news that was not fit to print. As my mother was not well, my father would entertain her by bringing home the ripest gossip and amusing her with it at meals.

But it was a staunch Presbyterian upbringing, too, inculcating an obligation to make sense of life that has fed into his fiction. He had to learn by heart the shorter Catechism:

Which was not short at all. By the time you've chewed through that, you've got a lot of answers to rather difficult questions. They may not be completely satisfactory, but at least they're something. A lot of people today are religiously illiterate. They think people who have religious beliefs believe stupid and impossible things. They've never looked into it to find out what they really do believe or why. So they're rather bereft. They're lacking any insight into one of the great concerns of mankind.

Going off to become an actor with the Old Vic in the 1930s made Davies something of a renegade. There he became a lifelong friend of Tyrone Guthrie, and was horrified to discover when he visited Annaghmakerrig, an artists' haven in Monaghan bequeathed to the Irish nation, that Guthrie's grave was overgrown with weeds. 'It looked like the neglected grave of a dog.'

He hardly had time to meet and marry Brenda, a stage manager and his wife of fifty years – 'It's been a long conversation' – before the war closed down all the theatres, forcing him to return to journalism in Canada, 'the family trade'. His numerous columns, collected as *The Diary of Samuel Marchbanks*, launched him as a writer:

People say that journalism spoils a writer's style. It's just baloney. I enjoyed the work and meeting people and knowing what was going on. A criticism I would make of some novelists is that they don't seem to know anybody but other literary people. They don't know a shopkeeper or a farmer or children or any ordinary people. It gives them a very squint-eyed view of life.

Davies is living out his last years in the countryside beyond Toronto, 'a very clean and orderly place which Peter Ustinov likened to New York run by the Swiss'. His neighbour, the director Norman Jewison, filming there because it was cheaper than in the US, had garbage dumped in the streets to make them pass for New York. 'When the property people returned from lunch, it had all been cleaned.'

Although he has a swarm of grandchildren, he doesn't get a chance to talk to them the way his grandparents did with him. 'It's very hard to pass anything on to them because I don't see them very often. And when I do they just smile and that's all there is to it.'

He feels compelled to continue writing fiction to keep memories alive for them. 'It's gone if nobody passes it on.'

• • •

Charlton Heston thought nothing of being John the Baptist, Moses, Ben Hur and Michelangelo, or even God. He played all roles with a gravitas that made him a Hollywood icon. But being himself was something else. 'Many actors are in fact shy people,' he says. 'That's one of the reasons why they pretend to be other people.'

We're in a lift in the Shelbourne Hotel on our way up to his room. It's late November 1995, long before Alzheimer's disease would purge all his memories and shut him off from the world.

He takes me to a couch by the window looking out onto St Stephen's Green. Perhaps his shyness has to do with growing up alone in the vast forests of the Michigan peninsula, where his father had a timber company. 'I had no playmates, but that's because there weren't any children nearby. I was happy roaming the woods, hunting and fishing. All kids play pretend games and I did it perhaps more than most, acting out the books I read.'

At ten his life changed drastically and forever. His parents divorced and overnight he was on a Pullman car heading south with his mother, sister and baby brother:

> It was the most traumatic experience of my life. But then again, if my parents had not divorced I'd never have gotten to Northwestern University and studied drama. I'd never have met my wife Lydia, who has made my life, and we wouldn't be talking here with the sun shining in the window.

At school in Wilomette, Ohio, he was a gauche kid from the backwoods, nervous even about crossing a paved street with moving cars. His parents' divorce was 'a dark and terrible secret I told no one'. It was only when he began acting in school plays that he felt at ease. Already by his late teens he had the gangling six-three build that, with his piercing blue eyes from his Scottish ancestry, distinctive broken nose acquired at high-school football and a deep voice, would make him a screen natural.

His later life has been lived with Lydia on a ridge in Beverly Hills surrounded by several hundred acres of Water Department woodland:

> The only thing I leave here for is to act. Actors have a public identity that they have to learn to be. I have been a public man for much of my life. It's the public man that's speaking to you now. I don't mean to imply that I'm a Jekyll and Hyde. But the public man is still a different kind of person, slightly more outgoing, more communicative.
>
> One thinks of actors as outgoing people, loving an audience. That's singers and comedians. They talk directly to the audience. Listen, they will say, looking right at you, and the next song I'm going to sing I heard in a little coffee bar, and I think you'll like it. But an actor on the stage is not relating to the audience. He's doing the play. The audience is watching. He's within the play. And of course in film, the audience is a year down the road.

Paradoxically, being a star is Heston's intuitive way of keeping a distance, as it is for Joan Allen, who is more readily thought of as the characters she plays than as Joan Allen. There is a sense in which she seems to live through who she becomes.

She's more comfortable being a suburban mother escaping conformity in *Pleasantville*, the long-suffering wife of a disgraced president in Oliver Stone's *Nixon*, or the wife in Nicholas Hytner's film version of Arthur Miller's *The Crucible*, who realizes that by lying to protect her adulterous husband during the Salem witch-hunts she has in fact damned him, than she is in being Joan Allen.

'I was raised in a conservative Midwest family,' she says.

> One thing you learn is that you don't talk about religion and you don't talk about politics. It was a kind of rule of thumb in my house. As a child I probably felt not very comfortable in how I was and like some people do, I tried to find a way in which I could express or pretend to be other people or to reveal aspects of myself in the guise of a character. I find a lot of actors are like that. They sometimes are very reserved in themselves.

She went through agony during the run-up to the Oscars in 2001 when Ang Lee invited her to present him with his American Directors Guild nomination for best director for *Crouching Tiger, Hidden Dragon*. Julia Roberts was going to introduce Steven Soderbergh for *Traffic*. Russell Crowe would be there to introduce Ridley Scott for *Gladiator*, so Ang asked me, because we knew each other so well from *The Ice Storm*.' She gives a shiver. 'It came off all right, but to be myself in front of people and make a speech and know that I was saying my own words was an incredible burden for me. I find it most difficult when I have to be myself.'

· · ·

Maybe interviewers are like actors in this respect. I was chronically shy as a child, hiding in daydreams. Books were an escape into other worlds reimagined in minutely detailed, painted comic strips or by modelling characters and land-scapes in Plasticine, turning their stories into plays performed by little cut-out puppets in a handmade cardboard theatre. Lying in bed, that child, who in memory seems like another person, fell in love with the contralto voice of his sister Jane's friend, Bernadette Greevy, as they practised duets downstairs to his mother's piano accompaniment. In the middle of the night he roamed the world, turning the dial on the radio and shifting wavebands, listening to a babble of languages, the lights out and the curtains open to the stars.

He typed out with two fingers on his father's upright typewriter stories with surprise endings, a formula assimilated from the collected stories of O. Henry, Guy de Maupassant and Damon Runyon, and found the courage to submit one to *The Evening Herald*. Seeing it in print and receiving a cheque for £3 – his pocket money at the time was six pence a week – emboldened him to embark on a book about how *homo sapiens* first evolved in Africa in the Olduvai Gorge, disproving the arrogant colonial claim that Africans were not intelligent enough to govern themselves.

Holy Ghost priests who were in Africa as missionaries spoke glowingly in class about their experiences. His father made journeys there accompanied by a publishing colleague from Macmillan in London, with the idea of translating the existing schoolbooks from English into Ibo, Swahili and other indigenous languages. Eager to learn more about this exotic continent that seemed so near, through his father's letters, he tried to make contact with revolutionary nation-alists who were struggling to win independence for their countries.

Months later a letter came back from a former mission school teacher, Julius Nyerere, typed out on five pages of flimsy airmail paper, introducing himself and spelling out his dream for a free Tanganyika. 'I was born thirty-seven years ago in Butiama in the Musoma district of the Lake Province. I am married and have five children. I now live in Dar es Salaam. I have no hobbies.'

Nyerere was leader of the Tanganyika African National Union (TANU), a party claiming to have 700,000 members, which had just won twenty-eight of the thirty seats for the legislative council. 'The elections are artificial because the constitution is an artificial one,' he wrote. 'The voters were required under law to vote for three candidates, one from each racial group. This device of racial representation was invented to emphasize and entrench the racial divisions in this country. We were opposed to it. When we failed to get it abolished we decided to use it to explode the bogey of race.'

He set out how he hoped to unite Tanganyika and persuade the British to leave through debate and reason rather than violence:

> I have a notorious reputation of being a moderate. I can distinguish between the ideal and the possible. I know that we cannot push the British from Tanganyika; but I know that as long as they allow us freedom of organisation they will soon find it impossible to govern us. I give them a maximum of six years. The people of Tanganyika don't want to wait one more minute. The question, therefore, is not whether the people of Tanganyika will wait that long, but whether the British will be stupid enough to wait that long.

This was April 1959. Nyerere was true to his word. Harold Macmillan made his famous 'Wind of Change' speech. Within three years Tanganyika peacefully achieved independence as the new sovereign state of Tanzania, with Nyerere as its first president. Writing this up in an article while still a student, a first attempt at an interview, failed to impress *The Irish Times*: they didn't even bother to send a rejection slip. Nyerere was little known. Africa was not yet on their radar.

Having just graduated in economics from UCD this would-be journalist left home for experience on a weekly paper in Clonmel, Co. Tipperary, then emigrated to England as a subeditor on *The Northern Despatch*. On the strength of the rejected Nyerere piece he was interviewed by Anthony Sampson for *The Drum*, a paper established in South Africa with black journalists to challenge the apartheid regime. UPI at the same time offered a job in their London bureau.

Instead he returned to Dublin to a staff job on the *Sunday Independent*, a rival paper to *The Sunday Press*, which his father edited, having been brought in to run *The Irish Press* in 1957 because de Valera felt its coverage of the IRA had become too sympathetic.

**Julia Alonso Beazcochea boating in the Isle of Skye, 1960.**

The chance to go to Africa was tempting, but a few months earlier he met a dark-eyed, vivacious 22-year-old Spaniard, Julia Alonso Beazcochea, in Darlington, England, to learn English. She was going back to Madrid. He didn't want to lose her. She joined him instead in Dublin and they married that summer.

• • •

Joan Allen says that an attraction to otherness was why she became an actress. Acting took her out of herself to become herself. Writing provides a similar release, allowing a way into other people's worlds, setting up encounters where it is possible to talk freely with a stranger and then make sense of it on the page. It can become, as it has for me, a life of getting personal with people you have never met before and may never meet again.

It's like stopping at a traffic light. You glance at the car beside you and glimpse a face behind the wheel, lost in thought. The lights change. The car pulls away. You wonder who this person is whose life has briefly touched yours but you will never see again. Yet out of billions of lives in the world and over time, each a link in its own chain of intimate but interconnecting memories and longings, the likelihood of meeting at random a person who knows you or someone from your past you didn't know you had in common is much greater than it might seem.

Shaking the hand of Robertson Davies, whose mother was a grand-daughter of a woman who escaped up the Hudson in a canoe in the late eighteenth century, meant that I, too, was touched by that history, reaching back through two centuries as if it were only yesterday. Paul Auster's memories of his childhood and of an uncle who hoarded books are as real to me through talking with him as any memory of my own. The song of a blackbird overheard by a monk in the Middle Ages is my song, also.

Attempts have been made to rationalize this sense of being just a few heartbeats apart from anyone else. The May 1967 issue of *Psychology Today* featured an experiment by the sociologist Stanley Milgram, which purported to show that everyone is connected by an average of six degrees of separation. Although the empirical basis for his conclusion was dubious, the idea caught on. It inspired *Six Degrees of Separation*, a tragicomedy by playwright John Guare in which, as Frank Rich enthused in *The New York Times*, 'broken connections, mistaken identities, and tragic social, familial and cultural schisms … create a hilarious and finally searing panorama of urban America in precisely our time'.

The plot pivots on the readiness of people to accept without question the idea that they might be connected with someone famous. A personable young black man turns up at a Manhattan apartment, distraught and bleeding from a slight stomach wound. He explains to the smart art-dealing couple who live there that somebody mugged him in Central Park. He made for their address, the only one he knew in New York, because he's a Harvard friend of their son and daughter. As he's cultured and articulate – and, he lets slip, the son of film star Sidney Poitier – they eagerly buy into his story, patch him up, and let him stay the night. When he turns out not to be what they imagined they feel betrayed, even defiled. But is he conning them or are they conning themselves?

Guare's play was a success on Broadway and the West End. His subsequent screenplay, directed by Fred Schepisi, didn't so much open out the story as provide the New York detail that was previously left to the audience's imagination. It launched the Hollywood career of Will Smith – then better known as a Grammy-winning rap artist – who was engagingly persuasive as the young man who so smoothly became a catalyst in the couple's safe lives, challenging their assumptions and those of all the 'haves' they represent. It enhanced popular belief in the 'small world' theory that, as Stephen Poole commented in

*The Guardian*, 'everyone is a new door opening into other worlds … Everybody on this planet is separated only by six other people … but you have to find the right six people to make the connection.'

It became a parlour game called *Six Degrees of Kevin Bacon* in which any Hollywood actor can be linked to Kevin Bacon in six steps. 'I thought it would have gone away a long time ago but it seems to have a tremendous amount of hang time,' Bacon said several years later. 'I was bugged by it at first and then I got used to it and came to see it as amusing.'

Amusing it may be, but hardly science. In the March/April 2002 issue of *Psychology Today*, Judith Kleinfeld reappraised Milgram's theory and found that its conclusion had 'scanty evidence' and could be just 'the academic equivalent of an urban myth', although the chances of making a 'six degrees of separation' connection were probably high 'for educated people who travel in similar networks'.

Since then the advent of Internet blogs and Twitter, Facebook and MySpace friendships and myriad other forms of online social intercourse have created a cyber world where anyone can plausibly connect with anyone they choose anywhere in the world. We experience through live satellite television the euphoria of being, say, with Barack Obama's family at the moment of his inauguration, or hearing the dying cough of a young Iranian woman gunned down during street protests in Teheran, or watching helpless as people are swept to their deaths in a tsunami.

Over a lifetime of interviewing it's hard not to feel a sense of being a link that, unknown to the subjects, in some way brings them together in a single consciousness where they play off each other, their experiences and their ideas forming a shared narrative. Their words rerun on a memory tape evoking resonances in unexpected ways, prompted perhaps by a snatch of music on a car radio or a film repeated on television, or a painting in a gallery, or picking up a novel or some poems while browsing in a bookshop.

An interviewer over time becomes like the angel portrayed by Bruno Ganz in Wim Wenders' elegiac *Wings of Desire*, a ghost wandering through the lives of others, listening and observing unseen, in the way a barman is unseen, someone to talk to but not really remember. The format of an interview allows freedom to talk close up with strangers with a freeness you rarely achieve with a good friend or family member.

The concept for *Intimacy with Strangers* emerged early in 2009 while completing *Citizen Artist*, the second volume of a biography of the painter

Robert Ballagh: the first volume, *The Early Years*, was published by Vincent Browne in 1986. Mirroring the way Ballagh bases his paintings on photographs of his subjects, the biography drew on years of interviews recorded with him and others who know him since our first meeting in 1977. It took the form of flashbacks while observing a particular work in progress, his portrait of Professor James Watson, the genetic scientist whose Nobel Prize-winning discovery with Sir Francis Crick of the double helix in 1953 led to the decoding of DNA and the secret of life. The observation of an artist's day-to-day engagement with society becomes a personal chronicle of the times: all art and literature is in one way or another an ongoing dialogue with the world in which it is created.

*Intimacy with Strangers* is an attempt to apply this approach to interviews with writers and artists whose work provides a cultural mirror of the good, the bad and the beautiful of recent decades, an alternative narrative. Its concept owes something to a series of documentary histories written by my uncle James in which he used contemporary reports and testimonies to provide a version of Irish history, in all its contradictions, through the eyes of people who lived it.

The art critic Adrian Searle argues that all photography has an undeniable autobiographical element. 'After all, the photographers had to be there, even if they were on assignment,' he says. Interviewing is subjective in the same way. In talking to others you find you are also talking to yourself. Moving back and forth through time and place in a life of interviews occasions all sorts of associations that mightn't have been apparent at the time but now form inter-weaving chains of unexpected connections, imbuing the past with a sense of the living present, an eclectic parallel history.

**Ciaran Carty on the Croisette during Cannes Film Festival, 2009.**

There is a strange intimacy about an interview that lingers on even if the interviewer and the interviewee never meet again. You can't talk in depth with someone without being changed by it. You imagine yourself into his or her life in a way that makes them characters in the story of your own life: the interviewer becomes, in some oblique way, the interviewed. This book is an attempt to give some shape and make some sense of years of such intimacy with strangers.

# WINTER

# one

Danny Boyle, Kieran Hickey, John McGahern,
Anthony Burgess and Chuck Berry

John McGahern at home in Mohill, Co. Leitrim, 1978.

'That's Bombay, movies and excrement. You smell it when you get there – there's no smell quite like it. But then it's gone and you smell jasmine, and it's like heaven ...'

Danny Boyle is talking on tape about *Slumdog Millionaire*, a rags-to-riches romance about a penniless shanty-town orphan who wins instant fame in India's version of *Who Wants to Be a Millionaire*. Never mind that up to now a foreign film, partly in Hindi with English subtitles and without box-office stars, would be unlikely to get a release in the US, let alone find favour with Hollywood. America, it seems, is losing its Bush-induced xenophobia. There's a growing curiosity about otherness. As 2009 rings in, *Slumdog Millionaire* is already building up Oscar momentum.

'One thing after another, those are the contrasts you get in Bombay, those are the extremes. It's an incredible setting for a thriller with its out-of-control money and corruption and this deity, these gods of Bollywood with all their glamour and wealth ...'

Transcribing a tape is the most tedious part of an interview, earphones plugged in, clicking on and off, winding back and trying to check what's said, reliving the immediacy of each moment. Pauses and unfinished sentences can be more revealing than the actual words. As you listen, ideas form, a narrative begins to take shape. There are times when you hear yourself interrupt a fraction of a second before the person being interviewed begins to say something unexpected, but then holds back to allow you to continue, and you mutter at your taped self, 'Shut up, shut up.' Interviewing is about listening, not unlike a priest in a confessional or an analyst beside a couch.

And always there's the problem of deciphering what you have scribbled down, perhaps in too much of a hurry. You check back with the recording, again and again:

> We think of these slums as being full of abject poverty. But they're not. There's poverty, of course. But what they're full of is business. Everybody is making deals. It feels like life is being lived to the maximum the whole time – they just go for it. There's movement and energy everywhere, and an extraordinary sense of dance and Bollywood dreamland …

Each tape can take two hours or more to transcribe. It's hard to stay focused. Right now in the garden below my window a bird is pecking at a rotting apple left on the grass from autumn. It only takes what it needs and then flies off. It will be back tomorrow for another bite. This is a seasonal ritual, an understanding that has developed. You don't think of birds as individuals but each one has a life of possibly ten or twenty years. They form a relationship with the garden and what they can expect to find there.

I first heard of Danny Boyle from Dublin film-maker Kieran Hickey when he was a drama producer with BBC Northern Ireland over twenty years ago. With virtually no funding for films available in the Republic, Irish filmmakers looked to Channel 4 and the BBC for backing. Hickey's *A Child's Voice*, a psychological thriller with T.P. McKenna as the demented victim of one of his own late-night radio ghost stories, was one of the few significant breakthroughs in Irish cinema in the late 1970s. The BBC screened it three times and it was acclaimed at Chicago and Melbourne film festivals. Yet it wasn't screened in Ireland until five years after its London Film Festival premiere in 1978. 'Nobody would put up any money,' Hickey told me. 'We had to finance it entirely ourselves. Making a film in Ireland is almost an afterthought to the effort of convincing people that you can make it.'

Hickey grew up in a terraced house off the South Circular Road in Dublin. He found James Joyce's *Dubliners* and *A Portrait of the Artist as a Young Man* an escape from the rigid nationalism and religious dogmatism drummed into him at school:

**Kieran Hickey, Dublin, 1987.**

It was immensely reassuring to know a writer who understood what urban life was about. I reached [out] to Joyce because he related to my own experience. What I had in front of me in his work was there in my everyday life. Something as simple as that was in its way more shattering than any other statement he could have made: the realization that there could be art in, as Joyce put it, naming the Wellington Monument, Sydney Parade, the Sandymount tram, Downes' cake shop and Williams' jam.

Hickey was exhilarated by how Joyce deconstructed time and space, using disconnected words to suggest incident and convey a psychological whole: he defied conventional 'clock' chronology, rendering transient impressions and relationships through the literary equivalent of cross-cutting and flashbacks. 'Joyce learned to look at the world in a cinematic way before cinema had really been invented.'

Hickey was reared on Saturday matinées, eventually graduating to the more refined offerings of the British Film Institute in the early 1960s, poring over *Cahiers du Cinéma* with another young film buff, David Thomson, who remained a friend for life and scripted some of his short fictional films. 'He was a terrific, eloquent talker – gruff, tender, lyrical, sarcastic,' writes Thomson in his invaluable *The New Biographical Dictionary of Film*. 'You could feel yourself starting to think better and faster in his company.'

Hickey first attracted critical attention in 1967 with *Faithful Departed*, a brilliant evocation of Joyce's Dublin drawn from a forgotten collection of over 40,000 Lawrence photographs he discovered buried in the National Library. 'They conveyed this frozen sense of time,' he said, describing his thrill on first seeing them. 'They recorded visually the images of Dublin Joyce had taken away in his mind and in his heart and later drawn on in his writing. They give us a glimpse of the Dublin that had become fixed in his memory.'

Although *Faithful Departed* was chosen to represent Ireland at the 1969 Paris Biennale, Hickey was only able to film it with the backing of the BBC. His later films, *Exposure, Criminal Conversation, A Child's Voice* and William Trevor's story, *Attracta*, challenging taboos of sexuality and political hypocrisy, all relied on BBC support, too. Ireland wouldn't have a proper film industry until Michael D. Higgins became Arts Minister in 1993, too late for Hickey. He underwent open-heart surgery that year. The bypass was a success but he died from an embolism soon afterwards.

Danny Boyle grew up in a working-class family outside Manchester, where, ironically, he had a more conventional Irish childhood than Hickey:

> I was brought up a very strict Catholic by my mum, who was from Ballinasloe. The iconography of the saints played a big part in my childhood. I was to be a priest, and went to the Salesian college in Bolton. I was an altar boy for eight years, serving Mass every morning. I remember the parish priest, Father McIvor, always had his slippers on under his vestments because he'd just got out of bed. At fourteen I was supposed to go to a seminary in Wigan. A priest warned me off it. Whether he was saving me from the priesthood or the priesthood from me I can't be sure.
>
> After that I started getting involved with staging plays at school. You'll find a lot of people in films, like Martin Scorsese or John Woo, flirted with the priesthood. There's a lot of theatricality in it, I suppose.

He found his way to the Royal Court Theatre, cutting his teeth as a deputy director on plays by Howard Baker and Edward Bond. He got the job in Belfast because no one would go there: it was the aftermath of the hunger strikes. 'I'd been there loads of times and it wasn't frightening at all,' he says. 'The BBC didn't want to appoint a local for political reasons. It was much easier to bring in an outsider, an Englishman, a Brit.'

Boyle had the idea of commissioning three original screenplays from three leading Irish writers, Frank McGuinness, Anne Devlin and John McGahern, to be screened on BBC 2 in autumn 1987. Since Hickey was already working on a film of McGahern's novel, *The Pornographer*, Boyle saw him as a natural collaborator.

McGahern was wary. Although it would be his first original screenplay, he had previously worked for the BBC on adaptations of his story 'Swallows' and of James Joyce's 'The Sisters'. 'Both were disasters,' he told me. 'The idea this time was to get writers and directors from theatre to create work for TV. All we had in common was that none of us knew anything about television.'

McGahern had always been drawn to films, maybe because they were hard to get to see as a child. 'Our visual senses were very deprived. The nearest cinema was seven miles away. There was a travelling cinema with a tent, but the generator would sometimes break down. I didn't see my first film until my father took me to Dublin for the All-Ireland final in 1947 and we saw Mickey Rooney and Spencer Tracy in *Boy's Town*.'

As a student in UCD he'd queue at the Astor on the rainswept quays to see continental films. He saw Becker's *Casque d'Or* several times. 'You can go back to a movie like to a book or a poem. It would be a brave man who would say that almost any novel was superior to *Monsieur Hulot's Holiday*.'

McGahern's screenplay, *The Rockingham Shoot*, the story of children beaten by a nationalist schoolteacher when they stay away from school to work as helpers on the local lord's estate during a pheasant shoot, comes from childhood memories, as does all his fiction: the mother dying of cancer in *The Barracks*, the small-town claustrophobia of *The Dark*, the bigoted persecution of the teacher in *The Leavetaking*.

Growing up in Cootehill, where his father was the garda sergeant, he remembers the British ambassador, Sir John Massey, arriving with all his bodyguards to take part in the annual shoot and ball in the big house at Rockingham. But unlike the children in the film, McGahern was never allowed to go there to earn the half-crown for beating out the birds. 'The hurt remains. We used to look at the lighted windows from away beyond the main walls.'

*The Rockingham Shoot* began as the draft for a story that didn't work out. 'The image was always in my mind and wouldn't go away. The idea of the ordinary life of a new order beginning outside the walls and, in a way, the old order being carried into the beginning of the new order.'

To this teacher, the survival of any trace of Ascendancy ways and the dependence of the village on the estate seems a betrayal of the ideal of a free Ireland. He only has to look out the window to see the gates of the Big House taunting him. Out of frustration and anger he conducts his class like a political meeting so that even a lesson on Goldsmith's *Deserted Village* is turned into nationalist propaganda.

THREE FILMS FROM
NORTHERN IRELAND

'NEXT'
NETWORK BBC2
8, 9 & 10th SEPTEMBER 1987

BBC
Northern Ireland

**A BBC Northern Ireland flyer for a 1987 series of Irish plays scripted by Frank McGuinness, Anne Devlin and John McGahern and produced by Danny Boyle.**

Hickey situated the action of the story in the early fifties with the teacher as a failed Clann na Poblachta election candidate. There is a sense in which he epitomizes the warped nature of much of Irish education of that period. But McGahern has something less specific in mind. 'The real idea behind it isn't of any period. It's that somebody who embraces an idea too literally or too passionately is always a danger to society peacefully functioning and to the natural order of things and to people's comfort. Lies are the oil of the social machinery.'

The irony is that the teacher is more intelligent than most of the people around him:

> Yet he gets enslaved by the nationalistic notion which he imposes out of some personal frustration on everyone else. Fascism is rooted in the way intelligent people like the teacher can get drawn into inhuman ideas. A narrow single thing – a dogma – can be more attractive, because it is easier to embrace, than actually dealing with the complicated difficult thing that experience is.

The local canon and the sergeant – symbols of Church and state – reject the teacher because they can see the dangers in his fanaticism. 'He never has to test his ideas in the real world. But they have real power and we have to see them as practical things. Even though they may be useful to them they have no illusions about them.'

Intimacy with Strangers: A Life of Brief Encounters

The brilliance of *The Rockingham Shoot* is that out of this familiar Irish situation McGahern and Hickey contrive a truly magical denouement. A troupe of travelling entertainers arrives at the school and puts on a performance of tricks and stories that captivates the children in a way the teacher never could. Music and brightness are brought into their lives for the first time and they respond to it in a way that overturns the narrow world that had been forced on them. Imagination triumphs over lies.

'These itinerant magicians were a permanent feature of the countryside in the forties. They were probably down-and-out actors coming to the schools to earn some drink money. They used to learn a bit of Irish to get by and infuriated the teacher with all their grammatical errors. But to us they were glamorous figures.'

• • •

*The Rockingham Shoot* was filmed in 1987, nearly ten years after my first meeting with McGahern, when he had just moved back to Ireland. He gave me elaborate directions on how to find his home hidden behind a hill down a boreen near Mohill in Leitrim. It was so sunny that hot June day that I drove from Dublin with the windows open, a cumbersome tape recorder on the seat beside me.

Although the magnetic-tape compact cassette had been introduced by Philips in 1964, it wasn't yet in common use. I'd borrowed an early-style tape recorder from an Italian friend, Fausta Hardy, to make up for my lack of shorthand and near-illegible handwriting.

I tried it out first in an interview with Anthony Burgess, without much success. There we were, sipping afternoon tea in the palm court of the Waldorf Hotel near the Aldwych Theatre, while a dapper young man played 1920s tunes on a white piano.

'I didn't know this still went on in London,' Burgess is saying. 'They even have a tea dance on Saturdays.'

He spends as little time as possible in England. He feels he doesn't belong there any more. Perhaps he never did. That's what comes of being a cradle Catholic. 'You're lucky in Ireland,' he says. 'You know where you stand. You don't have this damnable conflict.'

He now lives in an apartment on rue Grimaldi in Monte Carlo with his second wife, an Italian translator. 'I suppose I stay on there because I've too many books ever to be able to move out.' He's been accumulating books since he took up reviewing for *The Yorkshire Post* in 1960 and, at forty-two, became a literary celebrity overnight, writing his first five novels within a year.

'I'd been invalided out of the colonial service in Borneo with an inoperable brain tumour. I was given a year to live. When you have such a short time, you've no choice but to write very rapidly.'

He seems to have a superstition that if he doesn't keep writing the diagnosis might catch up on him. Over fifty books, including novels, verse, criticism, translations and children's stories, have poured from his typewriter since then. In between he's found time for numerous screenplays. He created the futuristic jargon for Stanley Kubrick's adaptation of his novel, *A Clockwork Orange*, and crafted an entire prehistoric language for Jean-Jacques Annaud's *Quest for Fire*. Burt Lancaster enthused about his *Moses* TV series: 'He made God a very tough customer.'

Yet he expresses bewilderment when people say he's prolific. 'I'm a very lazy person. I simply write regularly, one thousand words every day. It's a trade. Poet, learn your trade, Yeats used say. And why not?'

The pianist launches into Ivor Novello's 'Dream of Olwyn', a song my aunt used sing to my mother's accompaniment as I lay in bed upstairs as a small boy. It cues a flashback to Burgess' childhood. He grew up with music like this. 'My father played the piano for silent pictures in Manchester. We were a poor Catholic family. Music was all we had.'

His mother sang in music halls as 'Beautiful Bette Burgess'. Not that he remembers much about her. She died when he was still a baby. 'She gave me my Irish blood. Her mother was a Finnegan from Tipperary. I'm probably more Irish than English. Sometimes I even convince people that I am Irish.'

As he talks my eye is distracted by a glimpse of the tape snarling up. I prise open the cover but it spews out onto the table. I try to stop it but it keeps building up, like a pile of unstitched wool. I switch off the machine and reach for a notebook. Burgess is amused. Hopefully I'll have better luck taping McGahern.

As it happens, I didn't need the recorder. McGahern finds it an inhibiting presence. He'd prefer if I use a notebook or if we just talked. I leave it in the car.

That morning he caught a pike in Lough Rowan, 'a big one, five pounds at least'. It lies in the bath, like on a mortuary slab, its scales scraped off and eyes frozen in a final damp stare. He used to fish for pike as a boy before a scholarship brought him to Dublin to study at teacher-training college and at UCD. His mother had died of cancer: there was nothing to keep him in Leitrim.

He lived in London and Paris, writing *The Barracks* and *The Dark*. He married in a registry office because his wife had been married before, an act that led to his dismissal from St John The Baptist Boys' National School in Clontarf. The Irish National Teachers' Organisation refused to support him 'unless and until he had regularized his position in respect of his marriage'.

*Nightlines* and *The Leavetaking* brought international acclaim and lectureships in the States. But now his exile is over: he lives in a black slate cottage by the lakeside, seventeen miles from where he grew up.

He doesn't think in terms of having come home. He would consider it an insult to be called an Irish writer. 'I know that the colours, the sky, the particular qualities that I inherit are naturally Irish, but I feel that if one doesn't belong to the human kind first, one would be a very poor writer indeed.'

Where anyone lives is a matter of chance. 'If you happen to live on the moon, you'll learn to love it. It's the quality of the love of the place and not the place itself that matters. I'd be against the idea that it is better to live in one place rather than another. I don't think it matters. You don't change your life by changing the externals of it. The world that you write of is inside your head and you can take that anywhere.'

We talk in the small whitewashed room where he does his writing. The only furniture is a divan bed, a table of red Formica with a can of black biros, papers and typescripts, and shelves of books ranging from *One Hundred Years of Solitude* to *Huckleberry Finn*:

> All a writer needs is a cell. You create your own country, your own weather in front of a blank wall and the wall has always been the same, whether in Paris, Spain, London or here. The writer is not like a man selling turnips who has to be where the turnips are and not far from markets. His source of income isn't localized. He can live anywhere he wants.

McGahern has a deceptive manner. He can seem vulnerable in the city, a shy man trembling in a handshake. But here by the lake, the weather in his face, he conveys a sense of calm, undisturbed even by the ordeal of submitting to an interview. 'Get your confession over, and then we can talk,' his wife Madeline teases.

His soft speech has the same spare and considered exactness of his writing. There is a rightness about each word, but feeling, too, and every now and then the laughing lilt that you hear in voices from the area. He has an eye for the detail that illuminates life. He recreates experience with love because to him all that happens has meaning. 'I think either everything is important or nothing is important. A woman drinking a cup of tea is as important as the president of the country making a speech, because both are acts under the sky.' He sees the writer's function as tearing away the pall of the everyday, and simply saying: 'Look, it is exciting.'

We walk down by the lake, a flat mirror of water shimmering in the sun. The beauty of Leitrim is only on the surface. The soil is like Plasticine: it becomes too muddy in the rain, too hard in the sun. He quotes a local saying, 'When the crow comes to Leitrim, it brings its dinner.' It could be a microcosm of Ireland itself, so rich and so poor, rooted in tradition, wary of outside influence, 'that hard wind from Drumshambo'.

This was the primitive force he came up against in Dublin when the *Dark* controversy cost him his job as a teacher:

> I don't want to open old wounds. It's over. I've no bitterness. In some ways it happened to a different person in a different country. It was very unpleasant at the time.
>
> If I'd gone away quietly everyone would have been very pleased. I was glad that I did force them to sack me rather than do the 'decent' thing and go away quietly. All the pressure was to do that, including my own preference for a quiet life.
>
> People have accused me of exploiting the situation. I was approached by the Council of Civil Liberties to see if I'd be willing to take the authorities to the High Court. I refused. I had done all I wanted to do. I had drawn attention to it. People could make up their own minds.

He didn't grow up in a literary ambience:

> To me a person who was an author was like someone from Mars. One didn't think of it as something that would happen to oneself. I had been playing around with words in order to see. The way I can see is through language. I always had a feeling for words, words even beyond their meaning. Each word has a colour and a personality of its own.
>
> Naturally one is a reader before one is a writer. One is excited by other writers. The marvellous thing of my upbringing was that it was unselective. To get any book – like going to any film – was an enjoyable experience. The chance of there being a Protestant library near me led to me reading Scott and Trollope, but also Zane Gray. I didn't think of books as being by particular writers. They were just a way of living in an exciting, wonderful world, like going to the films. Then the thing deepens and it's a different excitement. You could call it the shock of consciousness, when you realize that these things are about your life.

Dinner now: we talk of other things, about Newcastle, where we both lived for a while, that dinosaur of the industrial revolution, a gorge ribbed with terraced houses and spanned by mighty steel bridges, the muddy Tees below. He wrote most of *Getting Through* there as a British Northern Arts Fellow. He finds it easier to write in cities than the country. 'You can disappear there. Here everyone would know where you had gone.'

We talk of films. He goes regularly to Dublin where his friend Kevin Lehane – who writes stories under the name Tom Corkery – manages the Ambassador Cinema. He fears the passivity cinema imposes. 'So much is done for you. In reading, you have to imagine your own screen. The reader's imagination is itself an artist in the way that I do not think the filmgoer's can ever be. The reader takes up where the writer leaves off, creates from the suggestion. A work is dead until it finds its true readers.'

• • •

Joanna Mackle of Faber has set up a photocall and several interviews with Chuck Berry, but he's refusing to go through with them. Even *The Times* has been turned away. But he makes an exception for me. 'Maybe it's your Irish accent,' Joanna says. 'Chuck likes voices that sound different.' So I'm sitting with him in his rooftop suite at the Royal Garden Hotel looking out over a wintry Hyde Park – it's early February in 1988 – and talking about why he dislikes interviews.

The more he reads what he's supposed to have said in interviews the less he feels like giving any. 'Everything keeps getting taken out of context,' he says, fixing me with his unwavering brown eyes, gauging my reaction.

It's as if people are only interested in writing what they expect to hear and if they don't hear it they'll write it anyway, all the juicy stuff about his times in jail and his womanizing, with only passing reference, perhaps, to 'Roll Over Beethoven', 'Johnny B. Goode', 'Sweet Little Sixteen' and the score of tunes that guarantee his place as the father of rock'n'roll. As John Lennon said, 'If you tried to give rock'n'roll another name, you could call it Chuck Berry.'

He's particularly wary of tape recorders, so I offer to put mine away as I did with John McGahern. 'We can talk more extensively without it,' he says. 'I've had bad editing experiences in the past. It's like taking a head from one photo and putting it on a body from another photo. You come out someone else.'

**Chuck Berry playing in Dublin in the last century.**

He's written his autobiography, word by word without the usual showbiz ghostwriters. 'To tell it as it was, without dramatizing, without shading the degradation. The worldly parts may be a contrast to my upbringing, but it's the truth.'

The result is a classy piece of writing, brilliantly catching the rhythms of his speech and thought and ironically perceptive of the often shoddy manipulations of the music business, a book not at all out of place under the imprint of Faber, publishers of Seamus Heaney, T.S. Eliot and other weighty names of literature.

Its publication coincides with the London premiere of *Chuck Berry: Hail! Hail! Rock'n'Roll*, a stylish Taylor Hackford film, which includes performances by Bruce Springsteen, Keith Richards, Eric Clapton, The Everly Brothers and others who owe their inspiration to him. It was shot during a concert to celebrate his sixtieth birthday in the St Louis theatre from which he was barred as a boy because he was black.

The black denim jacket he's wearing makes him look darker than he is: with his mother part Indian he was pale enough to pass for white in early publicity photographs, causing some Deep South promoters mistakenly to book him as a white act. So what happened when they found out he wasn't? 'They'd hire a band to replace me and sing my songs. I'd be paid regardless, so I coined the fortune without the fame.'

Growing up in St Louis at a time when even records were segregated – black singers could only be played on black radio stations – he'd been taught to know his place. 'Never let a white woman catch your eye,' his father cautioned when they'd decorate white homes. 'Black men have often dreamed their last dream where they thought they had a right to be.'

Not that he heeded the advice. Although married thirty-five years to Themetta Suggs, with a family of three children and ten grandchildren, he's never denied his numerous affairs with white women, one of which landed him in jail in 1958 on a racisit-prompted charge under the Mann Act for bringing an allegedly underage girl across the state line.

His mother and father sang in the Antioch Church Choir. 'Even before I learned to walk I was patting my foot to those Baptist beats, rocked by the rhythm of the deacons' feet.' His early vocabulary was picked up from the lyrics of gospel songs his mother sang doing the housework.

His first hit, 'Maybellene', which caught the high-school euphoria of taking girls for rides in his 1934 V8 Ford, was inspired by the country song 'Ida May' he'd heard as a teenager. Although it launched rock'n'roll, propelling Berry at the age of thirty from the local obscurity of the St Louis Cosmo Club to the Paramount Theatre in New York and the Apollo in Harlem, becoming the idol of bobbysoxers everywhere, he only earned a third of the huge royalties brought in by the record. His producer gave joint credits to Russ Frato and disc jockey Alan Freed as part of a payola deal: it took until 1986 to get all the rights back.

Yet the rip-off leaves him less than indignant. 'I signed my name,' he says. 'I was educated enough to know if you sign your name it's a bond. I was too enthused to notice the fine print or to consult anyone. I paid for it with dollars. I don't begrudge someone smarter than me taking advantage of me. I got smarter.'

He's even sanguine about racism he encountered touring Jim Crow states in the 1950s when he played to mixed audiences but had to eat and sleep in segregated premises. 'I can see why they should be biased towards me. You don't have to remain where you don't choose to be. Although I guess if I lived there I'd feel different.'

The irony is that he had the last laugh. By appropriating white hillbilly music and giving it a vibrant black beat, he became a Pied Piper for middle-class white teenagers in rebellion against their parents' conservative values, leading them out of the reactionary Eisenhower 1950s into the anything-goes tolerance of the hippie 1960s.

To him music has always been continuity, rather than the monopoly of any performer:

> From Nat Cole and Frank Sinatra to Muddy Waters and T'Bone Slim is quite a span in the eyes of some people, but in the eyes of music they all use the same notes. It's been said I've been an influence on others. But after I've composed and devised a piece and after it's on the market, I've no jurisdiction of it any more. The thing that motivates it and propagates it is the opinion of it. That's for other people, not for me.

What made him different was that he was in the right place at the right time with the right beat. 'I think I must have been in an opportune era. Because so many things were progressing and changing, and I came with the change of mind. I went along with the band, I guess, the changing bands. Hey …' he suddenly breaks off '… that's a good line. I probably won't remember it when I get in front of a typewriter.'

Although he admits to having read only six hardback books in his entire life, writing his autobiography has given him an enthusiasm for the written word. 'Half my vocabulary has come in the last five years.'

Feelings are what bring alive a word for him. 'You have to live with a word and experience it before it's yours. You can't know what caution is until you've stood on an upright rake.' The challenge in a lyric is to get the whole story in a line rather than a paragraph. 'Music is a short exhilarating way of telling a story. Music without lyrics is a melodic disposition of emotions. Jeez …' he again interrupts himself '… I've gotta get that down.'

He goes over to a bureau for a biro, moving across the soft carpet with a panther-like agility, a reminder that at sixty-one he can still career around the stage with his electrifying duck walk. There's a moment of silence as both of us note down what the other said. He amends 'a melodic disposition of emotions' to 'a melodic exploitation of emotions'.

Then he grins. 'I might improve on that when I get in front of a dictionary.' Does he have any difficulty reading scribbled notes afterwards? 'Only when I use abbreviations. The "exp." I've used for "exploitation" could get mistaken for some other word.'

He began writing his autobiography while he was in Lompoc prison in California doing 120 days for fiddling his tax returns. He'd mail the hand-written pages to his secretary to be typed up and proofread and sent back to him. 'Encourage all straight people to go to jail,' he says. 'It's a great education. I don't know whether I'm fortunate or freaky to have a philosophy that nothing is good or bad. When accidents or mistakes happen it's because of circumstances and conditions. To feel bad about it is not part of the deal. But to analyze it and deal with it is.'

He takes me to the door, putting his hand on my shoulder. 'If there is anything I can ever do for you, or anything troubling you, come to me and tell me,' he insists. Then he stops me for a final thought.

'Lis'en,' he says. 'That's the best thing I ever taught my children. Lis'en. Always lis'en.'

. . .

So I am listening to Danny Boyle, the tape spilling out his fast-spoken words as if infected by the breakneck momentum of *Slumdog Millionaire*. The film's premise is simple enough to have universal appeal. As the Indian teenager Jamal progresses in the quiz show, flashbacks from his life enable him to keep coming up with the right answers. 'It's the kind of idea where you think somebody else must have thought of that, but nobody has,' says Boyle.

As it turns out, the real story is not the quiz show but Jamal's determination to use it to reach the lost love of his life who may be out there somewhere, watching. 'It's not about winning money, it's about getting back his girl.'

Boyle held auditions for the role of Jamal throughout India, without success. Then his daughter Caitlin back in England suggested that he should check out eighteen-year-old Dev Patel, who plays Anwar in the Channel 4 cult series, *Skins*. 'As soon as she said that, I thought, yeah. And it changed the whole age span of the film.'

The flashback structure allows Simon Beaufoy's screenplay to veer intriguingly from neorealist tragedy to street comedy and from thriller to romance with a furious energy that gloriously epitomizes the spirit of Mumbai – or Bombay that was – a city of over 22 million that reinvented itself as the financial hub of India's transformation into a global economic power.

Along the filthy waterfront from this glittering citadel to capitalism, target of a horrendous terrorist attack only last month, is the illegal shanty town of Dharavi, where over a million people are crammed into less than a square mile without electricity, clean water or sewers.

Boyle encapsulates this Fellini-like collision of aspirations in a bravura sequence that brings together the shit and the stars in one startling image. There's a communal crapping area that entails paying a few rupees to walk out on some planks to a rickety makeshift shed perched on stilts over pits.

Cut to a Bollywood megastar making a flying helicopter visit to the town. Everyone rushes to be near him. Jamal – then a little boy – happens to be locked in the shed. The only way out if he wants to get the star's autograph is to jump down into the crap, which he does. He emerges, dripping filth. Everyone pulls back at the stench, enabling him to get to the front of the crowd. 'Please sign this autograph,' he says. And the star obliges.

Characters by chance coming into money that isn't necessarily a blessing are a recurring element in Boyle's films, right from the greedy flatmates in his 1994 debut, *Shallow Grave*. With the Catholic guilt-conditioning of his childhood, his narratives invariably pivot on some moral dilemma. Even *Trainspotting*, while seducing the senses, delivers a kick in the gut to complacency with its surreal plunge into the drug-crazed squalor of squats and bars in a tough Edinburgh suburb:

> The intention was not to make another drugs film, it was to make a truthful film. I think it's more effective than many more straightforward health-department messages. It's telling you that there can be an exciting side to drugs, but there's a really big price to pay as well. We wanted to capture the energy that's partly expressed and partly wasted by these lives on drugs.

His little-seen 2005 film *Millions* could almost be a dry run for *Slumdog Millionaire*. Take a wide-eyed, innocent, eight-year-old boy who believes in saints so intensely that they come to talk to him. 'So what's it like in heaven?' he asks. 'You can do what you like up there,' St Peter assures him, with north-of-England directness.

Having just moved to a new estate with his dad and older brother – they're trying to make a new start after his mum's death – little Damian is lonely and bewildered, hanging out by the railway in a cardboard den he calls a 'hermitage'.

As a train whooshes by, a bag stuffed with banknotes falls down on him, as if from heaven. He takes it as a sign to do good and feed the poor. His more worldly ten-year-old brother, catching him buying pizzas for the homeless

**Danny Boyle at the European Film Awards in Bochum, Germany, in December 2009 after SLUMDOG MILLIONAIRE won the People's Choice Award.**

and trying to stuff money through the letterboxes of the poor, appropriates some of the loot to buy a new Game Boy and a BMX bike, and even attempts to invest in property. The thieves who threw the bag from the train inevitably turn up to collect, just as he is playing Joseph in a school nativity play.

*Millions* might almost be a self-portrait of the Danny Boyle who as a child was caught up in the mythology of saints and saving the world. 'Although not autobiographical, lots of details in it come out of my life. I didn't have to check with anyone how things should be. I could drive them where I wanted to go.' It was originally to be set in the 1960s, 'but that would have been too personal, so we updated it. But it still feeds into my life.'

As does *Slumdog Millionaire*. Boyle lived in Bombay on and off for a year during filming. 'To go there as a film-maker is all you'd ever want. You cannot live there that amount of time and not get caught up in the music of it all. You cannot represent the city without the dance.'

Originally he thought of putting a dance number in the middle of the film. 'Like, arbitrarily and completely unjustified, a dance starts. And then it finishes and nothing is said about it. But we couldn't make it work.' So he came up instead with something even more astonishing, a surprise tour de force sequence rooted in the Indian musical tradition of representing the fruition of a couple, their physical union, through dance.

By a sad irony this sudden transformation into a gloriously apt full-scale Bollywood song-and-dance finale is staged in the Victoria Terminus, the train station that is a pivot of much of the action but was also tragically the scene of the appalling atrocity last month when a gang of suicide gunmen massacred 174 people.

'I was shocked how Western media reported what happened,' says Boyle:

> All the emphasis was on the idea that the terrorists were searching for Americans and British in the hotels, and that they were linked to al-Qaeda, sort of trying to repeat the Twin Towers or the Madrid bombings. But if you open up with AK45 guns in Victoria Terminus, you're not targeting Westerners, because there are none of them there apart from the odd backpacker. You're trying to kill everybody to create some kind of terror across the city. This wasn't a signal to the West. It was terror in Mumbai, and not for the first time.

Boyle still can't believe the euphoria his low-budget $10 million film with a largely underknown Indian cast has triggered. He's off to Los Angeles for the Golden Globes, and will return later for the Academy Awards where *Slumdog Millionaire* will go on to win eight Oscars.

What would matter even more is what he senses is a real swing back towards tolerance and fairness in the US. 'America has changed overnight with the election of Obama,' he says. 'Things are not going to stay the same there, and thankfully so for the world. So it seems right and proper that they should embrace a film that is part of that momentum.'

Boyle's mind is already on the 2012 London Olympics, a spectacular project that will draw on his theatrical skills as much as his filmic imagination. 'It won't be anything like Beijing, because what could be like Beijing? I don't think any nation could try something on that scale. We haven't that kind of money any more.'

So what has he got in mind for the opening ceremony? 'We'll try something intimate and remember its proper function, which is to welcome athletes to their Games. It will be an expression of a people's Britain rather than imperial Britain.'

The new Olympic stadium is nearing completion in a rundown area of east London, near his home, where he shot *28 Days Later*. 'So it's personal,' he smiles.

# two

Mickey Rourke, Ellsworth Kelly,
Donald Judd, Kim Basinger,
Guillermo Arriaga and Darren Aronofsky

Mickey Rourke and his dog Loki in 2005, drawing by Antonio Carty.

**m**ickey Rourke is sitting on a couch in front of a fire in the basement of Blake's Hotel in Knightsbridge, cuddling a gaunt hairless Chihuahua called Loki that accompanies him everywhere. He's savouring unexpected acclaim for Darren Aronovsky's *The Wrestler* in which he delivers a performance of heart-wrenching poignancy and subtlety many people didn't think he had left in him to give.

His portrayal of a has-been prizefighter, 'a piece of meat nobody needs any more', is so close to the bone it hurts to watch. It resonates with a sense of his own dashed hopes as a professional boxer, the Hollywood career he all but threw away, the wives he let down, the wasted talent. It's now won him a 2009 Golden Globe for best actor. Even better, it's won him back the respect of friends who stood by him. 'After all these years, I got a note from Al Pacino,' he says. 'That's enough for me.'

Rourke trained at the Lee Strasberg Actors Studio in New York with Pacino. 'I was just a kid from Miami. I auditioned and to everyone's surprise got in. This is where Monty Clift, James Dean, Marlon Brando and Paul Newman came from. I felt like I was somewhere. Then in Hollywood I realized it's not just about acting, and I wasn't sophisticated enough to understand how to play the game.'

He's wearing trainers and a black woollen cap. He works out every morning in the gym. He did all his own fights in *The Wrestler*:

> I'd seven months of weightlifting to put on thirty pounds of muscle to play this guy Ram, and then four months' wrestling training. When you get a guy twice your size picking you up and throwing you down, something is going to get hurt. If it wasn't my neck it was my arm or my knee. I spent more time limping around than I ever did when I was boxing. I'd no idea these guys took so much hurt.

Darren Aronovsky is making a comeback, too. After his breakthrough at Sundance in 1998 with *Pi* and critical acclaim for *Requiem for a Dream*, he flopped badly with *The Fountain*, a 'psychedelic fairy tale' starring his wife Rachel Weisz. Nobody would finance *The Wrestler* because he insisted on casting Rourke. 'We had $5 million and no distributor,' says Rourke. 'There weren't even chairs on the set for actors to sit down.'

Rourke got his old buddy Bruce Springsteen to write Aronovsky a title song for free ('he knows my trip, that's why if you listen to the song it hits you real hard') and another friend, Axl Rose from Guns'n'Roses, donated another song.

> Then we went to Venice and got an award and everything took off. We went to Toronto and got a distributor.
>
> Darren was relentless in his pursuit of wanting the best out of me. He knew how to push my buttons. He challenged me. He'd say, 'I want you to bring it more.' So I'd do a take again and I'd be thinking that with luck I'll make the bar for the last drink. 'Listen,' Darren says, 'BRING it, just look at me [and Rourke is now looking at me intently, gripping my arm] give it to me NOW.'

Loki noses his hand. 'She's seventeen, which is very old, and I had her mother and father before her,' he says. 'She comes everywhere with me. People make fun of us, Mickey and his geriatric Chihuahua. She's a doll.' I pat Loki's wizened head. 'Hey,' says Rourke. 'Don't I know you from somewhere?' So I remind him of Cannes 2005.

He's sauntering in from the terrace of a penthouse suite in the Hotel Martinez in Cannes. He is naked to the waist, his boxer's arms covered with tattoos, among them a shamrock and a tiger head. He's accompanied by a dark-haired girl young enough to be his daughter. She's wearing a bare-shouldered black dress that billows over her long tanned legs in the draught from the open window. She is carrying a small night case.

He beckons to the bellhop who brought her up. 'Can you translate for me?'

he asks. They exchange a few words and the girl hands the bellhop her case. He takes it into the bedroom and then escorts her out of the suite.

Rourke slips on a brightly coloured shirt and comes over to sit on a long leather couch. So who's the girl? 'I met her last night, I was drinking,' he says, sheepishly. 'During the night she slipped out to fetch some clothes. When she came back and knocked on the door, I was sleeping and didn't hear her. So I woke up this morning and it was like, where's the girl?'

Rourke is supposed to be putting his life and his career back on track. Hot out of Actors Studio in the early 1980s, he thought he had it all. He hit Hollywood as the new James Dean, first catching the eye playing an arsonist who teaches William Hurt to plant a car bomb in *Body Heat* and then as Kim Basinger's abusive lover in the erotic thriller, *9 ½ Weeks*. Then he blew it all in a series of bust-ups that made him unbankable. 'I don't know what went wrong,' he says. 'I wouldn't kick ass. I know I'm a good actor and I was very arrogant about that. I said, "It's the system, it's Hollywood," when it was me. I was the one that had self-destructed. It was just me pissing in the wind.'

Nobody could handle him. He was 'a nightmare to work with', recalled Alan Parker who directed him with Robert De Niro in the sexually charged *Angel Heart*. He just didn't seem to care, and abruptly – when his first marriage to Debra Feuer broke up – decided to quit acting altogether, walking out to fight professionally at thirty-five, an age most boxers hang up their gloves.

Rourke grew up in a dysfunctional family in a tough area of Miami known as Liberty City. 'I learned to fight or run,' he says. 'You have to. If you go too far you end up like my stepbrothers who are in and out of prison for the last twenty years. They have become institutionalized, they are only comfortable in jail. All the men in my family for three generations died in their thirties or forties, thanks to drink. I'm not going to fucking do that.'

He'd been handy with his fists as a teenager, working out his anger in the boxing ring where he scored seventeen knockouts as an amateur. 'I'd a couple of concussions. My mother freaked out. So I said I'd stop.'

But it kept nagging him that he'd quit. He felt he still had something to prove. He left Hollywood to make his professional debut in 1991 in Florida, winning a four-round decision over Steve Powell. 'I just wanted to give it a shot, test myself that way physically while I still had time,' he says. Sparring with world champions James Toney and Carlos Monzon, he scored several knockouts before retiring unbeaten in 1994.

'I was four fights away from a title fight, but they did a neural test and I failed it twice. The doctor said, "Mickey, you cannot get hit in the head any more times. You gotta stop." I was losing short-term memory. I have not known a fighter yet who did not want one more fight. I could not have one.'

He thought he could go back to acting. But it was not that simple. 'They didn't want me. I caused a lot of damage. They were afraid of me. I thought it was over. I did not think I would be invited back to the party.'

He found himself down and out in Beverly Hills:

Because when you fall from grace, you lose the house and the career and the money and the wife and the friends. You are alone. For a decade I had people kissing my ass. I had jobs whenever I wanted. Now I was a has-been. And it stayed that way for thirteen or fourteen years. I was living off selling my motorcycle collection and using up the money I'd made from boxing. And then I was down to nothing. I called a friend for a construction job. He was like, 'Mickey, I don't have time for your shit today,' and he hung up.

Francis Coppola, who cast him as Matt Dillon's wayward brother in *Rumble Fish* when he first broke into acting, helped him get back on track:

Studio guys were telling him to get someone like Mickey Rourke for the character of the bruiser in *The Rainmaker*. Francis said, 'But Mickey Rourke is still out there, still working, why not just get him?' The studio was hesitant, but Francis made it happen. He even ended up adding several scenes for me.

Now it's 2005. He's in Cannes because Robert Rodriguez has given him a juicy role in *Sin City*, a wildly over-the-top adaptation of Frank Miller's graphic novel. He plays Marv, a hulking, down-on-his-luck tough guy who gets lucky one night with a beautiful woman, but at dawn she is dead, leaving Marv determined to find her killer, no matter what the cost. According to Miller, when they met, Rourke lumbered into the room practically taking down the door jamb. 'I wrote down a note: Met Mickey Rourke. He IS Marv.'

Rourke admits he hadn't read any of Miller's graphic novels:

I'd never been in a comic store in my entire life and I certainly wasn't used to reading comic books. But when I read the story of Marv I was excited because here was this far-out looking cat with lots of interesting things to say and do, and I thought, wow, this is going to be really different and fun.

Hollywood seems ready to buy into the new, reformed Mickey Rourke, whose battered face looks as if it still has the prosthetics from playing Marv, but it's not yet clear whether Rourke is ready for Hollywood. 'I'm still working at it,' he says.

I guess right now it's paying off. I have consistency. Consistency was not in my vocabulary. I remember looking in the mirror in my bathroom and telling myself, 'No wonder it has all gone. You're a fucking animal.' I wanted to blow my brains out, but because I'm a Catholic, I didn't.

I have a priest I talk to in New York, being Irish and that. I walked into his church during the darkest hours and he's been there for me ever since. I'm not one too much for going to church on Sundays, but I pray all the time. We go down to his kitchen. He opens a bottle of red wine. We say grace and he hears my confession. He'll call me up. 'Is it going okay?' 'Yeah.'

'Listen, I read that shit they wrote the other day, don't worry about it, it'll blow over in a week.' On Thanksgiving or Christmas, if I haven't made plans, I'll go there and spend it with him. A lovely guy, Pete, you'd love him.

He's been with a psychiatrist for several years:

I used see him three times a week but I'm now down to once a week and a phone call. We don't want to let Marv out again. He wants to come out and play. And he can't. I cannot go through all the rejections, shame and humiliation again. It was like seeing Mike Tyson – whatever he does, there are those ghosts from the past and it is not very pretty. I brought that to the dance.

He's revered as one of the great American screen icons in France. Photographers follow wherever he appears in Cannes. On the red carpet for the premiere of *Sin City* he's greeted by hysterical fans waiting hours to see him. 'All this really started with *Rumble Fish*. It was in black and white, very arty-farty. Universal hated it. Nobody went to see it. It was a big disaster in America. I remember coming over to some premiere here. People were crazy about it.'

The same happened with *9 ½ Weeks*. The title refers to a torrid affair between a Wall Street dealer and a divorced SoHo art-gallery assistant who work their way through a variety of erotic sex acts, clips of which are still eagerly downloaded from the Internet. A particular favourite is a striptease in a rainy alley in which Basinger peels off a tuxedo to Joe Cocker's rendering of Randy Newman's 'You Can Leave Your Hat On'.

The film was savaged by American critics and grossed a mere $7 million. 'It was a huge flop, but over here it was a hit,' says Rourke. 'I've always got along well outside America.'

Thriller writer Michael Connolly makes passing reference to this popularity in his private eye novel *The Brass Track*. An attorney is trying to get some French cops to come to Los Angeles to testify in a trial. 'Fly them first class and tell them we'll put them in the hotel where Mickey Rourke stays,' he says.

'No problem. What hotel is that?'

'I don't know but I hear he's very big over there. They see him as some kind of genius.'

Rourke laughs. 'I must be doing something right. All I'm hoping is to be able to work. I think my best work is still ahead of me. I think all that I've gone through has made me a better actor.'

So what will he do tonight?

'Find the girl,' he says, buttoning up his bright-yellow shirt.

•  •  •

However high the temperature rises in Cannes, there's usually a cool Mediterranean wind to keep it tolerable. Summer in New York is even hotter, but humid too. Going out on the sidewalk is like stepping into a sauna. It's early July 1984 and I've flown in to interview some of the artists selected for Rosc, a major exhibition of international art soon to take place in Dublin.

The painter Ellsworth Kelly has his studio on a twenty-acre estate in the rolling hillsides of upstate New York, not unlike the New Jersey countryside of his childhood.

'I was very shy as a boy,' he remembers. 'I spent a lot of time alone in the woods, birdwatching near the Oradell reservoir. I was very much a loner.' His art teacher, Evelyn Robbins, recognized his talent for making pictures of what he saw and encouraged him to become a painter. 'I guess I wanted to communicate and this was a way I could be appreciated. Very often an artist becomes an artist because he can't communicate in any other way.'

All his life he has remained on the outside. He doesn't see himself as belonging to any ism although many lay claim to him. 'I don't think other art nourished me as much as nature. I'm fascinated by the randomness of shapes and forms in nature.'

He has gone his own way in rediscovering the essentials of abstraction – the actual process of perceiving the inner shape of things and giving it concrete form – almost like a naive artist. Painting for him ceases to be about objects: the painting itself becomes the object. Edge takes the place of line. Shape exists for its own sake. The smooth, flat, monochrome surface denies any suggestion of illusion or personal mark. Yet every image he creates is drawn from something he has actually seen. It is authenticated by what he has experienced. 'I use reality all the time,' he says. 'I see fragments of forms and lines everywhere and make them the subject of my painting. I need that validity.'

A mirror reflection of the arch of a bridge on the Seine is simplified into a geometric composition of two joined semicircles. Bathing costumes in a Rheingold Beer advertisement are reduced to their essential shapes and magnified into fused trapeziums in a free-standing aluminium sculpture. 'I have flashes. Like a glimpse out of the corner of the eye. I want painting to echo this thing. Too often we think what we see rather than see what we see.'

He's not trying to duplicate reality. His subject is the way reality is perceived rather than the reality itself. The shapes he abstracts from daily life are treated simply as shapes. All their function associations are stripped away. 'In my painting it's the structure that matters, not what goes on the surface. I'm not interested in telling a story.'

His low, white living room is furnished by Mies van der Rohe and Le Corbusier, all very austere. You think of Mondrian and the whole De Stijl movement towards the pure harmony of geometric abstraction. But being placed in this tradition makes Kelly uncomfortable. 'I don't consider myself geometric in that sense. I'm not really that interested in geometry, more in enlarged shapes.'

If he admits to any influence it is the Romanesque architecture he discovered as a GI in France. 'I was very much attracted to plain forms, the lack of decoration, the simplicity, the emphasis on structure.' Perhaps this is what brought him back to live in Paris after the war: the urge to reconnect with a tradition in Western art before the easel took over, when painting related to architecture rather than personal preoccupations.

He turned in those early years in Paris to the edge rather than line to define shape – cut-outs inspired by Matisse, reliefs and overlapping shapes. He'd structure a painting as a set of panels so that the wall on which they were placed in effect became part of the space of the painting. 'I wanted the viewer to sense how it works with what is around it rather than have the work self-contained with all the information within the four edges.'

He sees a painting in terms of sculpture as a shape floating in space on the big walls of a modern building. 'I don't make a separation between painting and sculpture. The glass and steel reinforced concrete structures have created a new form and a new space to work upon.'

Last year he visited Donegal (his family originally emigrated from there to West Virginia around 1800) and took a lot of photographs, including some of a stone cottage with a corrugated roof rusted bright orange. He frequently uses the camera to isolate shapes. Perhaps the cottage will eventually be recycled in some pure abstracted form. Nobody but Kelly is likely to make the connection if it is. You get the impression he prefers it that way. 'I'm not interested in personal handwriting,' he says.

That's why he avoids any suggestion of brushwork in his painting. All his sculpture is put together in factories according to precise specifications. His ambition is that his art should look as anonymous as possible, 'as if no one had done it'.

•　•　•

Returning to Manhattan, I surface from the subway at Washington Square. Donald Judd lives in a loft on the corner of Spring and Mercer, right in the heart of SoHo. The place is swarming with workmen hammering planks, welding metal, painting walls. 'This is a closed set, buddy,' I'm told. 'Isn't it Donald Judd's studio?' 'You looking for him?' 'Well, yeah.' The guy mumbles something into a walkie-talkie. Eventually a smartly dressed girl appears.

'I didn't know what I was letting myself in for,' Judd tells me upstairs. He has been talked into allowing *Flashdance* director Adrian Lyne use his studio as a location for some scenes in *9 ½ Weeks*. 'Some guy from Wall Street has an affair with this girl who runs a gallery,' he says. 'To make it look authentic they wanted a real studio.'

Having got a loan of the studio they're now proceeding to rebuild it, much to Judd's apprehension. 'This wasn't part of the deal. I'm afraid they'll wreck the place. They could do all this on a sound stage. They're spending $30,000 to put up a steel split-level floor, which they'll demolish after a couple of days. The whole thing is crazy.'

There is a curious irony in his predicament. Judd has sought to eliminate all elements of illusion from his sculpture. Yet now his studio is being manipulated to generate a make-believe setting in which two young stars, Mickey Rourke and Kim Basinger, can act out a series of sexual fantasies, or what Lyne terms 'an erotic drama'.

It was to get away from artifice that Judd gave up painting in the early 1960s. 'No matter what you put on a flat surface it seemed to me it was imitatory in one way or another,' he says. He felt restricted by the inherent illusionism of painting:

It's basically representational because that's where it comes from. Jasper Johns can do his flags as much as he likes but they're still representational. Someone else may just do brush strokes but they come from a hundred years ago too. Even abstract expressionism is a compromise between representational art and its meanings.

His paintings had related to Barnett Newman and Rothko: undulating lines on broad surfaces. 'The New York type of abstract painting,' he remarks, deprecatingly. 'Painting for me had certain meanings, which I didn't want in my work.'

The three-dimensionality of sculpture offered a way out through 'the specificity and the power of actual materials, actual colours and actual spaces in three dimensions'. Here was a form that corresponded to physical experience. It had the potential to be utterly impersonal, utterly inexpressive. 'Once I went into three dimensions everything seemed to open out.'

With three-dimensional freestanding pieces (rectangular box shapes in painted wood or lacquered metal or coloured plexiglass, aligned on a wall) he found a format that has been basic to his work ever since. To avoid any trace of illusion or expression – the mark of a sensibility so eagerly cultivated in traditional art – he has all his pieces made up in factories from industrial materials, which he regards as real materials as distinct from materials intended for art. 'They're there to be used,' he says.

Judd bought the five-storey Spring Street building in 1968 as a space not just to make his work but to show it in a more permanent manner than was possible in a temporary show. He rented a family house near Mafra in Texas, just over the border with Mexico and south of New Mexico, as an escape from the pressure of New York. The desolate emptiness of the desert offered a wonderful natural setting for his sculpture. Over the years he purchased abandoned military buildings nearby and giant cathedral-like hangars, which allowed his sculpture space to breathe.

He still keeps one of his first boxes in his bedroom at Spring Street, a bedroom big enough to be a gallery. A series of rectangular frames in coloured neon lights by Dan Flavin zigzag its full length. One of John Chamberlain's smashed metal pieces protrudes from a wall. A Claes Oldenburg piece stands by the window. 'They're friends as well as artists I particularly like,' he says. So much so that his eldest son is called Flavin.

We reach the bedroom in an old-style lift with folding grill doors. It's big enough to accommodate a desk: he uses it as his office. Living in this converted warehouse is partly a gesture towards preserving one of the few genuinely old parts of Manhattan. 'The city just wants to tear things down and build things up. It's just real estate.'

Judd comes from Excelsior Springs in Missouri ('rolling hills, rather like Ireland') but grew up in the Midwest. 'Art was pretty scarce there,' he says. He rejects the idea that there's anything intrinsically American about art produced in America:

> Jackson Pollock used to say it's American only because after all he's American, but primarily it's international. It's simply American by default. I wasn't brought up in Europe so obviously my work is not European art. But I don't intend to make American art. I'm against the whole nationalistic idea of art, which has again come back in vogue.

He doesn't like being labelled 'minimalist', either. 'The term is a mere concoction,' he insists. Defining art tends to reduce it to a verbalization. For Judd the object matters as much as the concept. 'I think about what can be done in the reality of the thing itself. I'm not very much interested in things that are just ideas.' He breaks off. A hammering sound is coming from beneath us. 'They're not supposed to do that,' he mutters, nervously. 'They'll set off the sprinkler system.' It seems the *9 ½ Weeks* workmen are trying to install another ceiling. The real studio they've hired isn't real enough for them.

Art for Judd is a fragment of the real within the real. For them it's a figment of the real.

• • •

Kim Basinger appears in a doorway in floppy white woollen socks. She's wearing a white bathrobe half-tied around her waist. Mickey Rourke looks up from a table by the window where he's slicing tomatoes. He comes over and caresses her damp blonde hair with his two hands. 'Close your eyes and just lie down on the floor,' he murmurs. 'Go ahead.'

He eases her down. She looks up at him. 'Close your eyes,' he repeats. He presses a black grape between her lips. Then some jelly. 'Stick out your tongue,' he whispers in her ear. 'Further. Further.' He drops syrup on to her tongue and she licks her lips. It drips down on to her bare legs. He kisses her hungrily.

Click on YouTube and you'll find this scene, which by 2009 has been downloaded by hundreds of thousands of viewers, many of whom probably were not even born when *9 ½ Weeks* first came out in 1986. Several other *9½ Weeks* scenes, showing Rourke pushing Basinger towards emotional breakdown with his sexual games, are equally popular. Although a failure in the US originally, it's a hit in cyberspace.

'More than probably any other actress, definitely not any other actress today, Kim has that old-fashioned glamour,' Curtis Hanson told me after she won a best supporting actress Oscar playing a Veronica Lake lookalike in his 1997 film noir, *L.A. Confidential*. 'Kim is the era of Rita Hayworth and Ava Gardner. She would have been a big star then as well as now.'

Basinger doesn't object to being seen in this way:

> You know … having sexpot attached to your name is a kind of compliment. It's the Europeans who made me realize that. Look at Sophia Loren. She is the world's sex symbol. Yet she's a mother. And she's intelligent. But when you venture back to the States, yes, your looks will open doors there. But the real doors of opportunity as an actress? Slam. Slam. Slam.
>
> I'm taken aback by the readiness of people – especially in America – to equate sex symbol with vapid, dipsy, unintelligent, all those horrible names. After a while you begin to get very self-conscious and very hurt by it.

As a schoolgirl she found looking too sexy could be almost as agonizing as being thought to be ugly or too studious. 'Believe me,' she says, giving a shudder and fixing her blue eyes on me through big, round, gold-rimmed spectacles. With her casual blue jeans, slightly short to reveal her ankles and socks tucked into sneakers, she looks less like a Hollywood icon than a teenage bobbysoxer. 'I was a very tall kid,' she says, 'and I had tremendous lips. And when they'd take the school photographs it was absolute agony for me.'

That was back in Athens, Georgia, where her father was a big-band musician who ran his own investment and finance company. Her mother, Ann, was a model and swimmer who appeared in Esther Williams films. The family is a mixture of German, Swedish and Cherokee Indian genes.

'They'd line you up for the photograph, not spending any time coaxing you or helping you look nice,' she says. 'Next, next, next … And I'd sit there in my little skirt and my white shirt and I'd suck in my mouth' – she demonstrates with an intake of breath – 'because I didn't want to have those lips. The kids in school called me derogatory names all my life because of those lips.'

She'd run home to her dad for reassurance. 'I'd cry and cry and cry and he'd tell me, "Don't you worry, Kim, some day those lips will make you money."' She gives a girlish shriek. 'And they did,' she says, but they lost me money, too. It's so outrageous the way people think about sexuality in America. I've lost jobs because I had this one word attached to me – *glamour*. I was thought to be too sexy. Isn't it crazy? You know, you're born the way you look. You can't help it. It shouldn't be such a big deal.

You feel you want to cuddle and reassure her. But Basinger is not that innocent. Her brother Michael (she's the third of five children) recalled how 'she was just hell-bent on where she was going, and nothing was going to stop her. She's as tough as nails, she really is.'

Basinger herself remembers being in front of the TV while her father was watching all the old 1940s and 1950s films. 'I saw Veronica Lake in *I Married a Witch* many times, and *This Gun for Hire*. I'd boast how I was going to be the biggest movie star in the world.'

Prompted by him she entered the town's Miss Junior Pageant. 'I did it to get out of Athens,' she says. Then she won the state's Miss Breck title, as her mother had before her, which brought her to New York and a modelling career with the Eileen Ford agency. 'It was the perfect time for a blonde blue-eyed girl to arrive. They were just starting the health thing. Every American was into working out. So I made lots of money. I looked up and said, Thank you, God.'

She was soon a regular in *Charlie's Angels*, *The Six Million Dollar Man* and *The Bionic Woman*, before making her screen debut as a would-be air hostess in *Hard Button*. She ended up married for several years to her make-up man, Ron Britton, a father figure nearly twice her age. 'A big mistake, he really was much more ahead of the game than me with everything.'

She breaks off, pursing her bee-stung lips. They're so full and lush-red they're almost a caricature of a pout that today might be mistaken for cosmetic enhancement. 'I think kissing is the most intimate part of sexuality, don't you?' she says. 'Sex is one thing. Sex is all over the place. But really getting intimate with someone, that's what kissing's for.' She giggles. 'And you know, I've had some pretty good kissers in my life, I must say.'

There was Mickey Rourke in *9 ½ Weeks*. She lured Sean Connery back to Bond in *Never Say Never Again*. She's the hooker hired to seduce baseball hero Robert Redford the night before a big game in *The Natural*, and in *Final Analysis* plays a patient pursuing a deadly affair with psychiatrist Richard Gere. Alec Baldwin proved so good a kisser that she married him soon after they co-starred in the goofy Neil Simon comedy, *Too Hot to Handle*. He was a playboy, she was a gangster's moll he keeps marrying again and again.

'I love to kiss Alec,' she says. 'He brings out the woman in me.'

By then forty, she married to have a baby. She even had Baldwin write into a movie contract that he could fly back to be with her at certain times of the month when she was fertile. 'She told me I had to wear boxer shorts and that I couldn't eat lots of stuff because it kills the sperm,' he said at the time. Eventually they had a daughter, Ireland.

Ireland? 'Because that's where we were going to go on our honeymoon, but we never made it.'

When Curtis Hanson sent her the script of *L.A. Confidential* she dropped it in the bin. 'That's all I was doing with scripts. I'd read a few lines and turn back to the baby. But then my agent rang and said, "You better read this one." And I did and I thought, what was I thinking?'

Hanson only knew her from her movies. 'But I thought she would respond to the chance to play the truth behind the Veronica Lake image,' he says. 'I thought she would bring out that image of Lake with the blonde hair over her eye, which is all people mostly remember her for. I thought she might blossom and show us something that we hadn't seen before.'

Basinger put herself completely in Hanson's hands during filming:

I'd just say, 'Did you get what you want?' And he'd say, 'Yes, I got it.' I'd say, 'Did you really get what you want?' He'd say, 'Yes, Kim, I got what I wanted, okay, now get outta here.' Maybe that's my insecurity, but as long as I had him on my side I was fine. I have to feel wanted on the set. I'd hate to be in a situation where a director or the studio or the producer didn't really want me.

Her need for reassurance worried Hanson:

It was actually almost unnerving the amount of trust she placed in me. Most actors who have been around a while kind of have an attitude that they can take care of themselves. And they do. They're used to asserting themselves. Kim didn't do that at all and I think it shows in her performance. There's an absence of any kind of technique. It's just she's there, which is fabulous for the movie because her character is its emotional core. She's the one character who knows the truth about herself and can see the truth in the others.

Basinger wasn't at all what he expected. 'You look at the posters. You see this striking beauty. But she's so different. She's like a tomboy. She'd arrive on the set in this beautiful gown but come clumping in, her arms swinging. She was funny, yet then when you roll the camera, suddenly, boom, she's so sexy.'

. . .

Out in the New Mexico wilderness near the border with Texas, not far from Mafra where Donald Judd's sculptures dominate the desolate plains, a trailer has been set ablaze. The black smoke-filled flames waft high into the empty blue sky.

Guillermo Arriaga is filming a pivotal flashback scene in *The Burning Plain* in which Kim Basinger dies in the arms of her lover. Much of the action of the film, which, like Arriaga's other screenplays, *Babel*, *21 Grams* and *Amores Perros*, cuts back and forward in time and space, seemingly at random, is set years later in Seattle where Basinger's screen daughter, played by Charlize Theron, runs a trendy sea-view restaurant but is haunted by her troubled past. Ten years after *L.A. Confidential*, Basinger is finding a new niche in older-women roles.

The unravelling of the narrative is triggered by a plane crash, just as *Babel* is about the unforeseen human ripple effect of a wayward shooting in Morocco, and the characters in *21 Grams* are brought together, without being aware of it, by a dreadful hit-and-run accident. A car accident links three otherwise unrelated stories in *Amores Perros*. Arriaga keeps employing the same non-linear structure, jumping backward and forward in time, introducing from the start recurring moments that turn out to come from later in the movie. Jean-Luc Godard famously proclaimed that a movie would have a beginning, middle and end, but not necessarily in that order. Latin-American storytelling, however, has always operated this way. The past and the future are present tense. 'We express always in disorder,' says Arriaga. 'We don't tell our stories chronologically.'

Cinema shares this capacity to break up time and space, existing in a parallel reality, the Orson Welles 'ribbon of dreams'. Too often film-makers fail to draw on this existential ambivalence, forcing narrative into a chronological straightjacket that doesn't relate to the random nature of everyday existence. Fragmented time becomes for Arriaga a way of confronting fundamental matters of life and death.

'The power of love and death is not only a redemptive thing, but the power of life,' Arriaga says. 'I'm not a religious person. I'm quite the opposite. I think this is our only life, our only chance. This is the place where we have to do things right. That's why I'm obsessed with decisions and consequences. Because I don't believe there will be a heaven where you can be saved. There's no more.'

He has a beard and, with his dark Mexican skin, could be mistaken for a Muslim: 'So every time after 9/11 I went to the US, they stopped me and took me away to a room for interrogation. All because of Osama bin Laden. Just think of it. Somewhere in the world right now something might suddenly happen that without you knowing it may later change your life.'

• • •

After days of torrential rain and flooding, the clouds have lifted in Marrakech. There's still a cold nip in the air, but an early December sun is casting shadows on the wide tree-lined Parisian-style avenue Mohammed V, where camels mingle with the traffic outside the opera house.

Darren Aronofsky is sipping a local Casablanca beer in magnificent pleasure gardens laid out by a Saadi prince in the eighteenth century but now the grounds of La Mamounia, a hotel evocative of the laid-back charm of the French colonial era. Such is their beauty Winston Churchill felt inspired to take up painting, telling Franklin D. Roosevelt that this was 'the loveliest place in the whole world'. Beyond the exquisitely laid-out orange groves, rose-beds and majestic palm trees loom the massive Atlas mountain snow-peaks, holding back the burning vastness of the Sahara.

Aronofsky is here with fellow directors Jonathan Demme and Matteo Garrone to give master classes at the 2012 Marrakech Film Festival, which, since it was established in 2001 – by mischance just weeks after 9/11 – has developed into a refreshingly open gathering of film-makers from all countries and cultures. This year it is celebrating one hundred years of Bollywood movies, which are almost as popular in the Arab world as in India. Shahrukh Khan and other Hindi superstars were mobbed by thousands of cheering fans, mostly young males, as they arrived for the gala red-carpet opening before being wafted off to a lavish party in the Taj palace, hosted by Morocco's king, who can trace his family back directly to the prophet Mohammed. 'I think it is quite fascinating for this to happen in a Muslim country,' said the festival's French director, Melita Toscan du Plantier.

Since directing Mickey Rourke in *The Wrestler*, Aronofsky has achieved further critical and box-office success with *Black Swan* and is now working on a $130 million biblical epic *Noah*, which has been shooting in Iceland and on location at Oyster Bay, Long Island.

It seemed he mightn't make it here when Hurricane Sandy whammed into the New Jersey coastline with 80mph winds and hurled a thirteen-foot surge of seawater at Manhattan, flooding its tunnels, subway stations and the electric system that powers Wall Street. But astonishingly, despite the *Noah* set being flooded, the film's 450-foot-long and 75-foot-high replica of Noah's Ark somehow escaped significant damage, as did a second ark, used for water sequences, which was moored in Boston.

'Like the original ark, they survived the deluge,' Aronofsky says. 'The whole area got whacked, but we were okay. The beach was thrown three blocks in. Some of the crew lost their homes. Everyone lost their basements. There was no electricity for days. It was a few weeks before we could get back on the set.'

**Darren Aronofsky, director of THE WRESTLER,
at Marrakech International Film Festival, 2012.**

Aronofsky grew up in that same neighbourhood of Brooklyn in the 1970s, the son of school-teacher parents who were conservative Jews. 'I was raised culturally Jewish, but there was very little spiritual attendance in temple,' he says. 'It was a cultural thing, knowing your history, having respect for what your people have been through. If you see my film *Requiem for a Dream*, it's filmed there. The whole area has been an amazing source for my films. So to see it take that kind of damage was really hard.'

He first pitched the idea for *Noah*, which stars Russell Crowe in the title role with Anthony Hopkins as Methuselah, back in 1997 after his precocious debut film *Pi*, which he shot for $60,000 with $100 donations from family and friends, became a surprise critical favourite, grossing $3.2 million at the box office. 'But I was very young then and had no idea what I was getting involved in. It's taken me a long time to get Noah together.'

It's been that way with every film he shoots. 'All my ideas seem to come from before I was making films. I was thinking of *Black Swan* and *The Wrestler* while I was still in college. The problem is that I'm running out of these ideas.'

*Black Swan*, a psychological thriller with Natalie Portman as a ballet dancer on the verge of a breakdown, emulated *The Wrestler* by gaining several Oscar nominations and grossed $330 million, giving him the clout finally to attract sufficient funding for *Noah*.

Maybe this will be his first film with a happy ending.

> Oh I don't know. *The Fountain* has a happy ending, even though he dies, but it's what he wants. And *Black Swan* is kind of happy too, because she gets what she wants, although she too dies. And it's the same in *The Wrestler*. Since I was a kid I always struck out against the kind of Hollywood happy ending. Aesthetically it didn't make sense to me that that was how life was.
>
> It might be the way I grew up. It was always much more complicated than just a happy ending. Some of the guys I knew ended up great and some ended up bad. It was hard to tell who was actually happy and who was unhappy. Film stories are great for making us feel that things will work out, but there's enough of that in the market.

Perhaps there'll be some dark new twist on *Noah*? 'I don't want to talk too much about the film at this early stage. I want to save that until it's ready for release in 2014. We're really shooting two movies. For the next year we'll be doing all the visual effects stuff.'

So let's talk about *The Wrestler* instead. He's amused to hear how Mickey Rourke has been singing his praises. How did he get Mickey to put together such a mesmeric performance? What has Mickey been up to since *The Wrestler*?

Apparently Rourke has recovered enough box-office clout to start making demands again. As the Russian villain in the franchise blockbuster *Iron Man 2* he insisted on not having to play 'a one-dimensional bad guy'. He wanted half his dialogue to be in Russian and decided to sport a pet cockatoo. 'Luckily I got Mickey when he was down and out of luck, at the bottom,' says Aronofsky. 'I didn't have to deal with him when he was coming back up. He's so talented and gifted, it's just getting him to focus that's the problem.'

He breaks off with a laugh.

This is a story I've never shared, but it's fun to humiliate Mickey now. There's this scene we were filming, *verité* style. We have the locker room filled with wrestlers and also the card girls, the pretty girls who hold up the cards with the different rounds.

Mickey is talking to one of these girls and the camera is trying to get in on him, but he keeps moving out of the shot and we keep trying to get around for a better angle.

And then I realize he's kind of deliberately blocking the camera so we can't see that he's asking the girl for her phone number. That's what was going on, right in the scene. That's how he is.

As with the guys Aronofsky grew up with, who's to say how Mickey Rourke will end up.

# three

John Updike in Chelsea, London, 1992.

he publicity director of the New York publishers Arnold Knopf has just issued a short statement nobody wanted to read: 'It is with great sadness that I report that John Updike died this morning at the age of seventy-six, after a battle with lung cancer. He was one of our greatest writers, and he will be sorely missed.'

Like the old Mexican farmer in Robert Redford's *The Milagro Beanfield War* who woke up every morning coughing phlegm before managing to mutter, 'Thank you God for another day,' Updike didn't let the nearness of death stop him writing. He told a *Kansas City Star* reporter shortly before the end that he didn't know what he'd do with his mornings if he didn't write. 'My memory isn't as good, I can't think of words. I might forget what one character's eyes are. Maybe each novel might be the last – but no, I'm not quite ready yet.'

My own father died in 1972 aged seventy-three in a somewhat similar frame of mind, writing doggedly to the end. A copy of Richard Ellmann's *Ulysses on the Liffey* was open on his bedside table in the Mater Hospital with notes for a review he was hoping to finish. Going through his papers I found a typed manuscript of a completed novel, his third. He smoked heavily throughout his life before a doctor friend, Tom O'Reilly, finally persuaded his to stop, at fifty-nine. 'It wasn't worth it,' he whispered to me, just before he died.

Updike died on 26 January 2009 in a hospice near his home in Beverly Farms, Massachusetts, about thirty miles outside Boston, where he lived with his second wife, Martha. Few people other than family and friends knew about his illness: he was never one to seek sympathy. He wrote so well and so prolifically that his brilliance was taken for granted, even underrated because he wrote in so many forms, always with wit and elegance and compassion: short stories, novels, poems and reviews of books, films, plays, art and music. Perhaps because of this he belongs among the really great writers not to win a Nobel Prize for literature.

*The Widows of Eastwick*, the last of his twenty-eight novels, was published by Knopf three months ago. It's a sequel to *The Witches of Eastwick*, which was filmed in 1987 by George Miller, with Susan Sarandon, Michelle Pfeiffer and Cher as a trio of promiscuous witches and Jack Nicholson their devilish seducer.

Updike made a habit of sequels, most notably with the quartet of *Rabbit* novels in which he observed America changing over four decades through the life of a small-town basketball star – the same age as himself – who never made the big time. He also wrote a trilogy of novels about another alter ego, Henry Bech. 'Sequels,' he told *USA Today*, 'can be a way to enrich the fictional reality by extending the time frame to see an entire life. They also save writers the work of imagining new biographies and names for their characters.'

Updike was disappointed by Miller's film of *The Witches of Eastwick* because 'it became Nicholson's film and dissolved into special effects'. The witches in his sequel novel are elderly widows who decide to revisit the scene of their sexual heyday. 'The cells of my body are getting impatient with me,' one complains. 'They're bored with housing my spirit.'

Here's a doomsday scenario that haunted Updike: the possibility of a world without books, a world without readers:

> I get letters from schoolchildren asking what they should do to become writers, what my advice is. I suppose it is to read. I'm thinking at the same time how hard it is for most of them to read. There are so many other more immediately grab-bing entertainments than reading available to them. The whole tenor of the times is rather gregarious, isn't it? It's not enough to want to read, you have to live in an era when reading is a kind of hot activity.

This was particularly brought home to him in December 1992 when he travelled by Tube from Heathrow:

I was struck by how many young people had Walkmans pumping music into their heads. What a different world they're living in than not just the one I grew up in, but the one I am living in now. How much are they *seeing*? How much of their attention is left to give to the actual world they're moving through? It's fairly scary. It puts you in mind of futuristic movies in which people are fully wired to some central command headquarters.

It's the morning after his Underground epiphany. We're in the study of a terraced house in Chelsea, loaned to him by his English publisher, André Deutsch. Although his jacket is off, his shirtsleeves are buttoned and he wears a tie. There is a courteous New England formality about him, a sense of dealing with the work at hand.

'Until around 3000 BC there was very little individual consciousness as we know it, very little sense of oneself as a separate individual with your own agenda and your own little ego talking to you,' he says, warming to the theory:

People were hearing the gods talking in their heads, somehow. The old myths, even Homer and the Bible, make sense if you realize people's hearing was wired differently. There was a kind of tribal unity enforced in this way.

The kind of self you or I grew up with – the little voice saying 'I' and looking for entertainment and reading books and sitting all enriched in the motion picture house – all of that may be just a phase of the human animal and we're moving back into a kind of pooled identity with the headsets.

Rock music in some way seems to melt identities, doesn't it? A sort of Dionysian emerging seems to be happening in a way that was not quite true with Bing Crosby or the Inkspots for us. It makes the whole idea of being a writer and advising younger writers a little gloomy. Because my deeper sense of it seems to me to be that writing, as I've known it and enjoyed it and practised it, is slowly on the way out.

Despite a popular perception of Updike as the epitome of urban sophistication – he made his initial breakthrough as a humorist on *The Harvard Lampoon* and then as a writer on the debonair 'Talk of the Town' column in *The New Yorker* – he has lived in small towns nearly all his life and deprecatingly refers to himself as 'a country boy'.

He relishes the seeming paradox:

In New York or Hollywood, the energy tends to come from outside, from people who have enjoyed the products of the machine and are enraptured by it. So yes, I was a country boy, but I was also one who had been poring over *The New Yorker* for years and who had idolized writers like James Thurber and Robert Benchley.

This raw energy from the outside is more important than sophistication from within. The fact that we have just elected a man from Arkansas (Bill Clinton) as president indicates again the need for bringing the barbarians in. The barbarians really are the ones who have the energy and the convictions. Any city or civilization needs to renew itself from outside the gates.

His mother used to tell a story about how as a five-year-old he would sit on the kerb outside their house in Shillington, Pennsylvania, watching the traffic. When she tried to get him to come in, he'd reply: 'No, I want to be where the people are.'

His fiction is at its heart a celebration of this everyday world that so fascinated him as a child but to which he was afraid to belong:

> Even before I began to write I had the sense that there was something more to be said about ordinary small-town life than American writers like Sinclair Lewis had suggested. I was determined to adopt a non-satirical attitude towards material of my own life.
>
> Of course, others had done this. James Joyce springs to mind as the supreme ennobler of the mundane and the ordinary, seeing the hidden middle-class life as full of heights and abysses, somehow conveying the fact that this is as significant as the deeds of a Greek hero. But a lot of my early energy came from this feeling that the attempt was worth making. There had been enough witnessed pain and excitement that my family and those around had provided that I wouldn't lack for material.

The only child of Wes and Linda Updike, he was born on 18 March 1932 – he smiles when I tell him my second son Antonio shares his birthday – and lived in the same house at 117 Philadelphia Avenue for the first thirteen years of his life:

> What was unusual about my childhood was that it was so stable. Even when we moved, it was only ten miles away to a house my mother had grown up in. It was all within the same county and I stayed in the same school system. When I read the writing of younger people I'm struck by their lack of a sense of place. They haven't lived anywhere long enough to have a feeling of place.

This apparent stability might seem to undermine his conviction that truly creative people tend to be monsters in some way, but he sees it as a confirmation. 'Creative people are deficient in a way that less creative people are not. To be a well-balanced, normal person probably means that you're not going to become an artist. Because you're not compensating, you're not exaggerating. For any artistic effect there has to be some overkill, some excess.'

For Updike, a chronically shy child growing up during the Depression, the monster was all in the mind, in his own worried perception of his inadequacies. It wasn't just that he had a stutter:

> The stammering was never so bad that it really was a handicap. I know several people whose stuttering really does make conversation with them quite painful. But if you only stammer once in your life, the sense of blockage, the sense of the throat not wanting to do what everybody else's throat does, is enough to make you feel you have to develop a special skill, a willingness to undergo some ordeal to make up for this set of lacks that you feel in yourself.

Much worse, he suffered from a skin condition called psoriasis, which, although neither painful nor contagious, caused him to come out in red spots, ripening into silvery scabs. He was so ashamed of his body that he never learned to swim because he was afraid of undressing in front of other people.

He became so worried about the way he looked and sounded, particularly as a teenager when the family moved out of town to the farmhouse where his mother had grown up, that apart from going to movies he'd stay indoors reading and imagining other worlds rather than go out to play in the real world:

> If I had siblings, or even if we'd stayed in the small town where we were living and where I had an inadequacy of playmates, I'm not so sure I'd have become such a reader and so introspective and so able to dwell on solitude. Those years between thirteen and eighteen when we lived in the country habituated me to what was to become the writer's life.
>
> There's a point at which a writer has to retreat from society. You can't really do this stuff with other people. The important part of your day is those hours in which you are alone. A lot of people who otherwise have all the gifts lack that particular ability to be alone for a stretch of time like that. They can't stand it.
>
> In a way it's a waste of a human being, isn't it, to sit in a room, writing. But for me it is a communication. The ideal reader, whoever he or she is, is there with me. It's much like the kind of companionship reading a book gives. You don't feel alone reading a book. To get on the other side of that transaction isn't such a change.

It's a reversal of roles that puts Updike among the handful of indisputable giants of contemporary literature, so respected that another novelist, Nicholson Baker, wrote an entire novel, *U and I*, humorously enumerating ways in which Updike impinged on his life. His four *Rabbit* novels, two of which won Pulitzer Prizes, provide a savagely accurate barometer of the ever-changing American way of life from the 1950s through to the Reagan era, the triumph of a writer, to quote Martin Amis, 'capable of doing just about anything he wants'.

Shillington is on the outskirts of Reading, now better known to readers as Brewer, home town of Harry Angstrom, the garrulous antihero of the *Rabbit* novels. Philadelphia was fifty miles away. 'We rarely went there and were rather afraid of it,' Updike recalls.

His father was the schoolmaster at Shillington High (Updike still savours its motto 'Learn to Live, Live to Learn') and inevitably something of a public figure, an aspect of the job he'd complain about. 'It seemed to me sufficiently painful that I didn't want any part of it. It gave me an aversion to public life,' says Updike. 'But as I have aged, my father in me has become more and more willing to undergo public ordeal. I find that once set up on a stage with a manuscript I tend to rather enjoy the feeling of holding captive a live audience. So the public dimension has claimed me after all.'

Updike, with his shyness and his complex about how he might seem to others, was more like his mother. 'She had failed as a teacher, and retreated from the public sector. She was a kind of recluse.'

For many years she'd wanted to write a book about Ponce de Leon, the discoverer of Florida:

> It was strange the way she fell in love with a sixteenth-century Spaniard, but she did. I remember growing up with this novel of hers. First she would write it in the first person, then the third person, and then she'd go back to the first person, never making a successful book of it, alas. I read it in a number of its versions and became a sort of literary consultant to her from the age of eight or nine. But I didn't especially want to be a writer then. I wanted to be an artist of some kind, a cartoonist like James Thurber.

It was this talent, and the jaundiced humour that went with it, that won Updike acceptance on *The Harvard Lampoon*, launching pad for so many American literary reputations:

> When I went to college I was terribly homesick and frightened. It was really a culture shock in a big way. I felt like an astronaut. I was suddenly away from Pennsylvania and away from my family. The first three months were traumatic, though I survived them. My own children had nothing like that wrenching sense of having left the known for the unknown.

He caught the attention of William Shawn, editor of *The New Yorker*, who promptly gave him the run of the 'Talk of the Town' column:

I was lucky to be looking for work and literary notice in the 1950s, which was a much less crowded era. The generation that came of age in the 1950s had been Depression children, so there weren't many of us. Jobs were easy to get if you were willing to work. Things like your first car and your first house came along naturally.

By twenty-one he was already married to Mary Pennington, with the first of their four children on the way. 'Having once found a comely female who forgave my skin, I dared not risk losing her and trying to find another.' Yet despite these responsibilities he gave up his *New Yorker* job after two years, moving with his young family to Ipswich, Massachussits, to write full-time.

I'd enjoyed the city but I could feel the desolation, the wasteland that lies under a modern city. I was trying to keep my own integrity alive and it was easier to try to do that in a small town. I think it would have gotten to me, the whole thing. I felt I would get to see a realer America outside New York than within. I felt I would draw closer to the secrets of my countrymen when I moved out of New York, where the people are all too canny and tend to be very work-orientated.

He'd published his first book, a collection of poems, *The Carpentered Hen*, and embarked on *Rabbit, Run* hoping to find in the dilemma of the high-school basketball star Harry Angstrom, trapped in a marriage he was too immature to cope with, resonances of the Eisenhower 1950s:

There was much to make me look on writing as not just important but as the only thing I could do. I took it much more seriously than many of my equally or more gifted contemporaries at Harvard in the early 1950s. There were many classmates of mine who seemed brainier and cleverer than I. But I really felt writing was my *only* option. I wanted to be a writer because I wouldn't have to go out and sell myself in the way more professional men and women do.

Now, ironically enough, it turns out that there's quite a lot of selling yourself in the business of being a writer after all. It wasn't quite the hermit's cave that I had pictured. Look at me now. Here I sit, talking away.

Ipswich was soon transformed in his imagination into Tarbox, the play-ground for the trendy wife-swapping suburbanites in *Couples* (1968), the novel that established his reputation as a ruthlessly frank observer of American sexual behaviour. Yet reality for Updike was somewhat different:

Being an only child I was innocent beyond my years. There was a lot about being a human being that I hadn't fully internalized or absorbed. So in my young adult-hood in Ipswich, I was really still growing up. Our set of friends, of other young couples, was very instructive. It was a kind of education that maybe a lot of people have acquired in their teens. I was excited to be in a small New England town, a young father, to be participating in all of the rituals. There was a lot of innocent non-sexual interplay, all of which was somehow very exciting to me, along with watching the children grow and the games adults play.

It was the heyday of the cocktail party. There was no real sense that drinking was bad for you. Sex wasn't bad for you either. It really was another world. It was a world in which women were not ashamed to be housewives. It was quite characteristic of our friends to have four or so children and for women to be unemployed. It was no disgrace. A wife didn't feel by and large she was missing anything by not being employed. It was the era of Julia Childs, French cuisine and learning how to cook, all that was somehow okay. And we were a little too old to get excited about Vietnam.

Updike came to terms with the darker, more violent side of the 1960s in *Rabbit Redux*, plunging his alter ego Harry Angstrom into the social turmoil that he largely avoided in the calm of New England. He angered Norman Mailer and other literary friends by refusing to sign petitions against the Vietnam War, his contrariness not unrelated to a feeling of guilt for being exempt from the service because of his skin condition. But it was rooted too in a small-town belief in American values.

There had been a large flagpole in his backyard in Shillington, where his mother ran up the flag on patriotic occasions:

The fact that our well-meaning and not inconsistent efforts to hold the 'commies' off in Vietnam was being so ungratefully regarded came as a surprise to me. Maybe I have a slightly unreal notion of the American virtues too, since I've seen the sunnier side of American reality. I'm aware of that intellectually, but in my gut I feel it's not so.

As an artist you're pretty much stuck with your instincts. In the end you have to trust your own sense of truth and not what somebody tells you is the correct attitude. There's a great deal of political correctness in the United States right now. If a creative writer took it seriously he would scarcely dare write a word because everything you write is going to be offensive to somebody or to some group. You have to just be a little hard-boiled about it. The fact that you are alone in your room in those hours of seclusion gives you more courage than if you were riding on a platform full of people who were reacting noisily to every sentence you wrote.

When a thing is generally accepted to be the case, my instinct is to doubt that it is the case. I've tended to be wary about the liberal consensus more than the conservative consensus, which by and large I have little personal encounter with. Writers are doubters by nature, and against the grain is where the vitality often lies.

Updike is a walking contradiction of literary stereotypes. Despite the clinical detail with which he has dissected sexual relationships in novels like *Marry Me* and *The Witches of Eastwick*, not to mention the infidelities of Harry Angstrom, who even near his deathbed in *Rabbit at Rest* seduced his daughter-in-law, he has remained all his life a churchgoer and believer in an afterlife:

> I never did put Christianity behind me. And it's healed me in some ways as a writer. It's given me something other than book sales and monetary reward to go by. In a way we all draw on religion whether or not we all subscribe to the somewhat fantastic dogmas that go with it. And it spared me any need to believe in human perfectibility. It freed me to observe human behaviour in all its darkness and futility.

He makes no apologies for the directness with which he has probed the sexual mores of his time. 'I'm a bundle of inconsistencies in my own behaviour. But you have to write about what interests you. And sex is interesting. You have to believe in a God of the living rather than a God of the dead. Since the living are so sexual, I feel no compunction about trying to describe them as that.'

He suspects that he may have lost some of the women readers he once had. 'It's hard to write about sex without being in some way politically offensive. But a fiction writer has to go where he thinks some light needs to be shed.'

Updike's second wife, Martha, is a psychiatric nurse whom he married in 1977 after the breakup of his first marriage. They're comfortable living in Beverly. 'It's a nice mix for me of country illusion with some urban conveniences. I've never lived on the West coast or in the Midwest and in that sense I am only a partial kind of American.'

He writes each day in a room looking out on the Atlantic, setting himself a quota of one thousand words a day, apparently undaunted by the fact that his writings to date run to over ten million words. 'I report for work in the morning like most other working people and do my best work from about nine to two.'

Having finally finished off Harry Angstrom in *Rabbit at Rest*, breathing his last in a Florida heart clinic – the novel was set in Florida in homage to his mother's long-running fascination with the place: she died just after he completed the first draft – Updike has embarked on yet another novel, *Brazil*, which is something of a departure. 'It takes place in a country where I've never really been. It's a bit of a fantasy. But I think basically I'm not really a fantastic writer. Because I miss the little touchstones that reality offers, the memory things. If you can't remember it exactly, it all begins to seem rather vague.'

For relaxation he plays golf or goes walking with Martha. 'But I don't really have much else to occupy me these days. My children are all long flown the nest, and my wife's children are out of the nest too. There's just the two of us leading an all-too orderly and sedentary life.'

What keeps him writing is the hope each time that somehow he'll do it better, much like Harry standing on the first tee feeling 'it is there, it comes back from wherever it lives during the rest of your life, endless possibility, the possibility of a flawless round, a round without a speck of dust in it'. Writing, like golf, is for Updike a sort of 'controlled letting go. When you're doing it at the highest level it feels effortless.'

It is typical of Updike that when he visited Ireland last year it was anonymously, on a golfing week organized by his country club, free of the fanfare that a major literary figure would normally attract. 'My wife thought we'd add on two weeks and we did, hiring a car and driving from Dublin to Cork. But there was still a lot that we didn't see.'

Rural Ireland was a confirmation of why he would never live anywhere but in a small town. 'They know your business to an extent, but they don't mention it to you. There's a kind of tact that obtains, so that you do have quite a lot of privacy. Certainly for a writer it has been nice for me to be left relatively alone.'

•  •  •

When John Updike conjured up a devil for *The Witches of Eastwick* he was perhaps thinking in terms of a man who was everything he wasn't, or to quote Michelle Pfeiffer's character Sukie Ridgemont, 'someone dark and dangerous'. If he wasn't thinking of Jack Nicholson, everyone else was, particularly director George Miller. 'It has to be Jack,' he said.

Such is the power of a Hollywood persona. The pitfall is that it can obliterate literary subtleties. Nicholson is aware of this to a point where he looks for ways to play against type, but no matter what he does or how he looks the camera still seems to love him. Even as Jack, the blocked writer in *The Shining*, hired as caretaker at a remote mountain hotel closed for the winter, going berserk in the eerie solitude and turning on his wife and little boy, a truly murderous scenario, you can't take your eyes off him and even retain a sneaking sympathy for him to the bloody climax.

Nicholson has got where he is by being likeable in unlikeable roles but unlikeable in likeable roles: the contradiction is his appeal, and he plays on it

Intimacy with Strangers: A Life of Brief Encounters

roguishly. Here he is in early February in 1997, about to turn sixty. He sits at a piano in the Dorchester hotel in London improvising the opening chords of 'Always Look on the Bright Side of Life'. Arching his thick eyebrows, he croons the jokey lyric – that's if a thick, tobacco-embellished croak can be called crooning.

The Eric Idle song from the Monty Python film *The Life of Brian* provides an ironic theme track for *As Good as it Gets*, a mischievous politically incorrect comedy romance that reunites Nicholson with writer-director James Brooks fourteen years after their Oscar-winning 1983 collaboration, *Terms of Endearment*. Sticking by friends like Brooks, better known for the innovative TV series, *Taxi, Rhoda, Lou Grant* and *The Simpsons,* than for his film work, might seem foolhardy in Hollywood, but it keeps paying off for Nicholson.

When he accepted a smaller up-front salary plus a percentage for the role of The Joker in *Batman* to help out director Tim Burton – previously untried on a big-budget production – his share of profits on admissions and merchandizing ultimately netted him over $60 million. *Batman* left him never needing to work again. He doesn't have to worry whether his agent will call. He accepts roles only when he feels in the mood.

'What I don't do is repeat something because it's been a success. That's what kills acting.'

*One Flew Over the Cuckoo's Nest*, which won him his first Oscar in 1976, was a one-off. So were Roman Polanski's film noir, *Chinatown*, and *The Shining*, Stanley Kubrick's adaptation of the Stephen King ghost story. 'You can have a lot of success by repeating the same thing, but when you do want to change, if the audience doesn't buy it, you're dead. It's one of the big pitfalls of being an actor: you've got to know about that or you'll get pigeonholed.'

Unlike other stars, Nicholson doesn't mind showing his age. He's put on weight. His face is attractively ravaged. His hair is thinning. He has weathered his notorious heyday of carousing, getting high and competing with Warren Beatty for women. Margaret, wife of former Canadian premier Pierre Trudeau, boasted in her autobiography that he had taught her 'just how much room there is in the back seat of a Daimler'.

'You know,' he shrugs, 'I can't be thirty years old any more. So why try?' He's wearing a gaudy brown suit and yellow shirt with a patterned red tie. 'Where's the ashtray?' he asks, lighting up a cigarette.

Although he loves music and can't be held back if there's a piano around at a party, he rarely gets a chance to show it on screen. So he welcomed *As Good as it Gets*, even if in his role as an oddly likeable manic-obsessive recluse he only gets to play one bar of 'Always Look on the Bright Side'. 'If only I'd been given my head …' he says.

Back in 1970 he sang the theme song in Barbra Streisand's *On a Clear Day You Can See Forever* but it ended up on the cutting floor. He got to play a few bars of Bach on a piano precariously balanced on the back of a van in Bob Rafelson's *Five Easy Pieces*. He'd rather not talk about his singing in Ken Russell's version of the rock opera *Tommy*. 'Just say I was better than Oliver Reed.'

'The thing is,' he says,

> they always make me do it a little worse than I do it. That's the problem. You're always in character. In *As Good as it Gets*, Jim didn't want me to give a clinical portrayal of manic obsession. The way we worked was that I'd just do it my way and if there was something that was too much, he'd say, 'Not too much disease.'

Nicholson prefers it that way, rather than use his clout to build up his role at the expense of the film. 'The moment he begins work, he becomes a servant,' says Milos Forman, who directed him in *One Flew Over the Cuckoo's Nest*. If he ever interferes on set at all, it's to support the director or his co-stars against studio interference.

'He helped me a lot when there was trouble on *Batman* and the studio freaked out,' says Tim Burton. 'He's always helpful. He'll do six takes if you want them and each take tells you something else. You'd almost wish you could play all six takes in the film.'

Recalling the troubled shooting of *The Witches of Eastwick* in 1987, Cher says, 'Jack would listen to us lovingly and then go fight for us.' Cher plays one of the witches, Alexandra Medford, who famously dresses down Nicholson's bed-hopping devil in terms some feminists might apply to him in real life. 'I think … no, I am positive … that you are the most unattractive man I have ever met in my entire life,' she tells him:

> You know, in the short time we've been together, you have demonstrated EVERY loathsome characteristic of the male personality and even discovered a few new ones. You are physically repulsive, intellectually retarded, you're morally reprehensible, vulgar, insensitive, selfish, stupid, you have no taste, a lousy sense of humour and you smell. You're not even interesting enough to make me sick.

Yet Alexandra is only one of a procession of women characters to be repelled by the rakish charm of Nicholson's screen persona only to jump between the sheets with him.

**Martha Stewart Divine denims Ace aphrodisiacs
Singletons rock School of rock Franz Ferdinand EST
Lunch for lovers 7 Day TV and Radio Guide**

**SundayTribune** 08.02.04

# Here's funny
Why Jack's back playing the joker

Jack Nicholson on the cover of the SUNDAY TRIBUNE magazine, 2004.

The joke in *As Good as it Gets* is that when Helen Hunt – the single mother with an asthmatic child he's been courting in his eccentrically gruff way – finally wants him to dance with her, he can't bring himself to say yes.

He's so busy hurting everyone in sight with gratuitously offensive remarks that no one realizes he's hiding his own hurt. Overhearing a gay artist played by Greg Kinnear tell Hunt about his abused childhood, he rolls his eyes and says, 'You think that's bad ...' but they just ignore him.

As with most of his roles, Nicholson is drawing on his own life. 'There's a deep hurt inside, and there's no way of resolving it, ever,' says his *Easy Rider* collaborator, Peter Fonda.

Nicholson never knew his father, although for much of his life he thought he did. It wasn't until the death of his sister when he was thirty-eight that he discovered she was in fact his mother. The alcoholic sign-writer in New Jersey he believed to be his father was his grandfather, which explains why he 'became conscious of very early emotions about not being wanted – a feeling that I was a drag to my family as an infant'.

Perhaps some of his sexual charm comes from growing up surrounded by admiring women. His mother, who turned out to be his grandmother, ran a beauty salon in New Jersey with his sisters, June – in fact his mother – and Lorraine. He learned the truth (and that his mother June had been abandoned by his real father when she was seventeen) during a TV interview: he's avoided TV interviews ever since.

This shock revelation was eerily anticipated in the climactic scene in *Chinatown*, where a traumatized Faye Dunaway, sexually abused as a teenager by her father, played by John Huston, reveals the truth to Nicholson – in his role of a disillusioned private eye – about the daughter she subsequently gave birth to, saying, 'She's my sister ... she's my daughter ... she's my sister and my daughter.' To add to the real-life parallels, during the filming Nicholson started an affair with Huston's daughter, Angelica, which gave an added edge to Huston's line, 'Are you sleeping with my daughter?'

Real life and make-believe keep overlapping in Nicholson's roles. 'Part of what's attractive about the job is you get to vent a lot of things inside an acting situation,' he says.

> Everything I do in movies is autobiographical. You can't really take the present time out of a film. There are always elements of your life at the time you are making a film that have attracted you to it and are somehow congruent to the piece and work their way in there. But I try not to let the characterization become

what the film is about. I want the film to be about the story. I concentrate on the storytelling elements of performance.

As the alcoholic dropout lawyer who befriends bikers Dennis Hopper and Peter Fonda in *Easy Rider* – the film that established Nicolson as an icon of his generation – he wore the same plain round glasses worn by his own father (or rather grandfather).

His character as the son who tries in *Five Easy Pieces* to reconnect with his father only when it is too late (the man is paralyzed by a stroke) was written from his own experience.

A key scene in *The Shining*, in which he sits at a typewriter manically repeating the same words, echoes his own frustrations as a young struggling would-be Hollywood writer, constantly being interrupted by his then-wife, Sandra Knight. They divorced after five years, but their daughter Jennifer has a small role opposite him in Sean Penn's *The Crossing Guard*, which also co-stars Angelica Huston, whom he hasn't spoken to since their break-up in 1990: he subsequently had two children with Rebecca Broussard, a waitress the same age as Jennifer.

Nicholson is wary about looking for patterns in his roles. 'I really think that every character I've ever done is separate,' he says. 'But I suppose there's a certain way that the text sounds the same way when it comes from the same person.'

When his sister June – his mother – moved to California, he went out to visit her, landed a job as an office boy in the cartoon department of MGM and got involved with a small acting group that also included Martin Landau. He became a regular in Roger Corman horror quickies, becoming friends with maverick film-makers Monte Hellman, Richard Rush and Bob Rafelson, who would be collaborators as his career took off.

Although many of his Corman films still have a cult following, he prefers not to look back:

Those I never watch and I recommend no one else does. When I worked with Roger – and I thank him because no one else would hire me – maybe that's how I got trapped in these devilish parts. But then I think about some of the straight parts I've played, like Eugene O'Neill in *Reds* or the teamster leader in *Hoffa*, and after all they're a bit devilish too. So maybe I'm just attracted to devilish parts.

He seems never to have doubted his acting ability:

I always felt good at it, I guess long before anybody else did. I felt like I couldn't do anything wrong, I was so hot in my own mind.

Polanski's *Chinatown* in 1974 was a kind of turning point, not just for me but for movies. The thrust of movies was away from narrative. I'd written a number of these non-linear movies. I started thinking it was too easy. You could write anything that way. *Chinatown* was really our move back to a more conventional narrative, a crime story with character values, one of the oldest forms but with a modern feel.

*       *       *

John Updike predicted a loss of individuality when he observed young people going around with earphones, listening to Walkmans. Now, not just TV adaptations of his work but his actual novels can be found on Google Books or as ebooks. Maybe it's not the same as having an actual book to be thumbed through at will, but it does mean Updike has become more readily accessible to millions of potential readers who might never have discovered him.

Marshall McLuhan talked of the world as a global village before it really was. The Internet finally made it so in the 1990s. In the next decade everyone from boatmen along the Nile to Inuits above the Arctic Circle logged on, acquired iPods and started to network and tweet.

Sitting at my computer I click on an item on the *Variety* website about a new ABC drama series, *The Witches of Eastwick*, based on George Miller's 1986 version of Updike's novel, which has just premiered nationwide in the US. No need to wait several months until some television programmer in UK or Ireland picks it up. Just check it out on your computer.

Updike believed every story had a natural form, whether as a novel, a play or a film. He was wary of adaptations, and was disappointed by the filmed *The Witches of Eastwick*. Watching this new TV version, it's as if he's at my shoulder and I'm judging it through his eyes as the characters he created, which I, and all his readers, imagined in their different ways, take on another life.

He has released a devilish genie that refuses to be controlled. So here's Darryl Van Horne, re-embodied by Canadian actor Paul Gross, arriving at the seaside town of Eastwick in a dark-windowed black stretch limo, a 'demon between the sheets' set on causing women's hearts flutter to his own malign purposes. 'Find your power,' he urges them. 'Use it.' And they do, making their innermost sexual fantasies come true.

'Of course, nowadays we know better than to believe in witchcraft,' confides a coy narrator. 'We call it silly superstition. But just for a moment, what if …?'

ABC's *The Witches of Eastwick* is a sophisticated entertainment in the fashionable manner of *Desperate Housewives* crossed with *Sex and the City*, easy on the eye, an adult giggle. Updike worried that Jack Nicholson's eye-grabbing charisma unbalanced the dynamics between the characters. Series creator Maggie Friedman gives the allegory a polished update, but it plays like a soap, the nuances lost in the rinse, the magnetism missing.

Ratings for the pilot and the early episodes were impressive, but ABC declined to order any additional episodes. Maybe Lifetime will pick up the show for a second season. Me, I'll stick with Updike.

. . .

Being a celebrity seldom bothers Jack Nicholson because he doesn't act the celebrity. 'It's just a part of life. I'm really good at sneaking around. If someone doesn't know me at a hotel, it suits me fine. And you can't get me when I'm at home.'

The trick is somewhat similar for an interviewer. You learn not to think of anyone as a celebrity. My luck was to discover this out of shyness. It was at the Cork Film Festival in 1965. The French director, Jean-Paul Rappaneau, was screening his first film, *La Vie de Château*. 'If you like it so much why not interview him about it?' Julia urged.

So it was set up. I walked around the hotel three times before having the nerve to go in, much as I'd done three years earlier at West Jewellers on Grafton Street before finding the courage to approach the counter and choose an engagement ring. But here's the strange thing. Once I was actually with Rappeneau and we were talking, it seemed completely natural. All the tension was gone. We were just two people in a room having a conversation. And it's been that way ever since.

It's like a golfer getting hung up about his putting to a point where it affects his whole game. The cure is to go unconscious and not think about technique. Just look where you want the ball to go and hit it, as a child might do. Picasso once said that he kept trying to paint with the unthinking innocence of a seven-year-old.

Jack Nicholson is happiest out of the limelight at a basketball game – at school he was known as 'that fat Irish kid who wasn't good enough to play so he managed the team' – or sipping margaritas in El Cholo's with friends, holding forth on work, life and politics.

Yet he was drawn to Hollywood in the first place because he was starstruck, like anyone else. 'Sure, I was starstruck then, I'm starstruck now. That would be a fair thing to say.' It's what keeps bringing him to the Oscars, whether or not he's been nominated. 'I love the glamour. My idea of a great evening is to be nominated for an Academy Award and know you're not going to win. It's happened to me often enough, and I love it. You can then party through the night.'

In the years after *As Good as it Gets*, which won him another Oscar in 1997, Nicholson reinvented himself with a string of grumpy-old-man roles in *The Pledge*, *About Schmidt* and *Something's Gotta Give*, where he dumps an adorable Amanda Peat for her fifty-something mother, Diane Keaton.

His role as a philandering bachelor who only dates women under the age of thirty – and ends up dandling a baby in his arms – was written for him by Nancy Myers. 'We talked a lot while she was writing it,' he says. 'I guess it gives some good examples of what my life has been like. You can only work with yourself as an actor. Everything else is stiff and conceptual.'

The way Nicholson tells it, his cavorting days are over – well, sort of. Never mind Kim Basinger giving him her imprimatur as 'the most highly sexed human being I've ever met, he's just the devil'. It's 2002 and we've met up again in Claridge's. 'You know, all good things come to an end,' he says, delicately nibbling a chocolate cookie. He's wearing his trademark shades and smoking a cigarette. A short-sleeved black jersey emphasizes the bulk of his barrel-like chest. Now approaching sixty-five, the nearest he seems to get to exercise is jumping out of his seat to cheer his beloved Los Angeles Lakers. 'I've been walking pretty slow upstairs for quite a while,' he says. 'I'm not much of a raver any more. I think it's sort of unattractive and inappropriate.' I tell him I don't believe it. 'Well, good,' he beams.

After the 9/11 attacks, he decided he'd turn to comedies for a while:

I don't want to depress anybody. I don't want to challenge them morally like I did. I sort of decided I was going over there with the clowns where I belong. Remember, it's show business. Just like shirts, fashion changes. Next year if I thought it would be theatrically effective to play an Ethiopian woman with a lisp and one leg that might be what I would do. But I'd still be myself.

He had dinner last night with photographer David Bailey:

We talk about movies quite a lot. He's always a good night on the town. He told me that if he was going to do a film on Picasso he'd cast me in the part. I asked him why. 'Because I know you would not try to act like Picasso,' he said. And that's the thing about acting for me. It's not about being the Hunchback of Notre Dame. It's what makes the movie register.

What attracted him to *Something's Gotta Give* is that it's romantic. 'At my age it's a pleasure to be associated with that adjective on any grounds,' he says. 'I don't have a lot of the evangelical left in me but I did for a while think that one of the things I wanted to concentrate on was to take sexuality in the movies into middle life. Because it's an area that's not broadly articulated in movies, or hasn't been.'

What he didn't realize when he started out as an actor was that he was giving his life over to movies:

> I just thought, oh well, it looks like that would be fun. Now look at me. That's the nature of the movie business. You're just 'the money'. They've got to know what you're doing twenty-four hours a day for whatever months you're doing a movie. So I have less flexibility than a surgeon when I'm working. I'm so heavily scheduled I've developed a kind of phobia about not making any dates. I don't know what I'll be doing right after talking to you, I don't know if I've another meeting. When I'm not working I like to leave everything open. One of the most common conversations I dread is someone who says, 'Well, shall I call you Wednesday then?'

If he hadn't been an actor, he might have been a painter. Instead he buys paintings. His collection of masterpieces by Picasso, Cézanne, Rouault, Chagall and Magritte spills from his Mulholland Drive home into the homes of friends, family and women he's known. 'I've given over two hundred away. I just buy what I love.' Picasso is a particular favourite. 'I always found it interesting that he never left the figurative. He went Cubist but never went into abstraction. I think it was some kind of connection with what he saw and what he put down.'

There's a parallel to the way Nicholson's roles tend to be rooted in some way or other to what he has lived. They offer different faces of the same reality, looked at from different angles, as a Cubist painting might. 'I always thought painting was going to evolve back into Cubism, because it's such an interesting form. If you paint at all, its tremendous fun to paint that way because you really see a painting that someone one else might not see.'

Nicholson paints a lot with his children. 'I wouldn't call it painting,' he says. 'I just want them to get into it. I want them to enjoy it.'

They watch films together, too. 'It's reassuring to see even the very young ones respond to human feelings and human situations, not just the special effects. It's become such a hip-hop youth generation, you wonder whether anyone cares any more.'

Not that he's all that pessimistic about Hollywood. 'It's a very Darwinian business. Relationships mean almost nothing. You can't make your relation a movie star. You can't make an audience like a movie they don't like. But because the business supports itself, they haven't been able to legislate it out of its natural vitality.'

Nicholson spans over six decades of Hollywood. *The Monkees* was a hit American TV series in the late 1960s. It followed the comic exploits of a psychedelic Beatles-like rock group. As a warm-up for *Easy Rider* he co-wrote a film version with series creator Bob Rafelson, who was making his directorial debut. *Head* was shown in Ireland as the second part of a double bill at Dublin's old Capitol cinema. As a critic, I welcomed it as 'an exhilarating cheeky collage of the weird, the wonderful and the daft, something completely fresh in American cinema'. It was the first time I'd heard of Nicholson.

We met casually in Cannes a few years later: all he could talk about was a bunch of exciting young directors who, he was convinced, were about to change Hollywood, in particular Steven Spielberg, just then making his debut with *Duel*, as well as George Lucas, Terrence Mallick and John Milius.

Then in 1976 I was in the audience at the Dorothy Chandler Pavilion in downtown LA to see him pick up his first Oscar for *One Flew Over the Cuckoo's Nest*.

We were both born in 1937, as was Morgan Freeman, who stars with him in *The Bucket List*, a darkly comic meditation on the nature of ageing and dying. Brought together in a cancer ward, where they're given a few months at most to live, they check themselves out and embark on a defiant executive-jet odyssey via the Pyramids, the Taj Mahal and the Great Wall of China in the defiant hope of catching up before they die on some of the things they've missed doing in their lives.

'When you have two actors as gifted as Jack and Morgan, it's like a couple of musicians picking up a score,' says Rob Reiner, who previously directed Nicholson in *A Few Good Men*. 'They can read right away what the tone needs to be and strike exactly the right balance between the humour and the emotion.'

*The Bucket List* playfully prompts reflections on mortality, something of a taboo subject in a Hollywood where youth is still everything and death is just a special effect in action films. It's what gets us talking the next time we meet up in February 2008 in Claridge's, a favourite Mayfair haunt. Nicholson has been spending an afternoon with Freeman, and they're sharing their thoughts on age with me, seeing that all three of us are now seventy.

Freeman experienced a dysfunctional childhood that makes Nicholson's seem almost normal. He was reared in segregated Mississippi by his seamstress grandmother and later by his mother and stepfather, after his alcoholic father walked out when he was four. He has four children by three different women, but has been with his second wife, Myrna, since 1984.

He was fifty before he managed to turn his up-and-down stage career into a Hollywood career with *Driving Miss Daisy*. Age gave him a gravitas that made him a natural choice to play a black president in *Deep Impact* and God in *Bruce Almighty*, and he's hoping eventually to portray his friend, Nelson Mandela. 'I didn't make bad decisions, I just didn't make the best decisions lots of times,' he says.

As for me, although married to a woman who somehow survived being born in a bombed palace that served as a hospital when Franco besieged a starving Madrid during the Spanish Civil War, I'm just a listener. 'In our different journeys we've got to this same stage in life,' says Freeman.

Nicholson has his hair shaved in *The Bucket List*, but what there is of it has now grown back. 'Hair is not my strong feature,' he says. 'They've being calling me balding since I was thirty. I fooled them.' As an actor he revels in his frailties, using them as props. Rather than insist on camera angles that show him at his best, he flaunts his double chin and his stomach and, if anything, makes himself seem even older than he is. 'I unJack myself. You can't be thinking of how you look and be a good actor.'

Although Freeman needed to be bald in *The Bucket List*, he was able to use a bald cap since he didn't have a scene being shaved. He has an impressive thick head of grey hair:

> I get it from my mother. I have her genes in every sense that you can think of. I don't look at all like my father, my biological father that is. I lived with him for about five months when I was eleven and then saw him again ten years later. He didn't know who I was. I was in an air force uniform. So I had a moment to look at him with some dispassion, just as a person. I didn't like him. I never did.

Ciaran Carty talks life and love with Jack Nicholson and Morgan Freeman as they all pass 70 **Review**

**Jack Nicholson, Ciaran Carty and Morgan Freeman being seventy together in London, 2007.**

He pushes up his sleeve and holds out his arm. 'My mother's genetic make-up is where I get this sort of lighter complexion underneath the skin,' he says.

That's how you look at black people. There's a yellow tone and a black tone and a red tone. My mother's background goes all the way to Europe and my father's more directly to Africa. He was dark-skinned and portly. I'm tall and slim. I don't think I have anything in me that you could point to my father and point to me and say, Oh yeah. My mother was very nurturing of me as an actor –

– he breaks off for a moment, his voice catching – 'She lived just long enough to go to the Academy Awards for *Driving Miss Daisy*.'

Nicholson quotes Winston Churchill, who was something of an optimist, because quite frankly to be any other way seemed to make it worse. 'I don't make lists,' he says.

I remember thinking once I'd like to live long enough to see the children graduate, stuff like that. I always wanted to speak another language. I wanted to learn to cook. I was once a short-order cook in New Jersey, but that was just hot dogs and hamburgers. A lady came asking for pancakes. I didn't get a lot of orders for pancakes. So they came out high. She just looked at them and said, what is this? I slapped them down with my hand. Make your own goddamn pancakes, I said.

Freeman has taken up golf. 'So most things on my "bucket list" have to do with golf,' he says.

Also I'm also very enamoured of a light business jet and I'd like to get it before it's too late. When I was a child in Charleston, getting an ice cream was a big deal. When I was in the air force – I signed up to escape – I got my first car, a 1951 Ford Convertible for $500. Now I have a Mercedes Benz C85 in Los Angeles and a BMW 750 in Mississippi.

I moved back to Mississippi in the early 1990s. I was living in the Caribbean, raising my grandchild. Her education was starting to slide, so we had to come

Intimacy with Strangers: A Life of Brief Encounters

ashore, put her in school. I didn't like New York any more, so we went back to where I grew up. When my career was stuck and I'd no work in 1981 and most of 1982, I figured my fifteen minutes were up and thought of becoming a cab driver, but kept procrastinating. I was afraid as soon as I stepped outside the door the phone might ring. And it did. I was offered a chance to fill in for a few weeks on a soap while the actor was in hospital. It's the luck of the draw. You're going to have down times in life.

What surprises is that life becomes easier with age:

I look in the mirror and have to remind myself that I'm seventy [says Freeman]. It's like, wow. Go back two hundred years and people were thinking of mortality at forty. Of course you have to take care. I was thinking the other day about my father, who died at seventy-nine. When he died his body was just fraught with all kinds of problems he probably never knew he had. He smoked three packets of cigarettes a day, so his lungs were shot. He'd wake up in the morning, sit on the side of the bed and try to clear his lungs before he reached for a cigarette.

Nicholson is sitting back in his chair, smoking. He has his sunglasses off. 'I've hundreds of them in drawers at home,' he says. He's wearing an open-necked red shirt.

People sometimes seem to be to be afraid to be happy. But the kind of life I've led almost every day, if there's not overwhelming tragedy in it there's some joy. I mean I'm happy that I'm alive when I wake up in the morning.

Years ago Walter Matthau nicknamed me the world's greatest old-timer. I played characters older or younger than I really was so that for much of my working career people didn't have too much of a sense of exactly how old I was. I always look for a vacuum to fill. When I could no longer go back to thirty-five any more I tried to bring sexuality to middle-aged characters. Of course I might have overdone it. When I read about somebody being seventy and you're supposed to take from that that he's elderly, it makes me laugh. That's a young guy to me right now.

He'll never be famous for being dignified, as perhaps Freeman is:

Certainly I'm not uncomfortable if somebody says, 'Jack, you're a womanizer', because I have been. But that's a matter of degree. The media enhance a reputation. I always say it's good for business. I'm not going to go around saying I'm not this or that, because I am an extreme person. But the last act of a gigolo is always written very sadly. That's one of the reasons I'm uncomfortable with my reputation. It just doesn't feel right.

So where does he find joy? 'I saw my daughter in a play just before I came to London. And I took particular joy in the faces of all the pundits who predicted that Hillary Clinton was dead in the New Hampshire primary.'

Freeman chuckles:

My candidate would be Obama. But if Hillary Clinton gets the nomination she gets my vote hands down. I don't think experience is what qualifies you for a job. Between Bush, Cheney and Karl Rove there was a hundred years of experience, and that prepared them for what? Nelson Mandela had no experience when he came out of prison and united South Africa as a nation. That's what you need, character, charisma and big ears. If you look at Obama, he's got big ears. That's what he's promising to use.

And joy? 'I think finding joy is finding yourself, being comfortable in your own skin. Once you're there, that's a joyful place.'

There's a parody of Freeman in Michel Gondry's *Be Kind Rewind*. 'My name surfaces in all sorts of places but there's no weight attached to that as far as I'm concerned,' he says. 'Mostly they're talking about some characters I played, they're not talking about me at all. Nobody knows me.'

It's like Nicholson's reputation for being funny. 'Comedy comes from the real,' he says. 'You can't try to be funny. I'm a funny person in a certain way but if you said to me to be funny I'd be at a loss.'

He's won the best actor Oscar three times, but lost out in 2003 with *Something's Gotta Give* to Adrien Brody's performance in *The Pianist*. There's a rumour he voted for Brody. 'Not true,' he says. 'I always vote for myself. And I'll tell you why. When I was a kid, there was a painting competition in my local dairy. When you bought an ice cream, you voted. Being a high-minded kid, I didn't vote for my own painting. It lost by one vote.'

As we part, he smilingly apologizes: 'I'm sorry I didn't give you shorter quotes.'

# four

Leonardo DiCaprio, James McEvoy, Chinua Achebe, André Brink, Doris Lessing and Terry George

Doris Lessing at home in Hampstead, London, 1994.

It's the day before Barack Obama's inauguration as president of the United States on 20 January 2009. In a few hours Leonardo DiCaprio has to catch a flight to Washington where he will be a guest at the ceremony. 'Our country has spoken resoundingly for a different future,' he tells me. 'I think Barack Obama has all the potential to do what he promised. We just have to give him the tools.'

DiCaprio is in London for the West End premiere of Sam Mendes' *Revolutionary Road*, a complex and engrossing adaptation of Richard Yates' generation-defining 1961 dissection of suburban American angst.

If Obama embodies the power of the American Dream, Yates shows its downside. Life is defined by the degree to which you compromise – or refuse to compromise – your ideals. Yates sets this timeless truth against the claustrophobic complacency and conformity of the Eisenhower era.

In the film DiCaprio and Kate Winslet are cast as an archetypal couple trying to break out of the rut of a failed marriage held together by a need to keep up appearances.

'Yates was so post-modern that he was simultaneously writing about the problems and dilemmas of post-war America while they were actually happening,' says DiCaprio, youthful in a blue open-necked shirt. He sits forward, using his hands to give emphasis to what he is saying. 'This was the suburbs of the white picket fence, of men going to work nine to five and women staying at home doing their job with the children, and of people not talking about their feelings – the whole iconic American image of proper family relationships.'

The sixties with its make-love-not-war psychedelic lack of inhibition was an inevitable reaction to this cosy conservatism, a celebration of free living personified by DiCaprio's own parents. They met as students at New York's City College, his mother an immigrant from Germany, his father a long-haired underground comic-book artist and activist in the counter-culture civil rights and anti-Vietnam War peace movement. 'My parents very much rebelled against that suburban existence. They'd seen it happen to people in their own families, and they wanted to run in the other direction. So they moved to a loft in SoHo.'

The marriage didn't last. They separated after Leonardo's birth in 1974 – he was named after the artist because his mother realized she was pregnant while admiring a da Vinci painting in Italy – and divorced when he was seven. He grew up with his mother in 'drug-infested' Echo Park in Los Angeles, where she supported him by working as a legal secretary. 'My mother understood *Revolutionary Road* to a T. She saw it happen time and again in her lifetime.'

DiCaprio got into acting with the help of the actor son of Peggy Farmer, a professional bodybuilder who became his father's second wife at a ceremony presided over by the psychedelic drugs guru, Timothy Leary. He quickly found his niche in a series of edgy roles – Robert De Niro's vulnerable son in *This Boy's Life*; Johnny Depp's handicapped brother in *What's Eating Gilbert Grape?*; the outré French poet Rimbaud in *Total Eclipse*; and a high-school athlete who degenerates into male prostitution in *The Basketball Diaries*.

All that changed in 1997 when he unexpectedly became every teenager's dream boy as Kate Winslet's ill-fated lover in *Titanic*, which confounded sceptics by becoming the highest-grossing film of all time. 'The *Titanic* romantic idol was as much a surprise to him as it was to the world,' says Ed Zwick, who subsequently directed him in *Blood Diamond*, a 2007 political thriller set in war-torn Sierra Leone.

Coming to terms with his sudden celebrity status was hard to handle:

There was a point after the film came out where I felt disillusioned with what I was going to do because there was such an immense focus on us. For both of us it was very much a departure from the type of films we'd done in the past. Both of us knew that. Both of us looked at it as this adventure we were going through.

We wholly realize it's going to be synonymous with our names for the rest of our lives and we're entirely comfortable with that. So much about being an actor is being able to control or steer the course of your own career. Not many actors are fortunate enough to be in that position. *Titanic* gave us that opportunity.

Both he and Winslet resisted pressure to reignite their onscreen chemistry in another film. 'We've taken so long to get together again because we knew that if we were going to do something again it had to be diametrically the opposite to *Titanic*.'

He sees *Revolutionary Road* as a throwback to Tennessee Williams and the Actors Studio era. 'It's two people trying to figure themselves out and a lot of angst happens in the process. The problem lies entirely within them. There's no big heist. There are no big explosions. Not a lot of films like this get made nowadays.'

*Titanic* has allowed him to get real at a time when Hollywood is becoming less wary about engaging with actual events or confronting challenging social and political issues. This new cinema of ideas ranges from the foot-in-the-door approach of Michael Moore's *Fahrenheit 9/11* to various forms of docudrama, which are faring less well at the box office, such as Robert Redford's *Lambs for Lions*; Paul Haggis' *In the Valley of Elah*; Brian de Palma's *Redacted*; Sam Mendes' *Jarhead*; and Kathryn Bigelow's *The Hurt Locker*.

With much of the US media playing along with White House spin during the George Bush years, and political debate reduced mainly to soundbites and doubletalk, cinema found the courage to become a form of journalism by other means, using drama to question the actions of governments and global corporations.

'Bob Woodward and Carl Bernstein, the *Washington Post* journalists who uncovered the details behind the Watergate break-in and cover-up that forced Richard Nixon to resign as president, were heroes in my house,' says Billy Ray, director of *Shattered Glass*, an exposé of media malpractice based on a real-life *New York Times* investigative journalist, most of whose stories turned out to be fabrication. 'I grew up in one of those classic Democratic liberal households where the idea of journalism as fighting for right was a really potent idea that we took very seriously. People don't feel that way any more. Journalism has gotten a really bad name.'

Working with former vice-president Al Gore, who made *An Inconvenient Truth* to provide a forum for the discussion of threats to the environment, DiCaprio identified with this movement by co-writing, co-producing and narrating *The 11th Hour*, a documentary highlighting the ravages of global warming.

So although Ed Zwick didn't write *Blood Diamond* for DiCaprio, once he finished the script he had no difficulty persuading him to play the role of a cynical Afrikaner mercenary who cashes in on Africa's vicious civil wars by trading arms for smuggled diamonds farmed illegally from rivers in Sierra Leone – an odious trade that supplied 15 per cent of the world diamond market in the 1990s.

'Leonardo is like Henry Fonda playing the bad guy in *Fort Apache* or John Wayne in *The Searchers* or Michael Douglas in *Wall Street*,' says Zwick:

> There's always this great moment where an actor relishes the opportunity to subvert the inherent sympathy his persona generates and do something that's antipathetic to that. The interesting thing is how they always maintain some transparency, some ability to see inside those characters. You see it in how Forest Whitaker in *The Last King of Scotland* is a monster and yet his vulnerability – his childishness and his fear – is also palpable. Those are the great villains. They're not only monochromatic, they're textured.

DiCaprio worked with orphaned children from the SOS Children's Village in Maputo, Mozambique, before filming began. He also spent time in South Africa, hanging out in bars with ex-mercenaries:

> I wanted to find their mindset and absorb their bitterness, to become like them. The character I play appealed to me because he was somebody who was learning to feel again, he was someone who was so scarred by the apartheid era that he saw the continent of Africa as a wasteland where everyone takes advantage of each other, turning a cold shoulder to the implications of their actions. He was technically a very difficult character to play because the accent was so alien to me, the culture was so alien to me, and the environment was so alien to me. I'd never spent more than a week in Africa in my entire life.

DiCaprio's character, confronted by brainwashed child-soldiers forced to fight because if they didn't their hands would be chopped off, finds he still has a conscience. 'Sometimes I wonder if God will ever forgive us for what we've done to each other. Then I look around and I realize God left this place a long time ago.' In Africa nothing is ever black or white: DiCaprio captures this moral ambivalence as a killer seeking redemption.

If his character is changed by the exploitation he finds in Africa, so was DiCaprio.

It changed all of us … The thing about Mozambique, where we did most of the filming, is that everything is there before you in the street, disease and death, sexuality and spirituality, everything is there before you. There's a certain detachment when you watch images on TV in the comfort of your Western home and even when you send a cheque. But it really gets to you when you actually go there and see the orphanages and realize how setting up a school can give a whole new lease of life to hundreds of children who lost their parents because of AIDS.

•  •  •

Idi Amin, a one-time boxer and soldier who bluffed his way to power as president of Uganda in a 1971 coup against the corrupt Milton Obote, is standing on an impromptu platform on the back of a truck, surrounded by sun-glassed bodyguards. 'I know who you are and what you are,' he tells enthralled villagers. 'I am you.'

Or rather it's Forest Whitaker in the role of Amin in the opening scene of Kevin Macdonald's 2007 film, *The Last King of Scotland*, a hard-hitting, soul-searching, gut-wrenching political thriller adapted from a novel by Giles Foden. The title is a reference to Amin's zany addiction to all things Scottish, which leads him to appoint as his personal physician a naive young Scottish doctor just out of college, Nicholas Garrigan. The character, portrayed by James McAvoy, is a composite of several Brits close to Amin, in particular his top adviser Bob Astes, known as 'The White Rat'.

'Basically I play an asshole; hopefully in a way you can still feel empathy towards him but not necessarily sympathy,' says McAvoy, who was born in Glasgow's Scotstown but brought up on a housing estate by his maternal grandparents and his mother, off and on, after his parents separated when he was seven: he's a young actor like DiCaprio with feet still on the ground. 'Garrigan is not an evil man, but just selfish and vain and egotistical. So when someone like Amin empowers him, that's quite dangerous.'

*The Last King of Scotland* is a cautionary tale of how easy it is to become complicit in the regime of a tyrant. Western politicians do it all the time, of course, for their own devious reasons: Neville Chamberlain with his appeasement of Hitler; Richard Nixon and Henry Kissinger in their support of General Pinochet's vicious coup against Chile's elected President Allende; Donald Rumsfeld when he gave America's support to Saddam Hussein against Iran in the 1980s: it's no wonder many ordinary people fall into the trap. Millions of Germans knew about the Nazi death camps but preferred to look the other way. Spanish tourism came of age during the heyday of Franco's vindictive dictatorship.

So who could blame Garrigan, fresh out of medical school and in his first job – giving injections to barefoot children at a Ugandan mission hospital – for allowing himself to be seduced by an offer from Amin following a bizarre accident in the bush involving the president's speeding motorcade and a wayward cow. After all, didn't the British Foreign Office, who helped put Amin in power, describe him as 'a splendid type and a good football player'?

McAvoy as the doctor provides a Western audience with a way into an alien world of kidnapping, assassinations and other unspeakable voodoo-driven atrocities. 'We tend to see the figure of the Westerner in Africa as being heroic, and I'm sure there have been good people from the West in Africa who have been selfless,' says McAvoy, after the film's London premiere in January 2007. 'But if you look at our history and our presence there over the last two hundred years, the main characterizing feature has not been selflessness, it's been selfishness.'

**James McAvoy with Forrest Whitaker shooting THE LAST KING OF SCOTLAND in Africa, 2007.**

Intimacy with Strangers: A Life of Brief Encounters

*The Last King of Scotland* is a rare film about Africa that doesn't have a white hero helping so-called natives who by implication are incapable of helping themselves. The only real hero is a black doctor who risks his life trying to smuggle Garrigan out of the country. 'Go home and tell the truth about Amin, they will believe you because you are white,' he says. By then we realize that if Garrigan does get out, he'll probably do nothing.

The curse of colonization is that the colonized are conditioned by the way they are seen by the colonizers. Man Booker award-winning writer Chinua Achebe, who was raised by Christian parents in an Igbo village in southeastern Nigeria, remembers reading H. Rider Haggard and John Buchan novels in the library of a college set up by the colonial administration in 1929 on the lines of an English public school. A scholarship boy, he found himself taking sides 'with the white characters against the savages ... The white man was good and reasonable and intelligent and courageous. The savages arrayed against him were sinister and stupid or, at the most, cunning. I hated their guts.'

Years later in 1975 in a lecture at Amherst University in the United States he caused controversy by arguing that Joseph Conrad's novel, *Heart of Darkness*, dehumanized Africans and was inherently racist, depicting Africa as 'a metaphysical battlefield devoid of all recognizable humanity, into which the wandering European enters at his peril'. In the course of preparing his lecture he counted the words spoken by Africans in another Conrad book, *Image of Africa*, and could only find six. Achebe also took Nobel Prize laureate Albert Schweitzer to task for reportedly saying, 'The African is indeed my brother, but my junior brother.'

On a visit to Dublin in 1988 for an International Writers' Conference on the theme of literature as celebration, Achebe is sceptical about the title chosen for the event: he finds it somewhat bland. 'I've noticed a kind of wariness toward politics by writers here,' he says, looking out over Dún Laoghaire Harbour from the lounge of the Royal Marine Hotel, a colourful figure in tribal robes and skullcap. 'There seems to be a feeling that writers can't do very much, that we just write poetry, that we talk to ourselves. But I think that's a very limited view.'

Even to deny that writing is political is in itself a political act:

Because language is not neutral, it's very much a political tool. It's charged with prejudices. So a poet who says 'I'm not in politics' is not being realistic.

To speak the English language is to become sexist. In my own Igbo language you don't use 'man' to stand for everybody. You don't say 'he' when you mean all of us. You say 'he' only when you mean a man. Otherwise you use a neutral pronoun that stands for man, woman or child.

English is a minority language in Nigeria, just like Igbo, Yoruba, Hausa and some two hundred other languages. 'Every language is a minority language in relation to the rest. But English is the biggest of them in terms of cutting across every barrier and every frontier. It's the only one that could be called the *lingua franca*.' That's part of the ambivalence of being an African writer. Colonialism lingers on through language. 'There's a sense of guilt about writing in English. About the fact that it is somebody else's language that comes to us with all kinds of bad memories. Yet we can't escape it. We have to use it even to talk to ourselves.'

Achebe, whose first novel, *Things Fall Apart*, dealt with the advent of white civilization in terms of its effect on an over-proud member of the Igbo tribe refusing to accept its inevitability, was already arguing these views in Lagos back in the 1950s when he worked in the talks department of the NBS, a radio network started in 1933 by the colonial government.

No doubt this had an influence in prompting Holy Ghost missionary priests there to approach my father with the idea of teaming up with the publisher Maurice Macmillan – a son of the British prime minister – to produce schoolbooks for African children in their own languages. There was a move towards independence throughout the African continent and, like in Ireland in colonial times, language was seen as a voice of freedom, an expression of identity. Africans wanted their children to be educated in the languages they spoke, not just the language of the white man.

Nigeria achieved independence in 1960 but a military regime under 31-year-old Lieutenant Colonel Jack Gowan was set up following a coup by northern officers in 1967. Thousands of Igbo living in the north were butchered in ethnic cleansing instigated by Muslim traditionalists. More than a million abandoned their homes and returned to their roots in the Igbo-dominated southeast, where vast oil reserves had been found in the 1950s. The military governor, 34-year-old Colonel Ojukwu, fearing the northern-dominated federal government would appropriate the oil revenues, in May 1967 declared the region an independent nation to be known as the Republic of Biafra. Achebe became its foreign ambassador, arguing the case of Ojukwu in the US and the UK.

The Gowan regime was backed by Britain and the United States and other Western countries, including the Irish government, which meant Biafra was isolated from the start, its independence recognized only by Julius Nyerere's

Tanzania, Gabon, the Ivory Coast and the Vatican State. Although about four hundred and thirty Irish priests and nuns remained in Biafra, there was little coverage of the war in the Irish media. Frank Aiken, then Minister for External Affairs and, ironically, an old comrade of my father – they orchestrated an escape of de Valera supporters from Mountjoy Prison in 1922 – indicated in the Dáil that he disapproved of Irish journalists going there. RTÉ was forced to abandon plans to send out a reporter. A subsequent *Seven Days* documentary led to a protest from the Nigerian embassy and attempts to muzzle its contents. It was suggested that the missionaries by providing medical aid to the Biafran refugees were getting involved in political and military matters.

Priests I had known at school in Blackrock College introduced me to missionaries who gave me photographs of maternity hospitals, schools and chapels strafed by Russian MiG jets in indiscriminate attacks on civilian targets. Father Sean Broderick from Clare told how he had gone to Awgu with twenty bags of food for refugees who were fleeing before the advance of federal troops:

> Two jet planes swept in three times on a small market where a few hundred women and children had gathered. There wasn't a soldier in sight, just the human target of women and children under the mat-roofed market. It was utterly senseless, utterly shocking.
>
> I reached Awgu hospital as bits of seventy-eight bodies were being piled in the mortuary. Two hundred more wounded filled the ward and the ground outside. Before I left, the death toll was over a hundred. An English doctor, Anne Seymore, came out of the operating theatre for a drink of water. She was covered in blood from head to foot, like a character out of the Apocalypse.

Another priest described what happened when Calabar fell to the federals. 'Over two thousand civilians were killed. Soldiers got tired bringing the bodies down to the river, so they made their victims walk there first and then shot them. The women were rounded up and put in a wooden shed, which was set on fire.'

It was clear that what was happening to ordinary innocent people was inexcusable and had to be made public. It was a humanitarian tragedy on an appalling scale that shamed the world but in which the world was complicit, whether openly by arming and supporting the federal army or by default by doing nothing to end the carnage.

On 17 March 1968 I filled a page in the *Sunday Independent* with the photographs and eyewitness testimonies that had been made available to me. It stirred the conscience of readers and two days later John and Kay O'Loughlin called a meeting to establish Africa Concern in order to raise money and get help into Biafra. This ad hoc organization later became Concern and a prototype for future emergency international humanitarian aid agencies.

The war ended in January 1970 when Ojukwu fled into exile. Between one million and three million people died in the hostilities or from disease and starvation. Biafra was in ruins with over three million refugees living off scraps. Aiken suggested that reporting what was happening was propaganda that only gave comfort to the Biafrans and prolonged the war instead of allowing the federal army a quick and decisive victory.

The innocent victims, in other words, were responsible for their own misfortune. Their real enemies were the people who tried to help them. Meanwhile the oil reserves were secure.

Achebe returned to a job at the University of Nsukka, his passport revoked. He continued to write novels dealing in one way or another with political change. He likes to quote a line from the Angolan leader, Agostinho Neto, which guerrillas sang while fighting the Portuguese: 'I wait no more, I am the awaited.' Even though taking on a political function, it remains good lyrical poetry. 'I think poetry has this possibility, which we cannot ignore.'

The former Western colonial powers have a wretched record of condemning the excesses of their protégés while at the same time allowing them to remain in power by default. This hypocrisy enabled Idi Amin to continue as president of Uganda until 1979 when his nemesis proved to be a simple unassuming former schoolteacher, Julius Nyerere. As president of Tanzania from 1961 to 1985, Nyerere may have failed to bring prosperity to his people with his unique policy of socialism rooted in village communes, but he provided much-needed moral leadership in the struggle for African independence.

Amin's final folly was to embark on a brief invasion of Tanzania in late 1978 that was easily repulsed by Tanzanian troops, who then pursued the invaders back into Uganda albeit in knowing breach of the principles of the Organisation of African Unity. Nyerere saw a chance to rid the oppressed Ugandan population of Amin, and took it. The capital, Kampala, was quickly overrun. Crowds took to the streets, chanting his name. Amin was forced into exile. The Tanzanian army withdrew soon afterwards, returning the country to its people.

I still have the letter Julius Nyerere posted to me fifty years ago in a hand-addressed envelope on which he stuck five shilling stamps and one twenty-cent stamp to make sure it arrived safely. It's before me as I write these words.

While Nelson Mandela was incarcerated on Robben Island, he was not alone. In December 1985 the peaceful change he would bring about in South Africa on his release four years later was already becoming evident, not just in the surprising moderation of the banned African National Congress but in a growing openness to debate among Afrikaners. Influential voices within the Dutch Reformed Church were pushing for radical reconciliation. With the economy collapsing, business people were seeking to work out an accommodation with the ANC. The stumbling block remained Prime Minister Botha.

'Once he is out of the way, perhaps someone with a bit more vision and understanding will take over,' novelist André Brink was telling me. What he failed then to predict was that the hoped-for man of vision would be black, but in nearly everything else he has been proved right.

'The government portrays the blacks as wanting to drive us all into the sea,' he says, but

> I've never yet heard a single black say that. Everyone in the African National Congress with whom I've had contact has been amazingly moderate. But it doesn't suit the government to get that image over because the longer they can persuade the electorate to believe that the ANC is a subversive terrorist organization, the longer they hope to stay in power. The irony is that the longer they go on with this, the more certain it is that they are going to lose power.

He speaks on the tape of our interview in a matter-of-fact voice with a slight Afrikaans accent that years as a student in Paris failed to erase. There is a sense of unreality about listening back to his voice talking to me over afternoon tea at the Gresham Hotel nearly a quarter of a century ago. The next day he was to be back in South Africa where the Botha government had clamped down on TV journalists attempting to cover riots in the black townships. 'It's almost as if they have a sort of death wish,' he says.

> The more this happens, the more writers need to take over some of the functions of journalism and to write in the guise of fiction things that are no longer allowed to be published in the press. There is so much distortion and silence and lies about what is really happening that it is imperative to keep people informed. The majority of whites in South Africa still don't know the extent of what is going on. Most of them, I presume, don't want to know. But that is precisely why and how apartheid is so effective: that if you don't want to know, you needn't know.

**André Brink in Dublin, 1988.**

Everything Brink is saying he has already written. He sees himself as giving witness in his novels and other writings, just as the African journalists working on Anthony Sampson's ground-breaking *The Drum* bore witness since the late 1950s: the word would make Africa free. An Afrikaner teacher in Brink's novel, *A Dry White Season*, tries to find out how a black worker he knew came to die in police custody: the very fact of his curiosity makes him a rebel to the South African authorities: 'Perhaps all one can really hope for, all I am entitled to, is no more than this: to write it down, to report what I know. So that it will not be possible for any man to say again: I knew nothing.'

Like the teacher, Brink is in this sense a subversive: his crime is to reveal through fiction the reality of what is happening under apartheid. The government banned *A Dry White Season*, but not before he succeeded in circulating it to three thousand private subscribers. His earlier novels had suffered a similar fate. Security police constantly harassed him, raiding his home, confiscating his notes and correspondence. When the black activist Steve Biko died in police custody, Brink recognized among the names of the interrogators involved some of those who had 'visited' him. He finished writing *A Dry White Season* a year later 'in pain and rage, but not in hate'.

Being an Afrikaner writer leaves him in a peculiarly difficult situation. 'If Nadine Gordimer criticizes the government, they shrug it off because she is English-speaking and she's only doing what they'd expect of her. But if someone from inside the establishment does it, it is regarded as a very vicious form of betrayal and you're branded as a backstabber.'

The irony is that in banning Brink the regime simply succeeded in making his questioning voice of dissent more widely heard. He was forced to start writing in English in 1974 after the suppression of *Looking on Darkness*, a novel in which he dealt with a coloured actor's affair with a white woman. But this meant that for the first time blacks could read him, too. He became internationally known and was twice runner-up for the Booker Prize. *A Dry White Season* was filmed by Richard Attenborough and won an Oscar nomination for Marlon Brando. 'More people read me now than if my books had been freely available,' Brink smiles.

Belatedly the government has come to realize that it was merely focusing attention on writers it hoped to silence. His books are now unbanned and it's even become possible for him to publish in Afrikaans again. 'It suits the government better to relax censorship and give the impression of relative freedom so that they can get on with the real business of repression behind the scenes.'

Brink didn't set out to be a political writer. But in South Africa being a writer is in itself a political act:

> I am basically concerned not with theories and polemics but with people and what a system like apartheid is doing to real people. But you can't escape from politics if you do that. I'd never like to see literature descend to the level of politics but rather elevate politics to the level of literature. If one is interested just in conveying propaganda, it would be more effective to get on to a political platform.

That Brink has become the writer he is suggests that South Africa is not without hope. He grew up in small villages in the very heart of the conservative, God-fearing Afrikaner laager:

> My parents have always being staunch supporters of the government. During the whole of my childhood and university days I simply never encountered any black person who was not a labourer or a domestic servant. Class and race are allied so very closely in South Africa that it never occurred to one that blacks could be teachers or lawyers. They didn't exist in those capacities. So there was no urgency to examine the values underlying the whole system.

Going to Paris as a postgraduate student at the time of the Sharpeville Massacre finally opened his eyes:

> I discovered for the first time what my people were involved in. I met with black students and discussed politics and literature with them and found that they knew more about many things which I thought I was an authority on than I ever did. It was an enormous culture shock just to sit down and have a meal with a black person for the first time. My world was opened up and it became much larger than before.

Which made it all the more difficult when he eventually had to return to a teaching job at Rhodes University in the Cape Province. 'In Paris you can exist like that and it becomes part of your natural way of life and then you go back and everything you've just accepted as natural is suddenly totally unnatural.' People who had been his friends didn't want to know him, particularly when he became the spokesman for a group of writers knows as Sestigers (Men of the Sixties) who were challenging the taboos of Afrikaans literature by writing of the actuality of life under apartheid. The prime minister even intervened to prevent him being appointed to an Afrikaans university.

He quit South Africa again for Paris, this time intending to settle. He arrived in the middle of the 1968 student riots. All his friends there were engaging in intense soul-searching about their situation in society. He did the same. 'After I'd gone back to South Africa the first time I was almost ashamed of my roots. So I didn't want to write about that. I wanted to write about Paris.' He did this in his first novel, *The Ambassador*. 'But then I felt if writing really meant something to me I had to do it at home. That the only thing I had which I could write about was precisely those roots, and I would go back and discover what had made me what I was and from what kind of society did I come.'

Even while he was banned from publishing in Afrikaans, he always continued to write in Afrikaans as well as English:

> It became a matter of preparing two versions of the same book every time. I usually start writing in Afrikaans, take it through several drafts, rework it into English and then sometimes translate it back into Afrikaans. It helps me looking at the same experience from completely different angles. It has become an almost indispensable double process for me now. I simply don't feel I've lived unless I can grapple with an experience on paper. It is only that second time when you've written about it that you really discover what it meant the first time, because language determines so much what one experiences.

Black, English and Afrikaans writers traditionally represented three totally separate streams of literature in South Africa. 'But more and more these streams have begun converging. There's nothing like a common enemy to credit solidarity. Even though much of this can't be expressed openly in terms of organizations, in terms of personal relationships we're all very close.'

In his novel *The Wall of the Plague*, which takes the Black Death of Europe's past as a metaphor for South Africa's present, one of the characters, a film-maker, remarks that 'a book doesn't weigh much against the violence of the world. It can never really become a substitute for reality. Yet what could have become of the world without the word?'

•   •   •

Chinua Achebe recalls touring East Africa on a Rockefeller travel fellowship a month after Nigeria achieved independence in 1960. He was required to fill in an immigration form in Kenya, indicating whether his ethnicity was European, Asiatic, Arab or 'Other'. On a bus to Victoria Falls in Northern Rhodesia he was challenged by a ticket-taker for sitting in front in a 'whites-only' section. 'If you must know,' he said, 'I come from Nigeria, and there we sit where we like in a bus.'

The patronizing racism of white settlers in Northern and Southern Rhodesia (later to become Zambia and Zimbabwe) mirrored that of Afrikaners in South Africa, but even they were not without dissenters, usually writers. The Left Book Club in Salisbury, now Harare, was a meeting place for those arguing for change in the 1940s, among them a precocious 24-year-old divorcée, Doris Taylor, with two children by her first husband, Frank Wisdom, but soon to marry 29-year-old Jewish lawyer and communist ideologue Gottfried Lessing, who had fled Nazi Germany in 1938.

'We really believed we were going to change the world,' says Doris Lessing. (Although she divorced her second husband in 1949 she retains the name under which she published her debut novel, *The Grass is Singing*, in 1950.) 'We were totally harmless and indeed rather pathetic. But put that fanaticism in another context and it's not very nice to think about.'

It's autumn 1994. For the last fourteen years her home has been a three-storey terraced house in Hampstead. She opens the door by pushing a buzzer. 'Come on up,' she says, peering down from a landing. At seventy-five she might no longer skip up and down stairs, but she still has the fresh complexion of a younger woman, rather in the way nuns never seem to age: put it down to her childhood on the veldt.

She certainly belies her intimidating reputation. For nearly half a century she has spoken out on everything from Stalinism, white supremacy and the Saatchi & Saatchi Tory advertising campaigns to the sheep-like conventionality of the English literary establishment. Her experimental sci-fi novel, *The Golden Notebook*, prompted Anita Brookner to dub her 'pioneer of feminist self-consciousness in its raw state'. *Time* magazine rates her as 'one of the world's greatest living writers'. But here she is, fussing about the house. 'I apologize for the dying rose. The builders are downstairs. I'm in a state of siege.'

We're in a great open room. Persian rugs cover the floors and hang on the walls. The couches are low, little more than cushions on the floor, as in a sheik's tent. Books are strewn everywhere, videos too, and a pile of CDs with Ella Fitzgerald's *Singing Cole Porter* on top.

This is the nearest she has come to settling down since she walked out on her parents at sixteen to work as a telephonist in Salisbury. 'Oh yes, it is home,' she says. 'Let's hope it sees me out. I've moved so much in my life.'

She needs the quiet. 'You have to be bored to write,' she says. She can see the countryside from the top floor. 'At night it's absolutely silent up there.' Once she even heard a cock crow, one of the first sounds she heard as a baby in Persia, where she was born. Her father, newly married to a nurse who cared for him when he lost his leg just before Passchendaele in World War I, shell-shocked and disillusioned with England, had gone there to work in the Imperial Bank.

She remembers their house at Kermanshah as a great stone building on a plateau surrounded by snow-topped mountains. Life was a round of legation parties and picnics. 'My mother didn't realize it, but that was as good as it was ever going to get.' Almost from birth she was in a state of flight from her mother, a devotee of the 1920s fad of never lifting a crying baby. 'This is your *baby*, she said when my baby brother Harry was born. What I resented was the lie. I was two and a half and I knew it wasn't my baby. I swear I could have killed her I was so angry.'

On a visit to England, her father was prompted by the Imperial Exhibition to become a settler in Southern Rhodesia, growing maize. It was like the American frontier days. They set off into the bush in an ox wagon piled with Liberty silks and Persian carpets, their way lit by hurricane lamps.

She stands at the bay window, looking out on the tidy suburban north-London streets. 'It took me a long time to realize how incredibly brave they must have been, leaving middle-class England without any money at all and landing themselves in this land full of savages and snakes, knowing nothing about it, hoping for the best.'

Home became a self-built mud house on top of a hill, with no electricity or water. 'My pity for them was mixed with anger and resentment. I knew they were victims, of course. I knew perfectly well they were having a terrible time. But they would have dragged me down if I hadn't got away.' As she did, at first by retreating behind the persona of Tigger from *Winnie the Pooh*, seeming to go along with what was expected of her, being a good sport.

'It was a protection,' she says. It was also the beginning of being a writer. 'I remember fixing moments, saying to myself, remember this, this is how it is, because they were trying to make me think their way.'

She became defiantly independent, able to drive at eleven and going out alone into the bush with a .22 rifle to shoot game, which she sold to the butcher so that she could buy material for frocks. She read voraciously and by ten already had a poem published in *The Rhodesian Herald*. At fourteen she quit the Catholic all-girls Dominican Convent High School, where the nuns tried to convert her, and moved to Salisbury, supporting herself working as a nursemaid and a telephone clerk. She married civil servant Frank Wisdom in 1939 without loving him, and soon had two babies. 'It was Tigger who married him. I really think that everyone goes crazy when there is a war.'

She walked out on her marriage and her children to become an active member of the Communist Party, which was banned, and was soon sleeping with the hard-line ideologue Gottfried Lessing, a period of her life dealt with in *A Ripple from the Storm*, part of a quintet of novels set in the fictional African country Zambesia. Her second marriage ended like her first, with her walking out and taking the boat to England with the manuscript of *The Grass Is Singing*, which dealt with the disastrous relationship between a white woman and her black servant. Gottfried moved to England, too, but soon settled in East Berlin where he eventually became head of the Africa section of the German Democratic Republic's foreign ministry.

She pours some jasmine tea. 'All fiction is autobiographical,' she says. 'It has to be.' *Under My Skin* is the first volume of her formal autobiography, which has been published by HarperCollins. Although it covers ground already touched on in her novels, she sees the past differently now. 'When you write an autobiography you realize how fluid everything is. You see it as an interim report, really, not definite at all.'

Gottfried returned to Africa as GDR ambassador to Uganda during the Idi Amin regime. He was murdered with his third wife in mysterious circumstances in the riots that led up to Amin's overthrow in 1979. 'One theory is that the KGB bumped him off because he had become an embarrassment,' says Lessing.

She refused an offer of becoming a dame of the British Empire on the grounds that 'there was no British Empire'. However she did accept the 2007 Nobel Prize for Literature, which she learned about while shopping at her local supermarket. Now aged ninety, she continues to write.

• • •

Paul Rusesabagina is an educated member of the majority Hutu ethnic group in the small, landlocked African country of Rwanda. In 1994 he was the trusted manager of the four-star Des Milles Collines hotel in the capital city, Kigali. With his wife Tatiana from the minority Tutsis, and their three small children, he lived in a suburban house furnished with the perks that came his way.

But when his country erupted in violence and the streets were bloodied by tribal genocide – up to a million people died in a hundred days – rather than escape with his family he stayed behind and allowed the hotel to become a safe haven for fleeing Tutsis. Like an African Oskar Schindler, he tried to buy off the rampaging militias with bribes of gourmet food and money from the hotel safe. By the time Tutsi rebels ousted the Hutu government, he'd saved over a thousand lives.

In *Hotel Rwanda*, Belfast-born director Terry George uses the story of this otherwise ordinary man to make comprehensible the unspeakable – much in the manner of the sceptical middle-American dad played by Jack Lemmon in Costa-Gavras' *Missing*, who becomes the conscience of the audience when he travels through Pinochet's Chile in search of his 'disappeared' aid-worker son. The atrocities committed in Rwanda, as in Chile, were all the worse because the outside world turned its back on what was happening, and UN troops on the ground stood by and watched, refusing to intervene.

George had originally intended to make a film about the Liberian Civil War, 'a cruel, bizarre conflict carried out by young kids who had this mixture of Western culture and voodoo and did the craziest things'.

Then he met Rusesabagina and heard his story.

> I knew I'd got a political drama through which I could explain the genocide. It had elements of suspense and a thriller, and the central romance of the relationship between Paul and his wife. It gives you a chance to take an audience inside an event – and for a character to become the story – and then walk them through it.

George utilized this genre before, the ordinary man who finds the courage to stand up against evil, in his screenplay for Jim Sheridan's *In the Name of the Father*, telling the story of the false arrest of the Guildford Four ('not so much through the character of Gerry Conlon, but through his father, Giuseppe') and also in *Some Mother's Son* ('through the Helen Mirren character, who's kind of bewildered by the whole hunger strike thing').

Terry George's own story is almost as incredible as Paulo Rusesabagina's. He was interned in Long Kesh (known as the Maze) as a Belfast teenager, and later served three years of a six-year sentence on a firearms charge. It was just before the establishment of the H-blocks and the Thatcher policy of criminalization that led to the 'dirty protest' and Bobby Sands' hunger strikes. He shared a cell with Ronan Bennett, who also went on to become a writer ('The Kesh was like a school for writers,' George jokes) and whose novel *The Catastrophist* was set in the Congo against the backdrop of the assassination of the charismatic nationalist leader, Patrice Lumumba.

After his release, George studied history and politics at Queen's University, Belfast, but never finished. Finding out that his name was on a Loyalist death list, he fled to New York as an illegal immigrant with his wife and two small children. He worked as a fact-checker at *New York* magazine, then as a researcher for Shana Alexander on *The Pizza Connection*, dealing with the criminal investigation of the Sicilian Mafia's control of the American heroin market:

> It was the longest mob trial in American history. I was working in the Federal Court in Manhattan with prosecutor Rudy Giuliani, who went on to become mayor, and with another lawyer who was later to head the FBI. So I was sitting in the middle of all these dudes, just waiting for the hand on my shoulder. I was terrified of immigration catching up on me.

We first met when he was Gregory Teer, an anagram of his name he used as a cover when his first play, *The Tunnel*, was staged by Jim Sheridan at the Irish Arts Centre. 'For God's sake keep it secret or he'll be done,' warned Sheridan. *The Tunnel* is about an escape from the Kesh. 'It's an allegory for the whole Northern Ireland situation,' says George:

They're digging this tunnel and by the time it collapses they realize they've almost dug their way back into the cage. The most likeable character in the cage, the joker who keeps everybody's spirits up, turns out to be an informer. We'd originally cast someone in the part who didn't think it was worth the train fare from Connecticut, so Jim played the role himself. Frank McCourt also had a role. So we've all done well out of the blarney, or whatever you want to call it.

George lives on Long Island. Americans think of him as American. 'I remember being asked did I not feel weird going to Africa and making this African film,' he says.

I said that as soon as I got to Rwanda I understood perfectly that the tribal division between the Tutsi and the Hutu was really an economic situation where the divide-and-rule colonizer says to one community that the other community is going to steal their land and their livelihood. Coming from Northern Ireland, I felt as much legitimacy as anyone else to make the movie.

• • •

Chinua Achebe's spine was severely damaged in March 1990 when his car overturned in the bush, crushing him underneath. He was paralyzed from the waist down and will require a wheelchair for the rest of his life. He continues to work as a professor in Brown University in New York and published his collected essays, *The Education of a British-Protected Child*, in 2009 and a memoir in 2012.

In his 1985 novel, *Anthills in Savannah*, he focuses on the corruption of ideals in a Sandhurst-trained army officer brought to power in a coup but suspecting betrayal everywhere after the failure of a referendum to make him president for life. 'The Nigerian security police were sniffing around while I was writing it,' he says. 'With the kind of writing we do and the kind of situation we have, it's absolutely impossible for me to appreciate the view that the writer has very little to do with politics. Even if you want to be left alone you can't. Everything you write and everything you say is regarded as a political statement anyway.'

# five

**Hugh Leonard, Mia Farrow and Woody Allen**

Hugh Leonard outside his apartment at Bullock Harbour, Dublin, 1999.

'What's the matter?' asks Julia, seeing me on the phone. The call is from Hugh Leonard's daughter Danielle. He's been in and out of hospital for months. We've being expecting the worst. Even so it's a shock. I try to speak, but the words choke. Then I tell her. 'Jack died during the night.'

He adopted the pen name Hugh Leonard when his first play, *The Big Birthday*, was staged at the Abbey Theatre in 1956. He was afraid that if it was known he was doubling as a playwright he'd lose his lowly job as a clerk with the Land Commission. The name stuck with him as a public persona behind which he could protect his private self. It became by default a distancing device to explore the humour and the pain of his life as if it was happening to someone else. Through it he could freely people his plays and novels with third-person reimagined versions of himself and of those he knew.

Hugh Leonard was his greatest creation, reaching a popular audience through the platform of his curmudgeonly and much-feared newspaper columns, but Jack was ambivalent towards the public person he had become. 'Anyone who knows me as Hugh Leonard doesn't know me,' he said. 'The name is something I don't answer to. You put it on the title page of a script. That's all it's good for.'

Our son Jack is called after him. We all holidayed together on the French canals. He loved coming to the house for Julia's dinner parties. He'd send her typescripts of everything he wrote, and dedicated *Rover and Other Cats* to her, an oblique mirror of his life through the misadventures of various cats he owned. He took pleasure in taking us to restaurants he had sussed out and enjoyed. We were invited to all his first nights. Of course there were tiffs. Jack could never resist a clever one-liner no matter who it might hurt. But the occasional falling out never lasted long. He'd listen to Julia, if not to anyone else, and soon all would be well.

The shock of his death is that although eighty-two he was so obviously reluctant to go. He suffered a terrible medical battering in his last few years but like the clichéd boxer in Hollywood movies who refuses to take the count, he kept getting up for more. His instinct, taking a cue from Monty Python's *The Life of Brian*, was always to look on the bright side of life, however sardonically. Even near the end when he could no longer type or write, he was talking of a holiday in the south of France. Age to him was a matter of how you regarded it, a truth encapsulated in an anecdote he told about two French generals walking along the Champs Elysées. 'They were both of advanced age, maybe about ninety. And this gorgeous girl walked past. "Oh," said one of the generals, "I wish I was seventy-five again."'

When it turned out that Jack's accountant and long-time friend Russell Murphy had swindled him out of £258,000, he quipped that it was wonderful he could afford to lose that much money. On the operating table for a triple heart bypass in 1994 he couldn't resist singing the Jeanette MacDonald song from *Arise, My Love*: 'Dream lover put your arms around me …' Calling in to visit him at the Blackrock Clinic a couple of days afterwards, we found him sitting up in an armchair with a bottle of Australian wine. Soon he was back at his typewriter, knocking off new opening and closing lines for his Mia Farrow film, *Widow's Peak*. 'Just to let American audiences know they're going to see a comedy and they've seen a comedy, otherwise they wouldn't be sure they're supposed to laugh,' he said.

His surgeon, Maurice Neligan, who had been at school with me, told him he could have two drinks a day. He used up his quota in the bar at the Abbey during the interval for his double bill, *Chamber Music*, a few months later. When the bell rang to return to our seats he noticed someone had left an unfinished whiskey on the counter. He downed it and told me, 'It doesn't count, it wasn't mine.'

Jack's unflappable optimism was nurtured by the happy endings of the films he watched as a small boy with his mother, or rather his foster mother: his natural mother Annie Byrne gave him up for adoption when he was ten days old. He was reared in a two-room cottage on Kalafat Lane in Dalkey by Mags Keyes, whose husband worked as a gardener for the Bewley family:

> I'd get off from the local national school at three o'clock, take the tram to Dún Laoghaire, get out at the Picture House, go inside and she'd be there in the front row of the middle stalls, and she'd have a packet of sandwiches and a Baby Power refilled with milk, my lunch.
>
> Going there was a wonderfully reassuring experience because it wasn't realistic. Everything was done according to a formula. You watched because it gave you a kind of confidence in the world. This was the way the world was and nothing was going to shake it. Because when you were a kid, that was all you knew of the world, what you saw in the movies. You talked them. You lived them.

Although he stopped going to films with his mother when he was ten, the habit stuck. The playwright he became was shaped by the forms and themes of films that stirred his childhood imagination. The germ of his Tony Award-winning autobiographical play, *Da*, can be found in *King's Row*, the Sam Wood melodrama about young people coming of age, which he saw when he was seventeen. 'You identified like mad. You said this could be my small town. The great thing about *King's Row* is that the town is never seen. So you were able to invent your own town in your head.'

*Da*, in which a successful writer returning for the funeral of his father is confronted by his younger self, shares this universality. Although Dalkey is the prism through which it views the world, the town is never named. One of Jack's first plays, *A Walk on the Water*, was modelled on the aimless youths in Fellini's *I Vitelloni* (The Drones). 'One of them eventually gets on the train and leaves. You get a marvellous tracking shot that takes in the bedrooms of the others and there is this sense of leaving them behind: they're sleeping and he's awake. Nearly all Fellini's films end with the start of a new journey. It's a great optimistic vein.'

His 1976 play, *Time Was*, began as a spoof for Ronnie Barker about two middle-aged men imagining they were Laurel and Hardy. *Moving*, which premiered in the Abbey in 1992, came out of an urge to write an Irish *Our Town*, playwright Thornton Wilder's evocation of birth, life and death in a small New Hampshire community, filmed by Sam Wood in 1940.

'Like Wilder's people, the Irish are so community-conscious, so aware of the past, and they don't like change. They cling to the importance of small things.'

However, once he started writing *Moving* it broke free of Wilder and became a completely different play. As in *Da* and *A Life*, the theme is memory and the interplay between the present and the past, between the characters and the places where they live. Although there is a thirty-year gap between Act 1 and Act 2, the characters moving into a new house do not age at all. They are the same people at the same age. The act of moving into a new house and the conflicting emotions it triggers becomes a teasing metaphor for the tug of the past and the promise of the future:

> It's the old Jimmy Stewart thing in Frank Capra's *It's a Wonderful Life*. What if I hadn't been born? Or what if I'd been born thirty years earlier? That's the game I'd like the audience to play. Capra's films were beautifully made. You just sat back and saw the master craftsman at work and every effect on the audience was beautifully calculated. He got the last juice out of a scene.

*Moving*, juxtaposing as it does the social attitudes and realities of Ireland in the 1950s and 1980s, is the nearest Jack came to a political play. He always had a loathing for theatre that peddles a political or a sociological view. As with Graham Greene, he kept his politics for his journalism. His plays aspire to no more than inviting an audience in out of the rain, entertaining them for a couple of hours and then sending them out feeling as good as when they came in. 'If I'm saying something, it's with a small *s*.'

He never felt comfortable in the role of an Irish literary figure, although it hurt him when his work was sometimes treated condescendingly by critics because of its accessibility and because, like Woody Allen, he was so prolific. He once joked that Bernard Farrell and himself were the only two talented playwrights in Ireland, all the others being geniuses.

Apart from being brought to the pictures by his mother, the biggest family treat was a tram ride into Dublin every Christmas to see the Jimmy O'Dea pantomime:

> And if my father was awfully flush we'd go to the Olympia as well to see Jim 'Howya' Johnson. It was the age before the microphone. I can still hear the principal boy smacking her thigh, this great whack, and her voice echoing loud and clear, 'I say, mother, what are we going to do now that the baron is coming?' And the mother would always be Jimmy O'Dea, whether as the Widow Twankey or as Jack-in-the-Beanstalk's mother.

The Queen's on Pearse Street, once home of the troupe of comics and singers, the Happy Gang, offered slightly more risqué pleasures than pantomime, particularly to an adolescent sneaking into the city with his pals:

> I remember being thrown out for smoking Craven A. The usherette said I was too young. The Queen's had the Queen's Moonbeams, who were poor cousins of the Theatre Royal's Royalettes. They had a routine where a building was on fire. It was all done by flicking streamers in front of the lights to simulate flames. Each girl was in tights and had a little hatchet – they were members of the fire brigade – and they went round and round in circles. One girl dropped her axe. We all waited for her to come around and pick it up and when she did her tights tore down the middle. She got the most brilliant ovation for a Saturday afternoon you ever heard in your life.

At the Theatre Royal he was once called up for Eddie Byrne's *Double or Nothing* quiz:

> The place was always full on a Saturday afternoon. I don't know what possessed me. I was fifteen and wearing my LDF uniform, a black coat that came three-quarters' way down. Byrne asked me four questions, on film of course. I was stuck on the last, 'What county was Brian Donleavy born in?' I knew the town – Portadown – but I didn't know the county was Armagh. But then I won the jackpot question, which was worth thirty-two shillings. My mother thought all our Christmases had come together when I went home with it.
>
> I'd never seen anything as vast as the stage of the Royal. As I sat there I could see little prompt boxes, and people looking out. And as I went off the stage, out of the darkness came a man's voice: 'Hard luck, kid.'

He went to the Theatre Royal every Saturday:

> The films were rotten, but it didn't matter: we went to see the variety. Noel Purcell and Eddie Byrne doing their married couple, very crude, Harry Bailey always in bad humour, the crooners Johnny Keyes and Babs de Monte, who used do exotic dancing, and Jimmy Campbell, with his little moustache, conducting the orchestra. We saw Danny Kaye and Edgar Bergen, and Tom Mix exhibiting rope twisting and using hand-mirrors to shoot over his shoulder. We never thought it could end. You couldn't possibly tear down a building the size of the Royal. But they did.

Frank Matchem's vast 4000-seat amphitheatre was demolished to make way for arguably Dublin's ugliest office block. With television usurping music hall as popular entertainment, the Capitol, which, like the Royal, combined live variety acts with a film programme, was replaced by British Home Stores, now Penneys. The Queen's survived as a stand-in for the burned-out Abbey Theatre before being closed, yet another sacrifice to the 1960s property boom.

Jack's 1994 forty-minute one-act play, *The Lilly Lally Show*, with Barbara Brennan as an old vaudeville performer auditioning in front of an unseen and unknown audience, is a homage to this lost era of music hall, a time of theatre as celebration:

> You see it in Fellini's *Roma*, the idea of the whole town coming together. We were all so innocent. It didn't matter if the costumes were shabby or the performers didn't know their lines. Once the lights came up, it was magic.
>
> One of the things I regret about theatre now is the virtual disappearance of the red curtain, the sense of never knowing what you were going to see when it went up. And I miss the footlights and the way they threw up the light, especially if someone came forward.

Ironically, television would become a natural outlet for the common touch and sense of comic timing he acquired hanging out in music halls. The success of his early plays, performed each year at the Dublin Theatre Festival, seemed to be leading him into films. He wrote a screenplay for his play *The Poker Session*. There were a couple of naughty English comedies, *Our Miss Fred* and *Percy* (banned, of course, in Ireland), in which most of his lines weren't used. But he soon realized that television offered a better opportunity to work with film without losing the control so important to a writer.

He brought to the new medium a meticulous craftsmanship that owes much to the Hollywood films he watched with his mother:

> The one thing movies did was give you a sense of form about your work. In the old movies, particularly the Warner Brothers in the 1930s, the scripts were absolutely honed down. If a Warner movie runs ninety minutes that's a very long movie. If the same film is remade today it runs two hours and fifteen minutes. But it's not only because they cut the script down. They had this wonderful stable of supporting actors like Ed Brophy, Hugh Herbert, Warren Hymer and Alan Jenkins. They always played the same part, just like in music hall. It was shorthand. They didn't have to build a character. You saw them and knew exactly what they were. And you were straight in the middle of it.

We first met around this time in 1971 through a letter Jack wrote to the *Sunday Independent* in my defence after a Galway priest took me to task for campaigning against Ireland's ludicrous system of film censorship and its routine policy of secretly mutilating or banning major films by notable directors such as Fellini, Bergman, Antonioni and Schlesinger.

'Art is not autonomous and art for art's sake breaks down when by intent and affect it is seductive towards evil,' claimed Fr James W. Kelly. He felt 'dirty' after seeing Jiri Menzel's *Closely Observed Trains*, which he denounced as 'an obscene film in conception with long moments organic to it of palpable sensuality and eroticism'. He argued that 'the art or quality film is much more dangerous than the cheap sex-violence stuff because it is by its very poetry more persuasive'. According to his warped logic, films were automatically objectionable if they were made by people leading 'immoral lives', in particular actresses such as Romy Schneider who spoke out in support of abortion and therefore 'had human blood on their hands'.

Anonymous phone calls were being made to my home at night while I was working on the late editions of the paper, threatening Julia and the children. Special Branch police called to the office over an article praising Andy Warhol's *Lonesome Cowboys*. The *Sunday Independent* was urged to dismiss me. So having Jack's unsolicited intervention in my support was helpful. 'It would probably never occur to our censors,' he wrote, 'that the facile happy ending, which portrays life as a boy-meets-girl-kills-the-villain-and-gets-rich daydream is the real pornography.'

Soon afterwards we appeared together on Gay Byrne's *Late Late Show*. We hit it off and he invited me with Julia to his house on Killiney Hill a few weeks later to watch the first screening of his play, *Stephen D*, which he had adapted for television. There were actors all over the place but we chatted mostly with his wife Paule, who loved movies nearly as much as he did. The daughter of a Belgian diplomat, she'd grown up in Hollywood and screen-tested as a child for *National Velvet* with Elizabeth Taylor.

She met Jack while he was acting in plays in the Land Commission drama group. They moved to England after their marriage where Jack became a top writer at Granada Television, making stars of Milo O'Shea and David Kelly with the hit comedy series *Me Mammy*. He scripted several films, writing *Great Catherine* for Peter O'Toole. *Interlude*, with Oskar Werner and Barbara Ferris, was undoubtedly his best film, a love story that wasn't cloying but had audiences reaching for their hankies.

They were now back in Ireland with their thirteen-year-old daughter Danielle, attracted by the Charlie Haughey tax break for writers. Their luxury Killiney bungalow was just over the hill from where Jack had grown up in Dalkey. Soon they would move to Colliemore Harbour, even closer to the village, before finishing up in Pilot View at Bullock Harbour just down the lane from The Club, his favourite Dalkey pub. Although Jack claimed it was just chance that drew him to Dalkey, the truth is that once back in Ireland a sense of the place and memories of his childhood would take over his imagination and flood into his writing to inspire, before the decade was over, his three greatest plays – the Tony Award-winning *Da*, *A Life* and *Summer*, and his classic memoir, *Home Before Night*.

*Home Before Night* is not so much an autobiography as a search for identity. The playwright Charlie, whose return from England for the funeral of his father sets up a dialogue with his younger self in *Da*, is now the narrator, Jack, trawling through memories of his actual childhood to make sense of who he has become. 'On his birth certificate his name was John Byrne, but in Dalkey he was Jack Keyes. His real self was somewhere between both names, for he had no wish to be the first and no right to be the second.'

By operating on two time levels – a favourite dramatic device used in *Da* and other plays – this real-life Jack confronts the immediacy of the experience of growing up in the 1930s with the balance of hindsight. The present tense 'I' de-romanticizes the 'he' that was. What might have been mawkish becomes savagely funny.

As a scholarship boy at Presentation College, Glasthule, he was followed home by boys who wanted to see for themselves the meanness of his cottage. When raffle books were being distributed in class the Brother missed him out, saying, 'No, Kizz, we don't want to be led into temptation.' Perhaps this was the makings of the columnist who would provide such biting commentary on the vanities of a middle-class Ireland that earlier rejected him but was now only too eager to suck up to his fame.

Although he eventually traced his lost mother, they never met. He couldn't bring himself to face her. It hurt just as much that he never knew his father. 'I used pretend Dennis Johnston was my father because he was a maverick. I felt in a sense a bit like him. If he'd ever found out he'd have been horrified.'

His cult column in *Hibernia* magazine achieved national notoriety when, over a paella – one of his favourite dishes, as long as it was cooked by Julia – he agreed to switch to the *Sunday Independent*, soon after Tony O'Reilly took over Independent Newspapers in 1974. The takeover provoked a massive sit-in that was eventually resolved by shrewd concessions to the unions involved. This emboldened the National Union of Journalists to blacklist Jack because he wasn't a member. The rules for membership of the union were designed to exclude non-journalists, effectively creating a closed shop. Arguing that this was a denial of freedom of expression I proposed Jack for membership, pointing out that he fulfilled the requirement that two-thirds of his earnings must come from writing. His application was approved.

When I quit the *Sunday Independent* in 1985 to become arts editor and associate editor of the *Sunday Tribune*, Jack was prepared to come with me. We agreed a deal with *Tribune* editor Vincent Browne over lunch at Patrick Guilbaud's restaurant. Tony O'Reilly was sitting a few tables away, a coincidence that Browne probably had engineered: he liked to get in people's faces almost as much as Jack.

A few days later Jack wrote to me, apologetically saying that he had received such a massive offer to stay at the *Sunday Independent* that he couldn't afford to say no. Vincent was shocked anyone could so quickly renege on a 'gentleman's agreement'. Julia was furious and wouldn't speak to Jack for quite a while. Ironically, when the *Tribune* got into financial difficulties some years later, Independent Newspapers bought into it with a 29-per-cent stake that kept it afloat until 2011.

A peculiarity of my friendship with Jack is that the only time we talked seriously to each other seemed to be in the course of interviews, of which there were many. Probably it had to do with his shyness and mine. We needed some formal context to allow us to open up. It may also explain his compulsion to reveal more about himself in his column than he ever did in conversation. Jack was generally more relaxed talking to women, and maybe it's the same with me, although not to the extent of the Jack who regaled readers of his column with accounts of lunches with glamorous women friends. Like all film buffs, he was starstruck. His Tony Award for *Da* gave him less of a thrill than the opportunity it afforded at the party afterwards to dance with Lauren Bacall.

'What do you know about women?' a friend asked in 1999 when he was writing *Love in the Title*, a play about three women. 'Well, I've been married for forty years,' he said. 'Exactly,' replied his friend.

The conceit of *Love in the Title* is that although the three women talk to each other as if it's the most natural thing in the world that they should be together, each of them is, in fact, living in her own time:

> I started off by having the two who are in period [costume] existing in the modern one's head. Then I said, to hell with this. Let them all talk to each other. No explanations. The audience will get used to it, like in the cinema. Once a

situation is presented for you, you say well it's there so it has to be true. So you accept it for what it is.

The device allows Jack to break down the generation gap that normally exists within a family and to arrive at unexpected truths by toying around with time and memory. Director Patrick Mason, who commissioned the play for the Abbey, encouraged Jack to become involved in rehearsals to a greater degree than he had with any of his previous plays, sitting down for days with his three actresses, Catherine Walshe, Karen Ardiff and Ingrid Craigie, adding and refining. 'Never did any of them say that a woman wouldn't say lines I had written. They accepted that these were women that could have been written by a woman.'

Arriving at such an intimate understanding of women didn't come readily to Jack:

I can remember a time when any woman in a play of mine was either a Madonna or a whore. You didn't see a woman as a person at all, you saw her as a conquest. You just wanted to go to bed with her, except there were no beds around when we were growing up. It takes a lot to leave that behind. It's a big achievement for any Irish man to get to like women. They've tended to see a woman more as a sexual machine. There's been a lot of Irish male hatred of women. When you start accepting a woman as a person you've actually to go back to square one, which alarms the woman to such a degree that probably nothing will ever happen. You only start getting to know women as people very late in life. It's very inconvenient and it's very rewarding. I wonder whether there are any happy marriages.

There's a line in *Love in the Title*, borrowed from Kierkegaard, to the effect that you have to live your life forward but you can only understand it backward:

Looking backwards I can understand a lot of my attitudes and a lot of my actions stem from the fact of having been adopted. With some people a feeling of rejection can result in taking revenge on women, as happened with Somerset Maugham who never really forgave his mother, whom he adored, for having died before he was ten. This may have warped his attitude to women. He really loathed women all his life. But other people who feel rejected may spend their lives looking for acceptance by women. When you look back, you know which one of these people you are, and you understand a lot of things about the way your life ran.

Some people faint at the sight of blood. With me, even the mere mention of it could trigger a sudden cold sweat. Seconds later I'd open my eyes wondering where I was. Coming out from a particularly gory B-movie at the Carlton I woke up abruptly thinking it was morning and I was in my bed, only to realize I was lying on the pavement on O'Connell Street with people walking by pretending not to notice. When Julia was pregnant with our first child there was a risk that because her blood was rhesus negative – a rare type prevalent among Basque women – she might need a massive blood transfusion on giving birth. It seemed a good idea to donate some of my own blood to the blood transfusion bank. All went well until in the waiting room afterwards a nurse gave me a gift pack with a blood-red pencil and pad and a brochure with colour illustrations of blood transfusions. I suddenly went hot and cold, and she caught me as I fell.

Thinking back it's possible that the swooning was caused by my shock as a small boy of dozing off one night to the reassuring murmur of adults talking downstairs only to be jerked awake by a shout of agony from my father. An ambulance was called and he was rushed to hospital with an acute appendicitis. When he came home a few days later, he began explaining in detail to the family the surgical procedure he had gone through. And I fainted.

The last time it happened was the first time I saw Mia Farrow. She was pregnant and lying naked on a bed. The tip of a knife scratched a line of blood across her stomach. The scene is early on in *Rosemary's Baby*, the Roman Polanski film based on Ira Levin's horror thriller about a gullible young New York housewife who dreams she is raped by the devil. The film was banned in Ireland, but this didn't apply to a private screening at the Guinness Film Society, which I attended as part of the campaign against censorship. Somehow I managed to stumble to the exit and the privacy of the bathroom before losing consciousness.

So here Mia is in real life years later in the summer of 1993, laughing with me about it. A brown mongrel terrier scampers about the hallway of a large mansion in its own grounds in the leafy Dublin suburb of Carrickmines, where she is living in secret with five of her eleven children while filming Jack's tongue-in-cheek murder mystery, *Widow's Peak*, her first film since separating from Woody Allen. 'The film is the result of a chance meeting between my mother and Jack during which she informed him that she had never made a film with me. So he said he'd write one for her. One's life is shaped by these accidents, don't you think?'

Her mother Maureen O'Sullivan is best known for her role as Johnny Weissmuller's scantily clad Jane in the MGM Tarzan films. Born in Roscommon and brought to Hollywood in 1930 by tenor John McCormack to star opposite him in the musical, *Song O' My Heart*, she retired from acting after her marriage to writer-director John Farrow but made a comeback in 1986 in Woody Allen's *Hannah and Her Sisters* and Francis Coppola's *Peggy Sue Got Married*.

Steeped in the aura of American films of his childhood, Jack naturally was enthralled by O'Sullivan. 'Maureen took me by the arm and said, you mustn't be disappointed if I don't get to do the film because I'm getting on. When the film finally came about and I met Mia, it was as if her card had been marked. Her mother had said I was alright, that she could trust me, that I was on her side.'

This was after Farrow sensationally ended her twelve-year relationship with Allen over his affair with Soon-Yi, her twenty-year-old adopted daughter from her marriage to composer André Previn. From the moment he heard about the break-up, Allen's name became unmentionable in Jack's presence.

By the time *Widow's Peak* finally got under way on location in Kilkenny, O'Sullivan felt she was too old. 'So I ended up playing the part intended for her,' says Farrow. Her character is a prim spinster in a town full of widows, whose ongoing romance with the local dentist is jeopardized by the arrival of a flirtatious stranger, Natasha Richardson. There's a twist ending prompted by Jack's addiction to detective stories, an addiction so strong that he and Paule would participate in 'murder' weekends at which hotel guests were given clues to a murder and invited to find the killer. 'All my life I wanted to write something that didn't make sense until the final sentence,' he said. 'This is like a John Dickson Carr murder thing, except that it's done for laughs.'

*Widow's Peak*, which had only moderate box-office success, wasn't his mother's sort of film:

> I think it probably wouldn't have enough action for her. But she'd enjoy the scenery. Colour films were few and far between in her day ... she'd been going to the cinema since 1906. The first colour we saw was *The Trail of the Lonesome Pine*. She told me, 'Oh, my eyes hurt.' She liked Westerns and gangster films best. She hated what she called the love stuff and codology.

**Mia Farrow, hiding out in Cabinteely, Dublin, 1993.**

Farrow scoops the little dog up in her arms. Its paw hangs trustingly over her wrist. 'She's called Tipp after Tipperary,' she explains. 'I got her in the dog pound. We'll be bringing her back to the States with us.' It will join a chaotic menagerie of pets already ensconced in her Central Park apartment across the street from Allen's: throughout their affair they never shared the same apartment. 'I have a dog, three cats, three birds and the usual rodents.'

A call from her lawyer in New York interrupts her. Her two months in Ireland are only a partial escape from the trauma of an ongoing battle with Allen for custody of their three children. He's now on his way to Dublin to exercise visiting rights. 'I have this powerless feeling at the moment, like watching television and I can't change the channel.'

Satchel, aged five – fathered by Woody and later to change his name to Ronan Farrow and be accepted at Yale Law School at sixteen, winning a Rhodes scholarship at twenty-three – can be heard playing around the house with Elisa, seven and Tam, twelve. 'They had their best time when we had a week in Kilkenny. They stayed on a farm. They fed lambs with a baby bottle, got eggs from under the hens, chased the chickens, and patted the cows and horses. They loved it. I feel that I've come home.'

She's not been back to Ireland since her mother brought her to Boyle in Roscommon to meet her grandparents when she was three. A garrison town, her grandfather was stationed there as a major. 'But the O'Sullivans originally came from Cork. There was a mayor or two, way back.'

She has haunting memories of her first night here:

I remember being so tired I had to be carried off the plane. There was an electrical storm and all the lights went out in the house. I was sitting straight up in my bed, staring out the window, looking at the lightning flashing. I saw this flickering light coming down the hall, a warmer light. A man was standing there. I didn't know who he was. It was the first time I'd seen a moustache. He was holding a candle and his other hand was in a black sling. His eyes were the saddest I'd ever seen. And he said, 'What are you crying for, a great big girl like you?' I said, 'I want my mummy.' He said, 'Mummy is tired, let her sleep.' And then I said, 'Are you Jesus?' He said, 'Not at all. I'm your grandfather.'

Mia was born in Los Angeles in 1945, the third of seven children. She was christened Maria de Lourdes, which became abbreviated to Mia because she couldn't pronounce it:

We lived in Beverly Hills and in the summer in a house in Malibu until I was twelve, when we moved to Spain. And then we moved constantly. It was wrenching. I was very upset having to leave my friends and the life I had made for myself at school … being snapped out of that. I look back on it as being idyllic, although I suppose it couldn't have been. But until about nine it seemed perfect. We had a beautiful garden. We had nannies. I read a lot. We were swimming all the time.

She was a Hollywood child, going to school with the children of other stars (her best friend at kindergarten was Liza Minnelli) but her parents didn't talk shop at home. She never saw their films although occasionally the children were taken on the set when John Farrow was shooting a Western. 'I remember sitting in John Wayne's chair. I had to be helped up onto it. He seemed like a mountain when he walked in.'

She worshipped her father. 'We'd go to bookshops and browse and walk home with a book under each arm.' He had converted to Catholicism when he married her mother. His Jesuit friends were always coming to visit. 'He was very tight with them. They'd come over and I had to pour two fingers of Scotch, straight into a glass. It launched an evening of philosophical debate. I'd sit on the stairs and listen.'

Farrow, who won an Oscar with his screenplay for *Around the World in Eighty Days*, was a writer on the side. He wrote a history of the papacy and a biography, *Damian the Leper*. 'The Damian book gave me a terror of leprosy. Even though there was no leprosy as far as I knew in Beverly Hills, I scoured my skin looking for the telltale signs, sure I was going to get it.'

When she was nine she was struck down, not with leprosy but with polio. 'That wiped the smile off my face. It changed everything. I see it as the end of my childhood. I was snatched out of that, into the public wards. I became aware of how many people were howling with pain.'

Coming home several weeks later was even more traumatic:

Even the grass had been reseeded to avoid contamination. The swimming pool had been drained. There were painters painting the house. All the carpets had been torn out. The sofa had been reupholstered. The dog had been given away and the children moved out to Malibu. Everyone was afraid they'd get polio. And I was terrified I'd give it to them. I had brought fear into the family.

Then her elder brother Michael was killed in a plane crash while training to become a pilot. 'He was the one in the family I could really talk to, the bright hope. It was my first death, and one from which I have never recovered. But as my mother always says, push on. She's been right there all my life.'

Some might say Mia's compulsion to have children – whether her own or adopted – comes from some longing to recreate her lost childhood. Although she had no children by her first husband, Frank Sinatra, whom she married when she was twenty and divorced two years later, she had twins when she married the composer André Previn in 1970:

The Vietnam War was going on and one was very aware that there were all these children needing homes. So we adopted wonderful little Park and that turned out so great another one came along. The next thing we had six and it's up to eleven now. People seem to think all my children are babies, but of course the first six have grown up.

Her original ambition was to be a paediatrician, working in Africa. But when she was seventeen her father dropped dead of a heart attack. 'My mother and I had to go to work. I never got back to school. I was lucky to get work right away as an actress.' She made her stage debut in 1963 in *The Importance of Being Earnest* and got a part in *Guns at Batasi*, which led to her role as the waif-like Alison MacKenzie in the television series, *Peyton Place*. But by then she'd fallen under the spell of Salvador Dali:

> I met him in the elevator in the St Regis Hotel in New York going to a party just before my eighteenth birthday. The doors opened right into the party on the top floor. I couldn't get out, the noise was too much for me. Then the doors closed and I noticed this strange man with a moustache who had come up with me. He said, 'Bonjour. One more time?' And I said, 'Alright.' We went up and down about three times and then he introduced himself. 'I am Dali. I'm completely crazy.'

The Spanish surrealist artist was living in the hotel with his wife Gala, 'a mysterious and wonderful woman with whom I also became friendly. We had many years of laughs. I remember him telling me that if I wanted a big change in my life, just put my shoes on the wrong feet. He gave me another way of looking at things.'

He tried without avail to persuade her to go to Spain with him. 'He had his time mapped out – a certain time in Paris, a certain time in Spain, a certain time in New York. He'd leave New York every year just before St Patrick's Day saying, "Everything is becoming too green."'

The anguish of her childhood and the death of her brother and father made her older beyond her years. Bette Davis, who met her in Spain when she was twelve, recalled: 'I saw a lonely little girl, Mia, who was born an old soul.' Lisa Minnelli sensed this too, saying: 'Mia has an uncanny sensitivity about people. She's so wise it's spooky. There's something so open and tender about her that people always want to protect her, but she is stronger than all of us.'

The playwright Thornton Wilder, author of *Bridge of San Luis Rey* and *Our Town* – the inspiration for *Da*, and one of Jack's favourite plays – became another father figure: she still has over forty letters he wrote to her. They were introduced by Ruth Gordon:

We all lived at Martha's Vineyard for a while every summer. I saw Thornton every day. If we didn't know something Ruth would say, 'Go and look it up in Thornton.' There was very little he didn't know. He loved hanging out in pubs. He liked to read out loud what he'd written that day. His sister would put a little lectern in front of him. He'd sit in his favourite seat, put on his glasses and read. He liked to hear it, I guess. And I liked to listen.

When she met Frank Sinatra while he was shooting *Von Ryan's Express* on the lot adjoining *Peyton Place*, she wasn't put off by the fact that he was thirty years older than her: if anything it was part of his appeal. Besides, he had the approval of her mother who told her, 'Age hasn't anything to do with romance.'
She knew little or nothing about Sinatra:

He hadn't really entered my world at all. I'd been at convent school in England since I was thirteen. We had only Gregorian chant around our house. I wasn't sure about who he was exactly. But I liked him straight away. I never stopped to this day. I think of how patient he must have been with me. I remember him referring to Tommy, and I said, 'Who's Tommy?' I just didn't know. And he explained very patiently who Tommy Dorsey was. He didn't get annoyed.

What did annoy him was her decision to appear in *Rosemary's Baby*. He didn't want her having an independent career and wanted her to film *The Detective* with him instead. When she refused he sent his lawyer to serve her divorce papers on the set in front of the cast and crew while she was shooting a scene for Polanski. Their marriage had lasted just two years, but they remained close friends. She refused any alimony, taking only a rocking chair.
Sinatra gave her a first taste of classical music: 'We'd listen to Vaughan Williams together. But my real introduction to classical music came from André Previn. A friend brought us together when he was living in London and separated from Dory Previn. Oddly enough he now lives near me in Connecticut. So I see him regularly. We salvaged hopefully what was best from our marriage.'
Soon after her divorce from Previn in 1979, Michael Caine introduced her to Woody Allen over supper in Elaine's in Manhattan. Although she'd made some significant films – Joseph Losey's *Secret Ceremony*, *John and Mary* with Dustin Hoffman, and Jack Clayton's version of F. Scott Fitzgerald's *The Great Gatsby* – her thirteen films with Allen established her as a serious actress. If *Annie Hall* was a graceful homage to his earlier muse, Diane Keaton, in *Purple Rose of Cairo* he imbues Mia with a similar immortality as a starstruck 1930s fan suddenly confronted by the lover of her dreams, who steps out from a film

to join her, but then the real actor appears and she's forced to choose between reality and fantasy.

Whatever about the pain and hurt of Mia's break with Allen, they are destined to be linked forever on the screen. 'I haven't thought about it like that, maybe because I haven't seen most of the pictures. Watching your own movies is a form of masochism. But I do have the movies we made together. He is a good film-maker.' It's obvious she can hardly bring herself to talk about him. 'There's so much out there flying around and none of it has been said by me. I am proud of that.'

A few days later Jack, who'd set up the interview and obviously enjoyed the covert nature of his role in leading me to her hideaway, invites us to a farewell at Roly's Bistro in Ballsbridge. Mia is emotional. She is leaving for the States the next day. 'If my mother hadn't made that remark to you about never having acted with me, we wouldn't be here talking about her, and who knows what else,' she says. Outside on the street we all embrace. She is so slight and soft I am afraid I'll crush her in my arms as we kiss goodbye. 'I'll be back,' she says. 'I think of living here.'

•　•　•

Woody Allen is fretting about the sunlight. It floods through the window of the Dorchester hotel in Mayfair, causing him to cringe. 'Close the blinds,' he pleads.

Don't you like the sun? 'Yes, but I don't *love* it.'

The room is now almost in darkness. 'You can open the blinds a certain amount,' he concedes. 'It's just that the sun was coming *directly* at me.'

With the blinds just a quarter open, it seems the sun is still too much for him. 'Close it a bit more … no, not that one, the other … that's fine.'

We shake hands. He's so thin and fragile with his pale freckled skin and big horn-rimmed spectacles, it's eerily like being with Mia: you fear you might damage him, too, just by touching him. One seems as vulnerable as the other.

As a small boy he hated the hot humid summers in Brooklyn so much he'd spend all his time in the dark of the air-conditioned movie houses, watching mystery movies. Or just stay home, reading. When he wakes up in the morning and looks out the window, he only feels good if it's raining, 'Because everything looks much prettier in overcast weather. If we go out in the morning and it's sunny, we usually go back in and shoot inside. If it's rainy, not too rainy but cloudy, then we shoot outside because the colour is much better.'

There's a scene in his comedy, *Bullets Over Broadway*, shot against a backdrop of flowers near the conservatory in New York's Central Park – a favourite location – in which budding playwright John Cusack fulsomely declares his undying love for leading lady Dianne Wiest, and she covers his mouth with her hand telling him, 'Please ... don't speak.' 'If we had shot that on a sunny day, the flowers would not have looked as beautiful,' says Allen. 'But it was a flat, cloudy day, so we got better colour saturation.'

*Bullets Over Broadway* is the third film 58-year-old Allen has completed since his break with Mia. He is still with her adopted daughter Soon-Yi. When I arrived at the Dorchester I saw her in the foyer, going out shopping. They are only briefly in London: a private jet is waiting at Heathrow to fly them back to the States in three hours' time.

Allen maintains that the furore surrounding their court battles and disputed allegations of child abuse levelled over his relationships with some of Mia's other adopted children was much less than it seemed in the tabloids:

> The perfect existential nightmare is that I go to the doctor and he finds a spot on my lung. But this wasn't existential. This was a civil matter. It wasn't as bad or as interesting as you would think from the outside. I got on with my work, completing our last film, *Husbands and Wives*. My lawyer had the most to do. But if you read the press accounts of it, you would have thought that the house was on fire and there were ambulances and, you know, it was Bosnia.
>
> It was a lot duller than that, just a couple of calls every day from the lawyer, a couple of things I had to sign now and then. And the proof is that I did my normal amount of work. It was not such a dislocation as you would think. It was not fun. But up until then, life was not so much fun either ... you know?

He is perhaps being somewhat disingenuous. Whatever about being a dull and tiresome experience for him, it was anything but for Mia. Her distress was particularly apparent when he arrived in Dublin with Soon-Yi and moved into a suite at the Shelbourne Hotel. His offence in her eyes was less that he was unfaithful than that he was unfaithful with Soon-Yi: this was to her a betrayal, which made everything else between them suddenly suspect.

The sheer brilliance of his films and his self-deprecating humour make it difficult to believe the worst of him, although ironically the theme of *Bullets Over Broadway* is that terrible things shouldn't be accepted from a person just because that person is an artist. 'I'm crazy about Leni Riefenstahl's films, but I don't excuse her as a person because she produced great art,' he says.

It's much the same point Jack made when he entered the censorship fray in my support, and argued that films shouldn't be censored just because people might disapprove of a director's or actor's personal life. So I didn't consider coming to the Dorchester to interview Allen to be a betrayal of Jack and his friendship with Mia, no more than he considered it a betrayal to fictionalize my family in his novel, *A Wild People*, which opens with a reimagining of one Julia's dinner parties.

Allen, like Jack, draws his material from what is close to him. His screen persona developed out of his stand-up comedy act at the Greenwich Village Duplex in 1961, 'You know, the standard fare, insecurity in life, nervousness and insecurity towards women, inability to have good relationships, fear and cowardice.' The dilemmas his characters experience are exaggerations of his own. It all gets mixed around in his imagination, coming out different yet familiar. Sometimes this may even anticipate life. *Husbands and Wives*, his last film with Mia, is about the break-up of a marriage over a young girl. 'It's strictly an act of imagination,' he says. 'I finished the script long before anything happened that you read in newspapers.'

He has lost none of his admiration for Mia as an actress, particularly for her performance as a Mafia moll who never takes off her sunglasses in *Broadway Danny Rose*, 'a very brave thing for her to do, because she had to act the whole picture without ever using her eyes'.

He surrounds himself with people he knows and can rely on. Over the years he has built up an ensemble of actors and crew, almost like a family, with whom he works again and again. All his films after *The Purple Rose of Cairo* were shot by the same cameraman, Carlo di Palma. Before that, going back to *Annie Hall*, he used Gordon Willis. He wrote his first two films, *Take the Money and Run* and *Bananas*, with Mickey Rose, with whom he used go to baseball games as a boy. Another close friend, Marshall Brickman, helped him write *Sleeper*, *Annie Hall*, *Manhattan* and *Manhattan Murder Mystery*. Doug McGrath, his co-author on *Bullets Over Broadway*, is a personal friend, too.

'Usually I write by myself. But every number of years I get lonely just sitting in a room, because I write at least one script every year, and it's an ordeal. So I like to collaborate with somebody, just for the sheer company of it. And I've always picked friends.'

Even the music he uses is culled from his own huge personal collection of records:

**Woody Allen on the cover of the SUNDAY TRIBUNE magazine, 1995.**

I have a million records in my editing room and we just look at the film and I get some idea of the type of thing I'd like and I put that record next to it and I look at it and either I was right, it's perfect, or it doesn't work at all and I try another, and another. Gradually, and it doesn't take long, maybe a couple of days, the scenes come alive. It's amazing the difference when you see a scene with a record and without a record.

If studios leave Allen free, allowing him final cut on all his films, he is equally free with his collaborators and actors. 'When I work with the cast of a film I always tell them that they can take my dialogue and throw it away. They can use as much of it as they want. They can change it or make it longer or shorter, whatever they like.'

That's why he shoots in masters, entire scenes that keep all the characters in view, just letting the camera roll and keeping it on the actors, catching whatever they do or say. There's no cutting or coverage. When he shoots a scene, that's the way it is, he won't fix it in the editing room. If it doesn't work, he'll reshoot the whole scene the next day. He's even reshot a whole film.

It's all to do with getting the script right and then finding the right actors and crew to bring it alive. 'I've replaced people. The problem is usually our own mistake and it's embarrassing. But I have found actors and actresses that didn't gel. They didn't get with it and they couldn't do it. Perhaps they gave a good reading, but when it comes to do it, they couldn't, or had some other problem, and we replaced them.'

With his track record for creating juicy acting roles, big-name stars are forever soliciting parts:

Sometimes they call up and say, you know, 'I'll do anything, I just want to be in your movie, big or small', and I'll send them something and they'll turn it down. But some of them are sincere about it. Jodie Foster just wanted to do anything in *Shadows and Fog*. I wish I had a bigger role for her. Madonna seemed perfect for the role of the prostitute in *Shadows and Fog*, but I didn't think we could ever get her, that she would want to do something that was so minuscule, but she was happy to do it. Sometimes it coincides with their schedules. They might say, well I do have two days in the next six months, it's perfect. If we'd offered Madonna a bigger part, it would have tied her up for some months and probably she'd have said no.

Although his films are invariably rooted in the upper-middle-class New York milieu he understands so well, he's frequently obliged to turn to non-American actors: Liam Neeson in *Husbands and Wives*; Michael Caine in *Hannah and Her Sisters*; Denholm Elliott in *September*; Ian Holm in *Another*

*Woman*; Jim Broadbent in *Bullets Over Broadway*. 'It's very hard in the US to find a regular man. We have these tough guys and heroes. Al Pacino, Bob De Niro and Jack Nicholson, they're kind of macho. But if you just want a regular man, the sort years ago who could have been like Fredric March, they're not so easy to find.'

He hardly ever parts with anyone. His two wives remained close friends: Harlene Rosen, whom he married in his late teens (they decided to divorce after a Bermuda holiday because 'the vacation is over in two weeks, but a divorce is something you have forever'); and Louise Lasser, who starred in *Bananas* – as has Diane Keaton, always one of the first to see his films.

It's all a bit too incestuous for some. 'God knows,' complained George C. Scott, 'many people say he's the funniest in the world, but I haven't been able to appreciate his humour. I find him neurotic.' But that's the whole point about Allen:

> You know, people come up to me at parties and say, 'What's wrong?' and I say, 'Nothing, it's just the way I am.' Generally I'm a gloomy pessimistic type and always have been. Let me put it this way. I wasn't happy when I was younger. I wasn't happy in my adult life. I wasn't happy last year, and I'm not happy now.

• • •

Jack is sitting awkwardly on a green leather couch in his Pilot View apartment above Bullock Harbour. 'I slipped on the bathroom floor going to bed and crushed the vertebrae,' he says. 'I don't know how when Laurel and Hardy fell down they never hurt themselves. It feels like a dead weight hanging off one's shoulders. It's a bloody nuisance. I've had to cancel holidays.'

He hasn't been himself for much of 2006 but is hoping to make it to a birthday tribute at the Pavilion Theatre in Dún Laoghaire on 9 November when he will be eighty. It's been arranged by Bernard Farrell and Margaret Dunne; Patrick Mason will direct excerpts from some of his plays and David Kelly will be the presenter. Probably no other Irish writer has created as many roles for actors in such a wide range of forms yet he remains something of an outsider in the arts world, more feared than admired. Brendan Behan's writer-brother Brian quipped once that 'Leonard has no enemies in Dublin, it's his friends who hate him.'

It took months before his fracture was diagnosed. 'I went to my GP because I wanted to get a signature for my bus pass. I ended up with a week in hospital and a man's hand up my backside. I woke up from a local anaesthetic and was told I had an ulcer and a touch of cirrhosis and a spinal problem.'

He sips from a glass of water without pleasure. 'I'm supposed to drink twelve glasses of liquid a day. Once in a while I feel I could use a drink. But I've been told not to, so I don't.'

There was a time in the casualty ward at St Michael's Hospital in Dún Laoghaire when it didn't seem he would survive, the cirrhosis was so far advanced, but he somehow pulled through. He was even well enough to come to lunch a few weeks later, although when he returned home he went to sleep and didn't get up until the next afternoon. But he made it to the opening night of *Da* at the Pavilion Theatre.

Paule died six years ago from an asthmatic attack. He points to the window looking out on the bay and across to Howth. 'There, by the door onto the veranda, trying to get some air while we were waiting for the paramedics. She was happy here. There was a good feel to it.'

She had her life and he had his. They were inseparable yet often quarrelled. The contradictions in their relationship were its strength. Like Groucho Marx he didn't belong to any club that would have him – and that included Aosdána – opting instead for the companionship of his own Dalkey local, The Club. He regularly has lunch at the Sichuan in Stillorgan with Farrell.

He preferred the company of women to men, and Paule understood. She didn't mind him taking other women to restaurants. It would all be in his column, anyway. If he strayed too far, she never knew or didn't want to know.

They loved to travel together or with Danielle, whether club class by air or a stateroom with a balcony on cruise ships, but were perhaps happiest dawdling on a barge along the canals of the Loire Valley. Paule would sit back in the sun chatting while Jack took the wheel, pulling in wherever he got the sniff of a good restaurant. One evening when we moored at La Belle Anguille, a group of singers from a local choir began singing impromptu *a capella* after their meal. Jack was so moved he broke into tears.

But that's all over now. 'I can't throw a rope and it really needs two hands to handle the boat,' he says.

He no longer keeps a diary. 'I found out that Paule was reading it, so I stopped. I'm sorry in a way, but there was no place I could hide it. The last entry I did was the day Paule died. I didn't want to do it any more. We had our

*Intimacy with Strangers: A Life of Brief Encounters*

fights. But we sort of became reconciled not long before she died.'

After her death he began an email correspondence with Kathy Hayes, a paralegal from Philadelphia they'd met on a cruise. Eventually, there were so many emails he thought it would be simpler if he just persuaded her to come and live with him:

> I don't know how I got Kathy. I found her in a game of Trivial Pursuit in Cape Town. I don't know what in the world persuaded her to come here. I think she saw *Da* on the stage with Barnard Hughes … that may have done it. She now knows more people in Dalkey than I do. She'll talk to anybody. But me, I don't take the trouble and as a result I'm regarded generally as surly, which I'm not.

In the months after his birthday interview, Kathy kept us briefed on his ups and downs. Her 13 January email reported that 'his decline since his birthday has been acute. He slept through yesterday and doesn't know he missed a day and is very confused and dehydrated. His GP told us that it is time to get him into a nursing home.' A day later everything seemed changed for the better. 'Unbelievably, I got him dressed this morning and we took him to Dali's for lunch. It was a so-so experience. He still doesn't know how bad he is, and was better today than he's been for a week.'

Four days later he was back in the respiratory ward in St Michael's. 'He kept removing the drip and they had to reinsert, but he did calm down after I talked to him and he slept through the night … when he wasn't trying to remove the drip.' Danielle gave up her job in London and moved home to help care for him. Jack was finally allowed home on 1 February. 'He is sitting on the couch as I type and delirious to be here,' Kathy reported. 'The cats looked up from the cradle and they smiled, but they all stayed put.' After a week he was 'as mentally sharp as back before this decline started in October. He is working on finishing his book.'

The book is *The Devil for Grandeur*, which, with *Home Before Night* and *Out After Dark*, would complete his autobiography trilogy. 'I've just a chapter to go,' he'd told me before his birthday. 'It sums up my mother. I wrote about half of it and then I said, wait a minute, it's high time my mother got a look in. So I'll write a book where she was the devil for grandeur. She always wore her best hat. She was a great one for the social graces thing.'

He gave up his columns in the *Sunday Independent*. 'I don't fancy going back to it,' he'd said, but it was so much part of him he couldn't resist writing the odd one whenever he had the strength. 'The deadline is a bit of a strain as you get old. I find it easier to write a book. There's no collaboration involved.

That's a great bonus, not to have a director and cast. I love actors, but not necessarily in my plays.'

His big disappointment was his failure to find a home for what he intended as his last play. It's called *Magicality* and is about the old theatrical fit-ups. 'It's a skit on Pinteresque dramas, the long pauses. People think highly of it but nobody wants to do it. The Abbey say they want a play about the new Ireland. They don't seem to realize that the new can be in the old.'

Plans were going ahead for his marriage to Kathy. She finally got approval for her two American divorce papers: getting the documents in Ireland had been a real stumbling block. For a while Jack was well enough to do his own emails again. 'Went to Woolworth's yesterday,' he wrote to me. 'Saw the Hope Diamond and bought it.'

Sally Anne and Derry at l'Ecrivain put on a celebratory engagement dinner on 2 June, the anniversary of Kathy's arrival in Ireland in 2001. Their plan was to marry in the registry office a few weeks later, but it soon became clear that Jack was too weak to make a journey into town. The registrar agreed to perform the ceremony at Pilot View instead. 'I cannot cancel now or Jack will be crushed,' Kathy messaged.

Two months later she returned to her mother in Philadelphia. 'I have finally broken, physically, mentally, emotionally and cannot take care of J. on my own. J. is in bits, but I am slowly convincing him that I am coming back – he doesn't really believe it.' That night he'd fallen out of bed onto the night-stand, almost losing his eye. He screamed in pain and had to spend three hours at St Michael's.

Yet again he improved. Only his body had failed him. In his mind he was as stubborn as ever. He was well enough to come to us for lunch, and even tell a few anecdotes. Kathy had returned, and he had Danielle. There were setbacks, of course. He went back to St Michael's for treatment. The New Year came and went. He tried to book a holiday in the south of France.

But his falls were becoming more frequent. The doctor warned such episodes would just keep happening. Early in November 2008 he fell on the pavement outside Finnegan's in Dalkey and gashed his head open. He was taken to hospital by ambulance and given eleven stitches over his eye. He had broken his arm, too high up for a cast. He was brought home with a sling. Kathy went ahead with plans she had made to return to Philadelphia at the end of the week. Her last email ended: 'They still think I am coming back.' She didn't.

It took Jack weeks to accept the fact that she was gone. But not even her loss dampened his will to live. The last time I saw him he was sitting in his green leather chair, his arm still in a sling. 'The only disadvantage is that I can't raise my hand in a Nazi salute,' he said. He spoke clearly. His mind had lost none of its sharpness.

Bernard Farrell was with him the day before he died on 12 February 2009. 'I was trying to tell him about *Slumdog Millionaire* but got the title confused. "That's not much of a title," he said. As Farrell was going out the door, Jack said, 'Goodbye, Bernard.'

Going down the stairs and out into the night, Farrell realized that Jack had never called him by his name before. It was a final goodbye.

# SPRING

# six

Liam Neeson, Natasha Richardson,
Brian Friel and Julie Christie

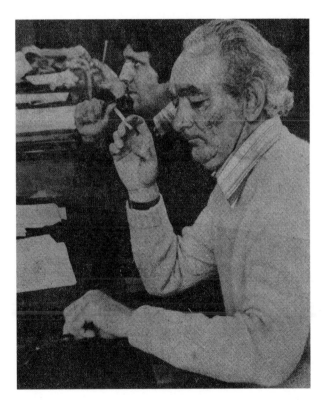

S pring breezes are blowing cherry blossoms from the trees out front. It's as if the pavement is covered by pink snow, a fleeting beauty revered in Japan as a metaphor for life. On my screen a video clip shows Liam Neeson as he makes his way onto a small podium at the British consulate in New York. He's wearing a flowing academic gown and moves with a loping grace unusual in so tall a man. He has just received an honorary doctorate from Queen's University, Belfast, where he majored in physics and maths in the early 1970s. It is his first public appearance since losing his wife Natasha Richardson after a freak fall on a Canadian ski slope two months ago. Sitting in the front row are their two sons, Michael, thirteen, and Daniel Jack, twelve. He gives them a wink.

He clutches notes of what he wants to say: whatever about actors never forgetting their lines, making a speech can be 'terrifying'. Then he looks up and speaks. He recalls arriving for classes at Queen's in 1972 the morning after the Bloody Sunday massacre in Derry, when British troops gunned down thirteen unarmed protesters, and being surprised to find the college largely empty. As he left to go home, striking students denounced him as a scab.

'I'd been totally unaware of the events the day before, and almost totally unaware of the larger grim struggle that was going on in Ireland,' he says. 'The message I took then was, "Boy, you've got to wake up. Get moving. You've got to get going." In a way, it's a message that a university always gives its students in the end: it's time to move on, get on with your life. I got on with mine, and I'm still getting on.'

An example of this is how just a few days after Natasha's funeral in New York he returned to Toronto, where he had been filming when he got the news of her accident. There were some scenes still to be completed in Atom Egoyan's erotic thriller, *Chloe*, in which he plays a man whose wife, Julianne Moore, suspects him of cheating and uses a call girl to catch him out. Neeson stepped back into character and did what was required. He then rejoined his grieving sons.

He quotes fellow Northerner Paul Muldoon on the restorative power of art, which 'builds from pain, from misery, from a deep-seated hurt, a monument to the human heart that shines like a golden dome among roofs rain-glazed and leaden'.

It's what he learned back in Northern Ireland from one of his first performances as an actor playing a young man trying to connect with his father in an amateur production of Brian Friel's *Philadelphia, Here I Come*, 'a play about the need to get on with your life, of the wrench of departure that comes with that need. I thought this is what I want to do for the rest of my life.'

Neeson was born into the Catholic minority in Ballymena, the Bible-thumping heartland of Ian Paisley. His parents worked at a local school, his father a caretaker, his mother a cook. The family lived in a small flat. 'You know how it was then,' he tells me. This is in 1994. 'Even to say the word sex was regarded as a kind of sin.' He jokes that the 1960s passed him by. 'All that free love and stuff? Forget it. I was locked away in my bedroom, reading *Hamlet*, I swear.' Well, maybe.

More often than not he was in the local state cinema, watching everything from a Sergio Leone Western to *Women in Love*, or training at the All Saints youth club where he developed a powerful left jab that, combined with his long reach and towering six-foot-four build, nearly won him an All-Ireland youth heavyweight title, but left him instead with a broken nose.

Perhaps because he grew up the baby in a family of sisters he was in no hurry to start dating, but when he did he made up for lost time, particularly when he was finding his way as an actor at the Abbey and the Gate in Dublin, where he'd hang out in Sheehan's pub with Neil Jordan, Gabriel Byrne, Garret Keogh and Jim Sheridan.

'Sure we all knew each other then, for heaven's sake. Dublin was a village. It still is.'

John Boorman saw his Lenny in *Of Mice and Men* and cast him as Sir Gawain in his Arthurian saga *Excalibur*. He fell in love with Helen Mirren who was playing Morgan le Fey ('She was so sexy. I thought, Gosh, that's Helen Mirren') and moved to London to live with her. Unable to get acting jobs, he killed time painting her flat while she was off acting. He brought her to meet his family at their tiny terraced home in Corlea Gardens. 'You couldn't imagine a family fitting in there, let alone a family of six,' she told friends.

Being cast as the mute in *Suspect* in 1987 brought him to Hollywood, where his quiet charm led to romances with a string of stars including Julia Roberts, whom he met on the set of *Satisfaction*. Natasha Richardson spotted him in Sam Raimi's cult horror hit, *Darkman*, as an avenging scientist whose face is disfigured and most of the time wears a mask. She was about to stage Eugene O'Neill's *Anna Christie*, a drama about a woman with a shady past whose passion is reawakened by a sailor. She was looking for an actor to play opposite her 'who is desired by every woman in the world – but who would fall in love with only one'. Their electrifying chemistry (critic John Lahr described him as a 'sequoia of sex') clicked offstage as well, leading to her divorce from producer Richard Fox.

Neeson moved from Los Angeles and they found a house in upstate New York. He became a father and settled into married life like, as Jordan remarked, 'a stallion brought to bay'.

Jordan, who made his directorial debut with *Angel*, a revenge thriller set in the North, had been the first to see Neeson as a natural flawed hero. He'd no hesitation lining him up for the title role in a Michael Collins film he'd written but was struggling to finance. Because of Collins' ferocious ruthlessness, he needed an actor with whom audiences would readily identify. 'Liam has an immutable likeability,' Jordan says. 'He could bury his mother in concrete and you would still sympathize with him.'

It would take Hollywood over twenty films finally to figure out this quality, and then only after Steven Spielberg, prompted by *Anna Christie*, cast him as the intriguingly ambivalent Oskar Schindler in the Oscar-winning *Schindler's List*. By now Jordan, with clout from the box-office success of *Interview with a Vampire*, finally had backing for *Michael Collins*. However, he hesitated about casting Julia Roberts as Kitty Kiernan opposite Neeson because 'she and Liam had been an item and one is always worried when actors have had a prior relationship, but here the worries were unfounded'.

**Liam Neeson signing as a freeman of Ballymena, Co. Antrim, January 2013.**

'Julia desperately wanted to do it,' says Neeson. 'The irony is that she first heard of Collins from me, because I'd known her off and on for ten years. And she worked bloody hard on it. I'd keep telling her, when I'd see her with her dialect coach, to take comfort in the fact that everyone was trying to do a different accent, not just her.'

His multilayered portrayals of Schindler and Collins brought offers of other real-life roles. But when writer-director Bill Condon approached him to portray Alfred Kinsey, the pioneering Harvard zoologist whose research uncovered the sexual secrets of Americans, it didn't feel right. 'I just didn't see the fit,' he says,

Intimacy with Strangers: A Life of Brief Encounters

but I've been a big fan of Bill since his James Whale biopic *Gods and Monsters*, so I listened to an audio tape of Kinsey delivering a lecture a year before he died in 1956. He's introduced on the stage in some huge auditorium in LA. He starts talking about sex. It's a very frail weak voice. But about five minutes in it takes on an extraordinary clarity. After twenty minutes, when the tape unfortunately cuts out, he's sounding like a thirty-year-old man. And that gave me the key. Of course … the man is a teacher.

Neeson himself was briefly a teacher at St Mary's teaching college in Belfast. 'A very bad teacher,' he insists. 'But I've two sisters who are exceptional teachers. That gave me enough of a link to think, oh yeah, that's the way in. He just loved disseminating knowledge. That's his *raison d'être*. It was a clue that got me into that whole process of building up a role.'

Having grown up in no-nonsense Ballymena, he is not inclined to make a big deal about anything he does as an actor. 'A role is just something to hang up on a rack when I go home at night and put it on again the next day.' He doesn't consciously dig into his psyche looking for neuroses to draw on. 'Of course for all actors there's some process that happens. But it's like a dog smelling where it's going. A thing feels right or it doesn't feel right, and that's it.'

Unlike Kinsey, who was in rebellion against the rigid purity of his home life, Neeson had understanding parents. When he was a teenager he found they'd slipped a Catholic sex manual between the pages of one of his boxing magazines.

To look like Kinsey, Neeson adopted the same short-cropped frizzy haircut:

That was the only resemblance I could get between him and myself. That and the bow tie. As he got older he became very weighty and doughy physically, a flabby kind of man. So I did the opposite. I lost weight to make me look frailer and more vulnerable, which is how he always was. He shouldn't have lived beyond eighteen. He had rickets, which leads to curvature of the spine as you get older. So there were things I could emulate there. But I don't look like him at all.

Although Kinsey concluded that there's no norm for human sexuality, which prompted him to explore his own bisexual nature, he was married to and lived his entire adult life with a smart freethinking student, Clara McMillen, portrayed in the film by Laura Linney who also played Neeson's wife in Arthur Miller's *The Crucible* and later in *Love Actually*. 'We're like an old married couple,' Linney once joked to me.

'The paradox about Kinsey is that he was blissfully happy,' says Neeson. 'He experimented with his own sexuality – although not as much as people thought – and used it as a springboard to empathize with people he was interviewing. But his marriage was absolutely bedrock. If anything, the film is a love story between a man and a woman.'

So perhaps Neeson has more in common with Kinsey than he recognizes. He, too, found happiness in marriage. Even when their careers took them apart, he and Natasha made a point of seeing each other every month. *Kinsey* was shot on location in Manhattan and New Jersey, which meant he was never far from home. He'd relax by taking off on his 1989 Harley Davidson. He hit a deer while motorcycling in Connecticut in 2000, fracturing his right pelvis and suffering multiple abrasions to his legs. A passing motorist found him crawling by the roadside. Although limping badly, it didn't stop him filming Martin Scorsese's *Gangs of New York*. 'You just get on with things,' he says.

• • •

When Natasha Richardson was four, her actress mother Vanessa Redgrave divorced her father, the bisexual director Tony Richardson, because he was having an affair with Jeanne Moreau. Two years later Redgrave had a baby by Franco Nero, who had played Lancelot to her Guinevere in *Camelot*.

Little Natasha was too young to understand. All she wanted was that somehow they'd become a family again. 'I remember I used to have a fantasy that if I saved up all my pocket money and sent red roses to my mum from my dad, it would bring them back together again,' she says

It's winter, 1998. We're at the Dorchester hotel in Mayfair, talking about *The Parent Trap*. Two eleven-year-old girls meet at summer camp and realize that they're remarkably alike, which isn't surprising: they're identical twins, separated after birth by the break-up of their parents. One was brought up in London by their mother (played by Richardson) who's now a top fashion designer, the other in California by their vineyard-owner father, Dennis Quaid. Naturally each wants to meet the parent they've never known so they swop places, pretend to be each other and go home to each other's house. Their dream is that they'll reunite their parents and all live happily together ever after as a normal family.

'What I longed for was the normal, too,' says Richardson. She's curled up on a couch, her long blonde hair swept back over her shoulder. 'My childhood wasn't the kind of one where your life is the same every day. There was the travelling, being in different worlds.'

Her mother had become a leading figure in the Workers' Revolutionary Party, taking part in Ban the Bomb and anti-Vietnam War protests. 'She wasn't always there with the tea on the table when I got home from school.'

*The Parent Trap* is a Hollywood eulogizing of the family ideal not just of Richardson's dreams but of most Americans. Never mind that the parents are played by fabulously beautiful stars and live fabulously affluent lives, or that the little girl – both twins are played by eleven-year-old Lindsay Lohan – has all the looks and savvy of the child star she is. Movie stars have always functioned primarily as romantic ideals. As American professor Virginia Wright Wexman argues, 'the relationship between Hollywood stars and their audience involves the stars' ability to model cultural norms and practices for a society that is largely bereft of more traditional modes of transmitting values'.

What's intriguing about end-of-millennium Hollywood is the way it has increasingly picked up on a white middle-class American longing for a reassertion of traditional family values and concerns. Time and again family groupings, put under threat, survive against all odds and are enriched by the struggle.

While this is blatant in *The Parent Trap*, it also underlies a surprisingly wide range of current American mainstream films. *As Good as it Gets* turns a pathologically antisocial Jack Nicholson into a suitable partner for single mother Helen Hunt. In *The Horse Whisperer*, trendy New York magazine editor Kristin Scott Thomas' obsession with her career puts her family in peril but in the end, brought to her senses by the homespun values of rancher Robert Redford, she returns to her patient husband (to the delight of her troubled teenage daughter, Scarlett Johannson) just as Celia Johnson did so tearfully all those years ago in *Brief Encounter*. Forget about the special effects in the 1994 blockbuster, *True Lies*, in which Arnie Schwarzenegger plays an American undercover agent who pretends to his wife, Jamie Lee Curtis, that he's just a computer salesman, and you'll find that it is essentially a £120 million exercise in completing (as sociologist Peter Kramer puts it), 'the simple dramatic feat of turning mummy and daddy and child into a happy family again'.

Where Hollywood stars once revelled in their extravagant lifestyles, they now increasingly proclaim their devotion to family. They fight to keep their children out of the public glare. The production schedules for *The Parent Trap* were arranged so that Richardson would not be separated from her baby sons Michael, who was born in Dublin, and Daniel. But then she has an understanding director. Nancy Meyers and producer Charles Shyer have children of their own. 'My eleven-year-old daughter is in the film,' Meyers tells me. 'For me as a working mother it was a way to be with her.'

Several of Hollywood's more popular films about family life have been produced by Meyers and Shyer. 'I think we're very limited thinkers,' she says.

> We have our own family and our work tends to come out of that. When I had my first baby we made *Baby Boom*, dealing with the dilemma of a woman balancing a career and motherhood. Now here I am directing an eleven-year-old girl just like my daughter. *Father of the Bride?* I'm not there yet but I was able to relate well to what the father went through in that film.

Like Richardson, Dennis Quaid tries to arrange his work around his family. He's married to Meg Ryan, whom he met in *Innerspace* (she refused to marry him until he went into therapy and kicked his drink and drugs habit) and they have a six-year-old son, Jack. 'There's a balance that has to be worked out,' he says. 'It's not just me any more.' While he was on location in Slovakia on *Dragonheart*, Ryan was in Paris with Jack filming *French Kiss*. 'Whenever I'd thirty-six hours off I'd go to Paris to be with them.' They divide their time between Santa Monica and Montana. 'It's not the Hollywood scene,' Quaid says. They go on family holidays driving around Europe. 'I'd like to take a bicycle ride around Ireland. My father's people come from Limerick. It's the only place I've seen pages of Quaids in the telephone directory.' He routinely says no to films that would keep him away from home. 'There'll always be another film but Jack's never going to be six years old again.'

One solution is to star together in the same films, as Natasha and Liam did in *Nell*. 'It would make family life easier if we could do it again,' she says. 'But we just don't want to work together all the time, although we've found a great little project, an adaptation of Patrick McGrath's *Asylum*, that we're going to do some time next year.'

The irony about family films is that they inevitably involve the use of child actors, yet starring in a film is hardly the ideal way to grow up. 'Although little Lindsay Lohan is terrific, it's not something I'd let my children do,' says Natasha, who was only five when she made her screen debut in her father's *The Charge of the Light Brigade* ('but that was only as an extra so that I could be with him'):

> Being a star is different. It's not a healthy environment for children. I don't think children should work. I don't think they should manipulate their emotions in that way. On a film set you're treated like a queen. You have people running around all the time doing what you want. It's hard to keep your feet on the ground – even as an adult. But for a child, it's very strange.

Hollywood's preoccupation with the idea of romantic love properly culminating in marriage is nothing new. A survey has shown that 85 per cent of all Hollywood films made before 1960 have romantic love as their main plot. D.W. Griffith was first to idealize the patriarchal family, devising the technique of parallel montage to show a man and a woman as incomplete by themselves but forming a satisfying whole when they merge with a kiss in the final frame. Although the Hollywood concept of the couple adjusted to suit shifts in social attitudes (it is now seen as more open, a coming together of equals) there is still nostalgia for the old simplicities.

Much of the fun of *The Truman Show* was the way it sent this up. Jim Carrey lives all his life in a TV soap without knowing it. He enjoys the epitome of an ideal married life: beautiful wife and child, wholesome neighbourhood, loyal friends. Yet there is an emptiness nagging at his soul. When he finally gets wise and escapes, billions of viewers watching worldwide break out in cheers. But has he really escaped? There's a teasing suspicion that perhaps he might have been happier living his sham.

*Pleasantville* raises similar doubts while appearing to dispel them. A couple of 1990s teenagers somehow are transported into a 1950s soap opera that propagates the ideal of a two-parent, two-child nuclear family diligently conforming to accepted norms of social behaviour, no matter what the cost. The awakening of the characters is signalled by their transformation from drab black-and-white to glorious Technicolor. The ironic twist is that when the teenagers return to the present, they bring with them a longing for a stable family.

It's a longing Hollywood shares, which is why the little girls embodied by Lohan in *The Parent Trap* succeed in bringing their parents back together. 'At first I thought, Oh I don't know, I shouldn't be part of the perpetuation of these myths,' says Natasha. 'But then I thought, Oh well, lighten up, this is a very romantic Hollywood film. Everyone knows it's not real.'

Nancy Meyers concurs. 'I don't think little boys or girls are going to watch and think they're going to bring their parents together. I think they know the difference between fantasy on the screen and reality.'

Cut forward nearly seven years. Natasha is back at the Dorchester. It has proved more difficult than she expected to persuade Paramount to film her Patrick McGrath project, *Asylum*, in which the neglected wife of a mental-hospital psychiatrist runs off with one of the inmates. The studio didn't think she was a big enough box-office name, even when Liam agreed to play her jealous lover. Just when she thought it might never happen she was offered the role of Anna in the Broadway premiere of *Closer*, Patrick Marber's ultra-smart play about couples switching partners. She couldn't make up her mind. 'At the time I loved the play but wasn't sure it was a big enough challenge for me,' she recalls. So Marber came back to her. 'If you play Anna, I'll write the screenplay for *Asylum*,' he proposed. 'So it was a bit of a deal,' she laughs.

*Closer*, in which she played the role Julia Roberts later took over in the film version, became an instant hit. Paramount still took persuading – by then Neeson was committed to *Kinsey* – but she wouldn't give up. 'It's a story of obsession and I guess I became completely obsessed,' she says,

> I don't think I had any idea it would take so long or be such a struggle. I just set my heart on it. I had a gut feeling that I just had to play this woman. I suppose I also thought this is a chance for me to explore on film the terrain that I have done on the stage. Although I've had some terrific parts in film – the kidnapped heiress in *Pattie Hearst* and the wife in Harold Pinter's adaptation of Ian McEwan's *The Comfort of Strangers* – I've not been given a chance to do what I do best. So I just couldn't let it go. It would have broken my heart if somebody else had done it, or if the film hadn't happened.

She feels a close empathy with the character Stella, a woman trapped in an unhappy relationship:

> When you're acting you draw on all sorts of things that are inside yourself or people close to you. I've observed friends who've suffered from nervous break-downs, alcoholism and depression. We've all had that feeling of shall I just blow it. Most of us thankfully pull ourselves back and don't. But some people do. They just blow up their lives and fall into the abyss.

*Asylum*, directed by David Mackenzie, is an extreme case of getting carried away by the passion of the moment. 'Reason completely goes out the door. That's why I think so many people can understand this story. We've all had those moments.' She had hers when she fell for Liam. As a four-year-old child, she'd witnessed the same thing happen with her parents.

Her black V-neck top is cut low, not unlike the dresses her character Stella wears. 'At one point the studio wanted to set *Asylum* in modern America instead of class-ridden suffocating English society in the 1950s,' she says. 'But if you take this story out of its time you don't have a story.'

If she identifies with Stella, now that she's a mother herself, she also feels close to the small son Charlie, caught in the middle of his parents' break-up:

It's horrifying as a mother to see what Stella puts Charlie through. The idea of leaving your child, I don't know how you could do it. How could you ever forgive yourself for what she allows to happen? I felt for little Gus Lewis, playing Charlie. His mother was around. I was thinking about her watching. I was thinking about my boys. Ughhh!

Yet growing up was also a magical time for Richardson and her younger sister Joely:

I suppose I fell in love with the acting world by being on sets. I followed my mother around while she was getting her make-up and hair done in *Isadora* and *A Man for all Seasons*. It was like being in an amusement park, in a way. Now my children come on sets. They're mainly interested in the little truck filled with snacks and chewing gum. That's their biggest treat.

She could hardly not have become an actress. She's the fourth generation of a family going back to Roy Redgrave, a star in Australian silent films. Her grandparents were Sir Michael Redgrave, who won an Oscar for *The Browning Version*, and actress Rachel Kempson. Her mother won an Oscar for *Julia* in 1978 and her aunt Lynn Redgrave, the loveable ugly duckling in *Georgy Girl* in 1966, has since won an Oscar as *Frankenstein* director James Whale's house-keeper in *Gods and Monsters*.

'Being the daughter of a famous actress and knowing what a struggle that was for me for a while because of the attention before you were ready for it, I hope my sons don't become actors. It would be awfully hard on them, although it's too early to tell yet.'

She has an apartment in Manhattan but her home with Neeson is in upstate New York. 'We have put down roots there and that would be very hard to leave. But part of me gets drawn back to England.'

George Devine, who ran the Royal Court Theatre and with whom her father launched the 'Angry Young Men' era with John Osborne's plays, talked about the right to fail and how this is so important for actors. 'There is in New York no avenue for the right to fail,' she says.

There aren't the subsidized theatres that there are in London. In some ways if I lived in England I'd be able to work more frequently in theatre and in a more diverse way. But I'm not sure about the whole notion of going back. Maybe it's because of being partly brought up in England and spending a lot of time in France, Europe and America, I'm one of those people who sort of belong everywhere and nowhere. I never feel entirely English and certainly not entirely American either.

She filmed Hugh Leonard's comedy, *Widow's Peak*, with Mia Farrow in Ireland and has worked with Pat O'Connor in *A Month in the Country*, as F. Scott FitzGerald's wife in *Zelda*, and with Paddy Breathnach in *Blowdry*. Part of *Asylum* was shot at Ardmore Studios. Yet she's never done theatre in Ireland. 'I've never been asked,' she says. 'I'd love to do a play in Dublin. Maybe Liam and I will find one, I wish we could.'

She was recently in China filming *The White Countess*, an original screenplay by Kazuo Ishiguro directed by James Ivory. It's a romantic epic set in the 1930s and reunites her with her mother, who last appeared with her in *The Seagull* in 1985. 'She plays my aunt and my real aunt Lynn plays my mother-in-law.'

Neeson brought their sons out to Shanghai for two weeks to be with her: 'After this I feel like it's time to recharge the batteries. I'll make my boys the priority. Working in theatre is so difficult in terms of school-age children. You can't get up with them in the morning. You can't put them to bed at night. I don't want to miss out any more on that.'

• • •

Liam Neeson strides on stage at the Guildhall in Derry, brandishing a surveyor's pole. He's playing Doalty in the 1980 premiere of Brian Friel's *Translations*, a character described in the text as an 'open-hearted, generous and slightly thick young man'. The setting is a 1830s hedge-school in Irish-speaking Donegal, where the British army engineer corps is carrying out an ordnance survey, mapping and renaming every nook and cranny of the country in English:

'The Red Coats were just across the foot of Croc na Móna,' bursts out Doalty. 'Every time they'd stick one of these poles into the ground and move across the bog, I'd creep up and shift it twenty or thirty paces to the side.'

'God!' says his companion Bridget.

'Then they'd come back and stare at it and look at their calculations and stare at it again and scratch their heads. And cripes, d'you know what they ended up doing?'

'Wait till you hear,' pipes Bridget.

'They took the bloody machine apart!'

'You must be proud of yourself, Doalty,' says Maire, a girlfriend of the hedge master's son Manus.

'What d'you mean?'

'That was a clever piece of work.'

'It was a gesture,' says Manus.

'What sort of a gesture?'

'Just to indicate … a presence.'

'I'm telling you – you'll be arrested,' says Bridget.

That *Translations* should be performed by the newly formed Field Day Company in the Guildhall – to say nothing of Unionist mayor Marlene Jefferson leading the applause – was understood by everyone there to be of historic significance. To the Catholic minority in the North this intimidating neo-Gothic building overlooking the river Foyle has always been a symbol of Protestant domination.

'This is theirs, boy, and your very presence here is a sacrilege,' says Skinner in Friel's 1973 play, *The Freedom of the City*. With two other demonstrators, Skinner is taking refuge from CS gas in the mayor's parlour after troops break up a civil rights march. Mistaken for an IRA assault force, they come under fire from the British and are shot as they surrender: a savagely ironic reference to Bloody Sunday.

But all that may be changing. The Guildhall has fallen to words rather than bullets. Despite violence and an economic recession – over 10,000 jobs have been lost in the area – a power-sharing city council offers Derry the beginning of hope. Friel's play is in keeping with the new tolerance. He hasn't written a polemic. Theatre for him has never been a soapbox. His plays explore the ambiguities and confusions that pervade ever-changing society: the truths of his characters are never more than approximations.

'The play found expression in the issue of actual place names,' he tells me.

It's a few days earlier. We're in the huge high-ceilinged and wood-panelled first-floor room of the Guildhall before a rehearsal. I'm just off the train after a meandering journey from Dublin, changing at Belfast and then continuing along the coast, stopping along the way at places with anglicized versions of once-Irish names. As the hedge-master Hugh says, 'It can happen that a civilization can be imprisoned in a linguistic contour which no longer matches the landscape of … fact.'

Friel plops a teabag into a cup of boiling water. 'I'm used to drinking tea in green rooms and it's always filthy,' he apologizes. He's a craggy-faced man with thick hair receding over a large forehead, his cheeks slightly ruddy. 'I think my concern is more with the whole problem that writers in this country experience having to handle a language that is not native to them,' he says.

There's a line where the hedge-school teacher says that they'll have to learn these names and they'll have to make them their home. And in some way that's what the play is about: having to use a language that isn't our own.

But I'm not talking about the revival of the Irish language. I'm just talking about the language we have now and what use we make of it and about the problems that having it gives us. The assumption, for instance, is that we speak the same language as England. And we don't. The sad irony, of course, is that the whole play is written in English. It ought to be written in Irish.

Much of the theatrical impact of *Translations* comes from Friel's inspired device of having all the characters speak the same language, with a translator – the hedge-master's other son, Owen, played by Stephen Rea – all the time interpreting what the English and the Irish characters are saying to each other: a recurring reminder of the fundamental differences that can be embodied in the same language.

As a playwright Friel has been conditioned by this experience as much as anyone else:

It's a problem dramatists here in Ireland never really faced up to, the problem of writing in the language of another country. We're a very recent breed. Poets and novelists, I think, belong to a less fractured tradition than we do. We've only existed since Synge and Yeats. There was no such thing as an indigenous Irish drama until 1904.

Dramatists from Ireland before that always had to write for the London stage, to pitch their voices in an English way:

They had to do that if they were to practise their craft. The whole Irish drama tradition from Farquahar to Behan is pitted with writers doing that. Ultimately they were maimed.

But there's a big change now. What many are doing is writing for ourselves. Not in any insular or parochial sense, but they want to be heard by their own people. And if they're overheard by anyone else, that's a bonus.

He's at pains, however, to dispel any suggestion of making a cult of Irishness. 'John McGahern once told you in an interview that he did not want to be considered as an Irish writer, and I can see the danger in that. But I think it's an appellation that other people put on you. So what the hell, you go and do your job.'

Which is how Field Day came about: to give life to the idea of writing for an Irish audience rather than primarily for Broadway or the West End. *Translations* will transfer to Dublin, followed by one-night stands in Magherafelt,

Dungannon, Newry, Carrickmore, Armagh and Enniskillen.

'But we're the most reluctant producers,' he says. He formed Field Day with Stephen Rea ('the company's name is derived from both our names'), and with the support of Seamus Heaney, David Hammond and Seamus Deane, because it was the only way they could get money from the Northern Ireland Arts Council to stage *Translations*. 'They only fund existing establishments, so we had to become an establishment.'

Now they find themselves into something much larger than anticipated, having to worry about everything from getting out contracts to putting up 'No Smoking' signs. 'It's not like going into the Abbey where everything is provided and all you do is sit in on rehearsal and that's it.'

Friel has lived all his life around Derry. 'We moved here from Omagh when I was ten. My father was a teacher, and I was a teacher too, but gave it up to write stories for *The New Yorker*. They paid such enormous money I found I could live off three stories a year.'

Tyrone Guthrie invited him out to Minneapolis to the first of the regional theatres he had started. 'I don't know what I learned there but I suppose it was some smell of what theatre was about.' Out of the experience came *Philadelphia, Here I Come*, which won a Tony Award and became the longest-running Irish play on Broadway, a record not matched until last year's triumph of Hugh Leonard's *Da*.

Since then he has had play after play on Broadway – *The Loves of Cass McGuire*, *Lovers*, *The Mundy Scheme*, *Freedom of the City* and *Faith Healer* – yet international success has failed to lure him away from the North. He continues to live with his wife Ann and four children a couple of miles over the border in Muff, Co. Donegal. All his plays are rooted in the Irish experience: that is where his material is. His plays give universal form to local particularities: the manner in which he expresses an idea invariably becomes an extension of that idea.

'The crux of a new play arises with its form,' he says. Thus *Philadelphia* has two actors to personify Gar's inner and outer selves. *Faith Healer* consists entirely of monologues, emphasizing the separateness of the characters. *Translations* is rooted in the varying nuances inherent in the same language on different tongues.

'A play offers you a shape and a form to accommodate your anxieties and disturbances in that period of life you happen to be passing through. But you outgrow that and you change and grope for a new shape and a new articulation of it, don't you?'

He boils another kettle, to all appearances like a tweed-jacketed teacher in some school common room. Derry is full of his former pupils, to whom he's known by the nickname Scobie. He is a meticulous craftsman, attending every rehearsal, never letting go of a play until it is a reality on the stage. 'The dramatist ought to be able to exercise complete control over the realization of his characters,' he says.

> The director can bring an objective view to the script that a writer can't have, but I'm very doubtful about the whole idea of a director interpreting a play in any kind of way that's distinctive to him. A good director hones in on the core of what a play is about and realizes that and becomes self-effacing in the process. A director is like the conductor of an orchestra and the actors are the musicians. They are all there to play the score as it is written.

If this makes Friel a conventional playwright, he's not bothered. He prefers to work within the possibilities of theatre rather than trying to make it something else. He has shunned the fashions of English theatre, avoiding both the Pinteresque concern with dramatizing mood and the Howard Brenton vision of theatre as a vehicle for politics. The English, he argues, can indulge in the rhetoric of propagandist drama because it's safe there: they're secure in a continuing culture that has hardly changed in hundreds of years. 'But here we're continually thrust into a situation of confrontation. Politics are so obtrusive here.'

He gestures out the window. The British army barracks dominates Derry from the opposite bank of the Foyle. Below, the entrance to the Guildhall is protected by a perimeter of barbed wire. The Catholic Bogside, scene of the Bloody Sunday massacre, remains a virtual no-go area for British troops. Many of its young inhabitants are interned and talking about hunger strikes. When I returned to my hotel last night after a party, the entrance to the grounds was locked as part of a de facto curfew. I had to climb over the wall to get in.

Friel is horrified. 'You could have been shot,' he says.

We stand there at the window. 'For people like ourselves living close to such a fluid situation, definitions of identity have to be developed more frequently,' says Friel. 'We've got to keep questioning until we find some kind of portmanteau term or until we find some kind of generosity that can embrace the whole island. That certainly is the ultimate aim, isn't it?'

• • •

'We have to fight injustice whenever we are touched by it,' Julie Christie tells me. Her way of doing so is not by speeches but by association. Despite the ongoing secret peace process that in the aftermath of the 1994 IRA ceasefire gives hope that political reconciliation may finally be within reach in Northern Ireland, the 1996 Foyle Film Festival in Derry has attracted few foreign film-makers. The exception is Christie. She's here for a special screening of *Don't Look Now*. She turned up alone, without the usual handlers that accompany stars.

It's snowing. She is being photographed under an umbrella in front of the city walls, within sight of the Guildhall, a shot reminiscent of *Dr Zhivago*. 'Except that *Zhivago* was shot in Spain in the sweltering heat with fake snow,' she laughs.

She didn't show any sign of panic earlier today when a 600-pound bomb had to be dismantled outside her hotel. A couple of minutes later she was out walking. She knows Ireland better than to be scared off by headlines interested only in violence and bloodshed.

She filmed William Trevor's *Fools of Fortune* on location in Connemara in 1990, a love story spanning decades in which she portrays a once vivacious young Anglo-Irish wife whose husband is murdered by the Black and Tans during the War of Independence in 1921. She was back in Ireland two years later to film Jennifer Johnston's *The Railway Station*, again as a widow but this time the husband was the victim of an IRA attack. While trying to get over her grief the widow meets and is attracted to a mysterious American – Donald Sutherland, Christie's co-star in *Don't Look Now* – who is working on the railways.

She poured much of herself into the roles, feeling a personal empathy with what it is to be Irish through times of sectarian violence and division. 'You *do* do that,' she says. 'You fill roles with yourself. To quote Hamlet's mother Gertrude, "To thine own self be true."'

It's an instinct – what her lover of several years, Warren Beatty, called 'her pathological honesty' – that caused Christie more than any other actress to be regarded as the personification of the permissive 1960s. As the free-living model Diana Scott in *Darling*, an Oscar-winning leading role created for her by director John Schlesinger and writer Frederic Raphael, she revelled in the independence of being a single woman out for a good time and having relationships with men on her own terms.

Julie Christie defying a bomb alert in Derry, 1996.

Intimacy with Strangers: A Life of Brief Encounters

This was provocative enough to cause public outrage, even in 1965. Christie didn't try to dodge it, either. She told reporters at the time that she didn't believe in marriage. 'Men don't want responsibility, and neither do I. Marriage is like signing your life away.'

Christie feels that Diana, like Gertrude in *Hamlet*, has been misjudged. 'I don't think she did anything wrong. There was masses of me in her. If I have some of her qualities, it's through no fault of my own.' She's keen also to put the record straight on Hamlet's much-maligned adulterous mother, whose hasty marriage to her husband's murderer pushed her neurotic son over the edge and led to her own death. 'She'd nothing to be ashamed of, I don't think she did anything wrong. I think she and Claudius rushed into marriage so they could be in bed together. It was lust. She didn't deserve to die for that. I personally don't see lust as something bad. I think it's joyful.'

Her steamy portrayal of Gertrude makes Kenneth Branagh's four-hour filmed version of the play, which updates it to the Victorian era, a controversial choice to open Belfast's new Waterfront Hall, an event intended as a symbol of the regeneration of the city after three decades of bombings and killings. Her support for a campaign calling for British troops to withdraw from Northern Ireland will do nothing to alleviate this controversy, although the fact it's all being debated is perhaps further indication that there is a return to normalcy.

What made Christie startlingly different in *Darling*, and in *Billy Liar*, parading defiantly through the streets of a typical north-of-England town as if she didn't give a damn, was that she was so un-English. Although she has lived in London and more recently in Wales much of her life, she's never really belonged. She was born on her father's tea plantation in Assam, India, in 1941, pampered by servants only to have it all snatched from her when she was shipped back to school in England after the war, much like Frances Hodgson Burnett's *Little Princess*.

> As I've blanked everything out, I think it must have been such a shock that it was unbearable. For a five-year-old girl to be sent away from the only country they've ever known, the only home they've ever had, the only parents they've ever loved, into a different country and a different climate, where they're with people they've never met before …

She shudders, and shuts her eyes: 'And then you find yourself in a horrible school where they beat you and do things to you. I think it's beyond a five-year-old's capacity to deal with. Therefore you shut down. I suppose everybody deals with such things differently. Fortunately I happened to turn into a delinquent.' For a while she found herself in a convent school in Hastings:

> Funnily enough, I loved that. I loved all the pomp and pageantry, the incense and the retreats and all of that. I was on the outside of it because I wasn't actually a Catholic. And I remember one day a girl saying to me, what does it feel like not to be Christian?
>
> I went to a lot of schools, because I kept being expelled. I can't say a convent school is worse than any other. Even sexually it's no worse, although it was bad in its distortion of sexuality, because you're at an age when sex is exciting. You're so full of curiosity. It's all you think about. And then to be punished for that in such terrible ways, as they do … It would make you peculiar.

A small role in the comedy, *Crooks Anonymous*, when Christie was twenty-one caught the attention of John Schlesinger who cast her in *Billy Liar*. David Lean saw it and liked the way she swung her purse:

> So I got a call to test for *Dr Zhivago* in New York. Michael Caine came with me. He didn't get his part – Tom Courteney did – but I got mine. I don't remember any feeling of excitement or anything. I don't think David Lean meant very much to me then. But I wanted to learn to be an actress, and I knew it was going to take some doing because I wasn't a wonderfully talented natural.

It was to be the first in a succession of roles in which she played women whose love defied convention. She attracts three different men in *Far from the Madding Crowd*. She tumbles in the hay with Alan Bates in *The Go-Between*. She tries to have an adulterous affair with George C. Scott in *Petulia*, the film that brought her to Hollywood and into the arms of Warren Beatty. During their prolonged affair, when they shared a small cottage on Vancouver's Howe Sound, they starred together in *Shampoo*, *Heaven Can Wait* and Robert Altman's *McCabe and Mrs Miller*.

So what about Beatty's claim that she's pathologically honest?

> He says things like that. It tells you a lot about Warren. Of course I'm also incredibly dishonest. If you're pathologically honest you're bound to be a pathological liar as well. But I know what he means. I do try … and that's why I'm so halting in my speech … to get things right all the time, instead of having delightful skilled conversation, which is nothing to do with getting it right. It would be very nice to have those skills, but there you are, I don't.

We've moved indoors and are sitting at a warm fire. She's dressed casually in blue jeans and a sweater. Her blond hair is swept back and her blue-grey eyes are surprisingly shy. All her life she's felt woefully shy. That's what stopped her having an affair with Francois Truffaut when he was directing her in *Farenheit 451*. 'We were both pathologically shy. There were definitely strong feelings between us. But we were so shy. There was no way of bridging that.'

Her bed scene in *Don't Look Now* with Donald Sutherland has been called one of the most erotic ever filmed, but she gives all the credit to director Nic Roeg. 'Films are the director's vision, not the star's. They are all to do with the camera and the scissors.'

Being with Beatty politicized her, although she didn't realize it until after they split up and she returned to England:

> I don't ever remember being political before that. But then I've got such amnesia about the past. I can't even remember lines from my films. But I am told by people who are still my friends that I was on the Aldermaston anti-bomb marches. I doubt that I was on them for any other reason than maybe a good band was playing or my friends were going there or there were some nice boys. I can't believe that I had worked things out by then.

Becoming an instant icon in the 1960s never went to her head: she did her best to ignore it.

> I don't think you know these things are happening when they're happening. I really didn't have much of a clue. I mean, I've always resisted being swept away, particularly by the money level of things. All it meant was that I could at last do what at that point many young people of my age were unable to do. I could actually buy myself a house, a modest house, but it was the most incredible thing I'd ever done.

Fame was easier then; it didn't get in the way of leading a private life:

> Nowadays there's much more Puritanism. Famous people are condemned for stepping out of line. When I was famous, you were let off the hook a bit. I used to feel that I was physically safe because I was famous. Now it's almost the opposite. You're a target. I don't think anybody can have a normal life any more if they're a celebrity. If you have an unconventional relationship you immediately come under this ghastly surveillance. Nobody understands that we're all different human beings and we have to operate in a way that makes our life best for us. We can't all conform to one norm when there are millions of differences between us all.

Last year she returned to the stage in *Old Times* by Harold Pinter, with whom she had taken part in several Nicaragua Solidarity Campaign protests in the 1980s. 'I think it's a very fine thing that Harold does, which is to maintain his ideals with a passion and fury that can't be obliterated by the stamp of public opinion. He's so angry. And he doesn't mind if he's laughed at or looked at as a kind of dinosaur.'

•   •   •

You don't expect to be sitting out on the Falls Road in Belfast, sipping cappuccino. It's a measure of the success of the peace process that we are. It's August 2009, two years after the DUP's Ian Paisley and Sinn Féin's Gerry Adams shook hands and went into government together. Bobby Ballagh has driven up from Dublin with me to give a talk at the West Belfast Féile, a festival launched in 1988 in the aftermath of some of the worst violence of the Troubles when a Loyalist gunman mowed down mourners at an IRA funeral just down the road ,and two British soldiers were later pulled from a car and murdered. Back then, secret talks had already started between Adams and the nationalist leader, John Hume. 'We were trying to piece things together,' says Adams, who agreed to be interviewed for my biography, *Robert Ballagh: Citizen Artist*.

The Féile was started to channel the rage and defiance of young people into painting murals rather than throwing stones and Molotov cocktails. Ballagh was involved from the start, giving workshops and presenting prizes for the best murals. The murals have since evolved from strident military symbolism into a call for civil rights throughout the world, epitomized by a recreation of Picasso's *Guernica*.

It was painted by two artists from opposite sides of the political divide. Mark Ervine is a son of the former and now dead UVF paramilitary David Ervine who, after abandoning violence, became leader of the Progressive Unionist Party and played a key role in bringing about the Loyalist ceasefire in 1994. Danny Devenny, a Republican who started painting as a prisoner in Long Kesh in the 1970s, is best known for his mural of the hunger striker, Bobby Sands.

We get talking about films. During the Troubles, Adams used slip down to Dublin to go to the cinema: he'd have been shot if he tried to do so in Belfast. But now that it's no longer dangerous, he hasn't the time. 'I haven't seen a film for ages,' he says. He's heard good things from Danny Morrison about Steve McQueen's *Hunger*, in which Michael Fassbender portrays Bobby Sands. He's

Intimacy with Strangers: A Life of Brief Encounters

curious about *Five Minutes of Heaven*, directed Oliver Hirschbiegel whose film *Downfall* portrayed Hitler's last days in his bunker.

Liam Neeson plays a former UVF paramilitary, now an advocate of peace and reconciliation, who meets up on a TV show with James Nesbitt, the brother of a Catholic he assassinated. It was shot on location in Belfast, Lurgan and Newtownards and is based on two men who in real life never met, so it is an imagined situation that personifies the moral dilemma of a violent society coming to terms with peace.

*Time* magazine once labelled Neeson apolitical because he didn't play on sectarian politics in his Northern roles. The fact is that he always instinctively looked for things in common instead of focusing on differences, a stance conditioned by his upbringing in Ballymena and his work with Brian Friel, a private writer reluctant to be drawn into the political domain.

Stephen Rea, who played the brother who acted as translator for the British soldiers carrying out the ordnance survey in *Translations*, recalls the play's groundbreaking Field Day production in Derry's Guildhall in 1980: 'We were very easily categorized as a bunch of Northern nationalists, but we wanted to be a unifying influence. It was in no sense that we wanted to say that the nationalist experience was greater or more interesting than anybody else's experience.'

A few weeks before my encounter with Julie Christie in Derry in 1998, a city where the hope of peace that was in the air at the *Translations* premiere in 1980 had been dashed by the hunger strikes and Margaret Thatcher's intransigence but took heart again with the 1994 ceasefire, Neeson was talking to me about his portrayal of Michael Collins in the Neil Jordan biopic. 'Everything people say about Collins is true,' he said in that soft Northern voice of his. 'He was a thug and a bully. And yet he was damned likeable. I'd love to have been able to meet him.'

Meeting Neeson is near enough to what meeting Collins might have been like. He has much the same spontaneously engaging presence. It comes from his childhood:

> We grew up on a street with Catholics and Protestants. My buddies were nearly all Protestants. And once a year we weren't allowed out on the Twelfth. It confused me, but I just accepted it and the glee of looking out the bedroom window and seeing these extraordinary bands with their sashes coming up and down the street.
>
> But that wasn't being apolitical. It's funny, you know … Americans are always trying to pick up on black or white issues. But all the Protestants on our street

were from the exact same background as us, genuinely struggling some months to pay the rent and get the bits and pieces at Christmas for the kids – we were all in the same boat. That's one of the great sadnesses for me about the North. Protestants and Catholics have so much in common, but the British, as they learned from the Romans, have a divide and rule mentality.

Now in 2009, despite the demands of Hollywood, Neeson has found time to narrate *The Leap of Faith*, a documentary by Patricia Reagan and Jennifer McShane ('they mortgaged their homes to finance it'), which follows four or five Protestant and Catholic families who make the decision to send their children to the new integrated Cranmore primary school, just off the Malone Road in Belfast.

'God, it's brilliant,' he says. 'They're the real heroes, people who are realizing a terrible wrong in their society that has affected them and they're damned if it's going to affect their children.'

# seven

Pedro Almodovar, Carmen Diez de Rivera,
Carlos Saura, Luis Berlanga, Juan Luis Cebrian
and Antonio Buero Vallejo

Julia Alonso Beazcochea in Madrid, 1943.

'*h*ollande?' It seems the girl in the press office at Cannes Film Festival hasn't encountered an Irish journalist before. She's wearing an almost transparent white blouse, casually unbuttoned. Being topless is no longer burn-your-bra feminist bravado: Yves Saint Laurent has given it his imprimatur.

'Non, *Irlande.*' She looks again at a letter from my editor Conor O'Brien seeking accreditation. She gets up from her desk and goes to another room, looking back with a reassuring smile.

The year is 1972. You could arrive in Cannes at the last moment as I did, without accreditation or even accommodation, and still be made welcome. I'm led down a bustling corridor to meet the head of press, Louisette Fargette, who not only produces a pink badge, admitting me to all press screenings, but makes a few phone calls and finds me a room in the nearby Hotel Cavendish.

The Palais des Festivals is a graceful turn-of-the-century villa on an elegant palm-shaded promendade, known as the Croisette, which forms a crescent around the beaches where onlookers swarm in the hope of glimpsing a starlet posing for publicity shots, a ritual initiated in 1954 when Simone Sylva walked up to Robert Mitchum while he was being photographed and dropped her bikini top.

Nearby, a massive billboard for Fellini's *Roma* obscures the stately facade of the Carlton Hotel with a gaudy picture of two naked women on their hands and knees, each endowed with three breasts to evoke the she-wolf that suckled Rome's founders. A few days later it is sprayed with red paint by American feminists led by Eleanor Perry, who scripted *The Diary of a Mad Housewife*. 'We all revere Fellini,' she says. 'We just want to protest the way his movie was being promoted.'

The festival is still small enough to allow such free-spirited actions. Tented restaurants don't yet clutter the beaches. Stars like Jack Nicholson can move about freely and chat with journalists over a beer. Publicists and handlers are relatively few in number and only too eager to arrange interviews, much to my relief as part of my brief is to meet leading directors like Hitchcock, Bergman, Pasolini and Antonioni whose work is routinely cut or banned by the Irish film censor.

To file copy you have to type it out and get one of the wire-operators on duty at the Palais to transmit it back to your paper. An American critic suggests it is a good idea to slip them a bottle of whiskey early on to ensure that you're put at the top of the pile.

There is no sign of the armies of bouncers and squads of riot police that today take over the town for two weeks and seal off streets each night so that dark-windowed limousines can deliver sequined stars to the red carpet stairway a few hundred yards from their hotels.

If Cannes, all these years later, has changed for the worse in terms of lack of accessibility – a custom-built, fortress-like bunker beside the marina replaced the original Palais in 1981 – the chance to be surprised any time of any day by films from anywhere in the world remains and keeps bringing me back to a small attic flat above the noisy restaurants on rue des Frères Pradignac, lent to me by an architect friend, Kate Quinn. She and her former partner, who designs yachts, laid it out using the wooden roof beams to simulate the ambience of a cabin. One of their yachts was used in the Philip Noyce thriller, *Dead Calm*, with Kate standing in as Nicole Kidman's double in some of the more violent scenes.

So now it's May 2009. Pedro Almodovar is here with *Broken Embraces*. The *enfant terrible* of Spanish cinema, he's become something of a Cannes regular, first as a member of the jury that gave the Jury Prize to Victor Erice's *El sol del Membrillo* in 1992 and then in 1999 winning best director with *All About My Mother*. He opened the 2004 festival with *Bad Education*, throwing one of the festival's more memorable parties at which he carved Serrano ham for guests and danced through the night in the company of gorgeous women and a variety of transvestites: at times it was hard to know one from the other. He was back in 2006 with *Volver*, which won best screenplay while the best actress award was presented to his entire female cast.

He's sitting in the shade of a large canopy by the beach. His trademark mop of black hair is now a dignified grey. 'But essentially I haven't changed. The circumstances have *changed*.' Although he speaks good English – picked up from Andy Warhol, who identified him as a kindred spirit on a visit to Madrid in the late seventies – a translator sits with us, not sure when to translate as Almodovar keeps straying into English while I sometimes find myself talking in Spanish.

After seeing a Richard Brooks film version of Tennessee Williams' *Cat on a Hot Tin Roof*, Almodovar, then a twelve-year-old choirboy, vowed that he would lead 'a life of sin and degeneracy'. So has he succeeded? 'I did have a period of debauchery, which was perhaps from 1977 to 1978,' he laughs. 'That was enough. I think I fortunately also had a vocation to write and make films, and that in some ways removed me from all the risks and dangers that come attached to such a life.'

Although his name is synonymous with the frenetic explosion of creative energy in Madrid after the death in 1975 of the dictator Franco, whose regime of moral and political repression stalled Spain in a cultural doldrums for forty years, everything he does is coloured by his experience of growing up in a small town in La Mancha, surrounded by women.

He is in some ways a Spanish equivalent of Federico Fellini who, although fascinated with the Rome where he lived, was haunted by memories of his childhood in Rimini. Madrid is Almodovar's Rome. The theme song of *Volver*, recurring like the Nino Rota folk melody in Fellini's *Amarcord* to evoke a longing for a home left behind, is from a zarzuela or street opera, *La Rosa del Azafran*, which he remembers his mother singing with women from the village while washing clothes in the river:

> Neighbours are very important in little places like the village where I was born. I remember my mother leaving me with the neighbour across the street. There was a kind of solidarity.
>
> When these women moved from their villages to Madrid, they brought this with them. You will find it in the poorer neighbourhoods of Madrid, where Penelope Cruz's character Raimunda lives with her daughter and her sister. It's

as if they've reproduced the village in the city. I know that because my sisters behave with their neighbours exactly like my mother.

In *Volver* (the translation is 'to return') Almodovar takes us back to his village roots, but as always in his films the autobiographical elements are ambivalent. His alter ego is not a man but the strong-willed Raimunda, who returns from Madrid with her teenage daughter to visit a blind aunt who reared her after her mother's death. But Raimunda is also a version of Almodovar's own mother, as in different ways are all the women who inhabit this wonderful ghost story: the timid older sister Sole, the protective neighbour Augustina, and the mother herself, who comes back from the dead because she is 'lonely'.

There's a running gag – despite its theme of murder and sexual abuse, *Volver* is a comedy – in which the characters keep sensing the presence of Raimunda's dead mother. 'This house still smells of my mother,' Raimunda says when she arrives at her aunt Paula's house.

'My mother is to be found in all the characters,' says Almodovar:

> It is very much my mother speaking. It really carries her scent. We filmed in places where she used to be. Those patios in La Mancha, the windswept streets, the neighbours that Penelope's aunt spends her time with – these are very much my mother's situations. It established a dialogue not so much with my memories but with my very origins, and this was something that was totally unexpected.

Cruz first caught his eye as a wanton teenager in the Bigas Luna film, *Jamon, Jamon*, in 1992. 'I didn't meet her until years later, but I knew then I wanted to work with her. I realized she was the kind of actress who suited my films. But the parts I was writing were all older than she was, up until the first time we worked together on *Live Flesh* in 1997.'

He cast her in *All About My Mother* in 1999 as a nun who becomes pregnant by a transvestite who gives her Aids. 'I gave myself to Pedro,' she told me at the time. 'Pedro loves women. He focuses everything on women because I think he knows us very well. He allows you to be a woman, not just a symbol.' She hadn't worked with him since then, so *Volver*, in which she plays a mother whose husband molests their daughter just as she was once molested as a young girl by her own father, is also a coming back for her, as it was for 61-year-old Carmen Maura, in the role of the mother, whom Almodovar met in 1977 performing in an underground production of Jean-Paul Sartre's *Dirty Hands*.

**Pedro Almodovar, Cannes Film Festival, 2009.**

She was the star and I was at the bottom. We'd spend hours together in her dressing room. When she brushed her hair and made up, I'd tell her the stories I was writing. She started working with me in Super 8 films. She pushed me to make something bigger and with other actors asked for the money that got *Pepi, Luci, Bom* made. So she was my beginning.

Maura, in rebellion against her upper-class family and a husband who thought he owned her, did everything from measuring penises in *Pepi* to discovering via an automatic answering machine that her boyfriend in *Women on the Verge of a Nervous Breakdown* was dumping her. She broke with Almodovar in a tiff over not having a good enough seat at the 1989 Oscars, but made up with him for *Volver*. 'It was very moving for me that even if we hadn't worked together in the last eighteen years, our relationship didn't change at all,' he says. 'It was like we were working the day before.'

A decade on from *All About My Mother*, Cruz still feels she belongs to Almodovar. She was in junior school when he was the flamboyant outsider shaking up Spanish cinema. 'I always wanted to be an Almodovar girl,' she says. 'I was obsessed with it.' In *Broken Embraces* she gets to be several Almodovar girls at once in a role that requires her to be different perceptions of the same woman. The film noir plot unfolds in flashbacks as a film director, blinded in a car crash on the volcanic island of Lanzarote fourteen years before, recalls the love of his life, a young would-be actress he seduced while directing her in a film financed by her wealthy lover.

The film-within-a-film titled *Girls and Suitcases*, a favourite narrative device Almodovar employs to draw on his own life while avoiding the auto-biographical, is a pastiche of *Women on the Verge of a Nervous Breakdown*. 'I did it because it was cheaper, not in any sense of self-tribute.' Cruz is observed both in her role as actress and as the character the actress is playing, while all the time the geeky cameraman son of her jealous lover spies on her under the guise of a 'making of' documentary, the silent rushes of which are scrutinized by his father each night with the help of a lip-reader to detect evidence of infidelity. 'The wonderful thing about Penelope is that she has so many characters inside her and some of them are even unbeknown to her.'

In *Volver* his camera is all over Cruz, lingering on her deliberately exaggerated cleavage as she scrubs floors, closing in on her bottom as she struts through the neighbourhood and zooming in on her wide lush lips as she talks. He sees her as being very much in the sensual tradition of European icons like Sophia Loren and Anna Magnani. He dresses her in the same straight skirts and cardigans associated with their earthy persona. He even has a clip from one of Magnani's films playing on television in the background in *Volver*.

'Penelope is a very different person to her character,' he says. 'She's a very refined girl, but she's much better at playing down-to-earth characters than sophisticated characters. It is a huge pleasure just to look at her as she is performing. The director is the first spectator. I think I became a director just because of that.'

Almodovar may not be the first gay director to devote himself to actresses – think of George Cukor and more recently François Ozon – but he's certainly the most outspoken. 'The fact that I'm seen as a director of women I often think is simply due to numbers. There are always more women than men in my films.' He concedes that men may have been the main protagonists in *Talk to Her* and *Bad Education*, as well as *Matador* and *Law of Desire*, in which even the girl played by Carmen Maura was a man. It's also true that Spain's two leading male stars, Antonio Banderas (whom he spotted as an extra and cast in *Law of Desire*) and Javier Bardem, undoubtedly owe their breakthrough as international stars to him. 'But I'm more interested in women than in men,' he insists, pouring some water. 'I grew up in a very female universe.'

He was born the son of a carter in the small village of Calzada de la Calatrava in La Mancha, the country of Cervantes and Don Quixote. He didn't have any relationship with his father, who died when he was young. 'To me La Mancha represents my mother and I could never forget her.' His younger brother Augustin, with whom he created the production company El Deseo in 1986, has revealed how, after their father's death, Pedro became head of the family: 'If my mother had been a young woman today she would have bowled everyone over. She was really bright. Unfortunately she could only go to school for a year, just long enough to read and write. But she wrote beautiful poems and she's very liberal in outlook on things and is very open.'

She'd write letters for villagers who couldn't read, and read out loud the letters they received back, adding in things to make them feel happier. 'I first learned about fiction from her,' he says. She encouraged him to move to Madrid in 1967 when he was twenty-three. He got a steady day job in Telefonica, but in the aftermath of Franco's death began making outrageous mock pornographic Super 8 films that he presented in clubs and bars as happenings, imitating the programme of a real cinema with fake newsreels and fake adverts, and also providing a running commentary.

It was the birth of the *movida* – a sexual and cultural revolution beyond anything experienced in London in the so-called Swinging Sixties – in which young Madrileanos, encouraged by the left-wing mayor, Enrique Tierno Galvan, rejoiced in the hedonism of the moment, music, drink, drugs and sex. Suddenly there were no rules or restrictions any more in Spain. Everything seemed permissible. There was an upsurge of unashamed excess.

His mother gamely stood by him, even playing small roles in *What Have I Done to Deserve This* and *Women on the Verge of a Nervous Breakdown*:

> She could have been a character that I wrote. La Mancha is a very matriarchal society where it's the women who take the initiative, who get things done. This is the quality I remember from my childhood. They were very strong women, much stronger than the men. When my father died my mother was living in Extremadura and she wanted to come back to her origins. And then she started living again in the same street where she lived when she was a child. And all the girls she had played with then were widows.

He was soloist in the school choir:

I'd spend all day practising for Mass. One of the priests had the idea of presenting the headmaster with a surprise on his patron saint's day. It was a version of 'Dream of Sorrento' with a new set of lyrics, sung by me. They brought me to the priests' dining hall where they'd all had a bit to drink and had unbuttoned the tops of their habits. I sang the new version describing our headmaster as a gardener and his pupils as flowers whom he cared for with the flame of his love.

The incident – the small boy being offered up like a sacrificial lamb – becomes the pivotal scene in *Bad Education* that involves a paedophile headmaster:

The film is exactly like when I was the age of the protagonist. I wasn't sure about my faith when I was ten. I asked myself about what are we doing here in this world. I was waiting for some kind of sign. I waited a year for God to manifest himself to me, but he didn't. What manifested instead were the delinquent acts of his representatives on earth. I knew the enormous amount of abuse that was going on and allude to it in *Sisters of the Night, Matador, Law of Desire* and *What Have I Done to Deserve This*.

I think faith is a privilege that God grants his believers and I simply was not one of the chosen. I would have loved to have faith. It would probably have resolved many nights of insomnia. But unfortunately I never had it. And life is tougher without faith. But it is something you can't force.

He got the idea for *Broken Embraces* nine years ago on a visit to Lanzarote, soon after his mother died. 'My spirits, still in mourning, found reflection in the blackness of the island, a kind of soothing energy.' He took a photograph of the black volcanic Golfo beach, not realizing until the print was developed that he'd captured the image of a couple embracing, dwarfed by the landscape. He began imagining fictional explanations for their furtive embrace:

I wanted to use this photograph because it was full of mystery, like the photograph in Antonioni's *Blow-Up*. I had the feeling that the island was hiding a secret, something I had to find out. Since then I went almost every year to Lanzarote, trying to think of a way to include the island and the photo in a script, but they wouldn't fit.

The solution was to have Cruz and her director-lover escape to a remote bungalow on Lanzarote. As they lie in each other's arms, they watch Rossellini's *Voyage to Italy* on television. Ingrid Bergman and George Sanders are visiting Pompeii and witness the excavation of the bodies of a man and a woman smothered as they slept by lava from the eruption of Mount Vesuvius:

The lava set their embrace and their love for eternity. This prompts Penelope's character to say, 'When I die I want to die like this, in the arms of my lover.' She wouldn't mind at all if at that moment Timafaya erupted on Lanzarote and they too would die in each other's arms. Her lover sets up a camera on automatic, capturing their embrace in a photograph, a photograph that fuses their embrace for eternity. Of course, someone will then come along and tear up that photograph, hence the title *Broken Embraces*.

Quotes from other films are frequent in Almodovar's films, whether *Duel in the Sun* in *Matador*, *Double Indemnity* in *Bad Education* or *Johnny Guitar* in *Women on the Verge of a Nervous Breakdown*:

> These references are an essential part of the writing process from the very beginning. But I don't include them as a tribute. A tribute is something very passive and it would stop the story. These are a dynamic part of what is happening, as memories are.
>
> You are always discovering the story. Even when you finish the script and you start rehearsing with the actors, there are new things you didn't know before. The actual and the imagined become one, like a mirror.

* * *

Given the haphazard nature of foreign-language film distribution, it's not uncommon to become familiar with directors out of sequence through their more recent films before discovering their earlier work. Dublin audiences were introduced to Almodovar in 1989 when *Women on the Verge of a Nervous Breakdown* became a hit at Maretta Dillon and Neil Connolly's pioneering Light House Cinema: for a few glorious years this flourished on Middle Abbey Street right in the city centre before being demolished to make way for a department store development, but would later be reincarnated in Dublin's Smithfield Square.

He so flamboyantly captured the *jaleo* or buzz of a Spain I'd come to love through Julia that I tracked down as many of his earlier films that I could find – in particular *Law of Desire*, *Matador* and *What Have I Done to Deserve This* – and became his champion, so much so that the Spanish Cultural Institute, later the Cervantes Institute, invited me to give a lecture.

Maeve Hillary, the wife of the Irish president, indicated that she would attend. Eleven days before the event my mother fell ill. Despite two burglaries she still insisted at eighty-three on living alone with her cats and piano in the house on Sandymount Avenue where we grew up. Her GP finally managed to get her to agree to be admitted to St Vincent's Hospital. He told me she was unlikely to survive more than a few weeks.

Her relationship with Julia had initially been somewhat spiky, perhaps conditioned by her long-held distaste for de Valera or 'that Spaniard'. But just as she finally forgave Dev when he visited my father on his deathbed, a blind, 93-year-old president saying farewell to a loyal friend, she came to love Julia the more they got to know each other. Julia would bring her hot food and take her to buy her groceries on days when it was too wet to cycle to the village. She loved having the children around and played Chopin waltzes while they danced. She even came to Spain with us.

Each night she lay in hospital, drifting away before our eyes. The morphine administered to ease her pain opened a flow of increasingly incoherent memories where she seemed to find peace, memories of heading off to Paris in the late twenties with her friend Beag and the swagger of the men on the boulevards with their hats and their walking sticks, memories of her father with his stock of white hair and how she always had to provide him with his bottle of Guinness when he came to play bridge, even though she disapproved of drink, but mostly confused memories that made sense only to her: it was as if by reliving life she could somehow hang on to it.

I stopped by the hospital on the evening of the Almodovar talk. She was sleeping. The talk passed in a daze. The many references to Almodovar and his mother took on a poignancy that made it hard to go on. By the time I got back to the hospital it was nearing midnight. A nurse didn't expect any change so I kissed my mother on the forehead and left. As I opened the door at home the phone was ringing. She had passed away in her sleep. Julia returned with me to the hospital. We stood by her bedside, comforted by the sense of calm.

Julia was seventeen when her own mother died of cancer. Her father was seldom around. She was an only child and had taken on the responsibility of running the apartment where they lived on Andres Mellado in Madrid. She remembers bringing her mother to the doctor and being told there was no hope. She didn't tell her mother but she knew she knew; neither wanted to worry the other. She shared her mother's bed almost to the end so that she would not be alone in her pain. One night her mother told her to go to her own bed, and closed her eyes forever.

Much like Almodovar, her mother Estefania grew up in the country, the eldest of four children whose mother married when she was fourteen. The husband worked in Logrono, capital of the Rioja region. When he arrived home on his horse to the tiny mountain village of Pradillo and found his wife skipping, he inquired about his dinner. 'Don't bother me,' she said. 'Can't you see I'm playing with my friends?'

When the Republican government came to power in 1931 and introduced sweeping land reform and rights for women, her mother found work in Madrid and encouraged her two brothers and her sister to join her: she was the head of the family they had learned to rely on. She was forty-one when much to their disapproval she married Julio Alonso, a man of striking dark looks and several years younger.

A few days after their marriage, civil war broke out. Madrid was under siege. The university area around Arquelles where they lived suffered the worst bombardment. Julia was born in a palace that had been converted into a makeshift hospital. All her mother's jewellery had been pawned to buy food. They fed on cats. Her father was cut off outside the city driving trucks that gathered the bodies of the dead. He eventually got back after Franco's victory emotionally scarred and restless, living only for the moment. He never settled down. He missed Julia's First Communion. She overheard someone complaining that he was with another woman.

The family was divided in the relentless purge of Republicans launched by Franco. One brother married the daughter of a Franco supporter and made a small fortune with a franchise for Otis lifts; the other brother, a champion at the Basque game of *frontón*, had to hide for two years in the attic. Her sister Carmen fled with her husband and two children over the Pyrenees to France, where they lived as refugees for several years.

Julia grew up in an education system run by the Catholic Church as a propaganda arm of the fascist regime, self-proclaimed as the 'world's spiritual repository'. She remembers girls in her class wearing gold bracelets with little swastikas. The school took its cue from the all-powerful Seccion Feminina of the fascist Falange group that urged young girls 'not to burden themselves with books ... there's no need to be intellectual'. Girls should not 'take sport as a pretext to wear scandalous costumes'. It was compulsory for everyone to line the streets whenever the self-styled Generalisimo with his goose-stepping troops made a public appearance. Her mother warned her never to speak of anything that she heard at home.

She found work at the American air bases after her mother's death. Her father had remarried and she was an outsider in her own home. She wanted to go to England to learn English but couldn't get a passport without her father's permission until she was twenty-one. By then his second wife had left him, taking most of her mother's things. Through an agency she got a job as an au pair with a family in Darlington. To be allowed travel outside Spain she had to sign an undertaking that when she returned she would do her 'Social Service', a form of female military conscription that obliged young women to supply free labour for hospitals and other social institutions. She got a train to Irun, another to Paris, and then another to Calais where she got the ferry to Dover, another train to London and then finally another six-hour train journey to Darlington, afraid to sleep in case she was robbed or missed her station. She'd never been out of Spain before.

And so we met. I'd stuck a pin in the jobs section of *World Press News* and found a newspaper in Darlington that was prepared to give me a start in journalism on the basis of my degree in history, politics and economics. As Paul Auster says, everything is born out of chance. Relationships are formed at the throw of a dice.

An ex-RAF pilot who ran the paper's photography department took me under his wing. He was married to a Catholic and told me the best place to meet girls was at Sunday Mass in the town's only Catholic church. I followed his advice and was immediately lucky. The only time Julia was allowed off was to go to Mass on Sundays. She was a friend of Joan Maguire who worked with me on the paper. They'd met at a bus stop. She was looking miserable. 'What's wrong?' Joan asked. 'I've no friends.' 'Well, I'll be your friend,' Joan replied. She was with Joan that first Sunday, dark-haired and dark-eyed in a light-blue coat, and we got talking over coffee.

Her time in Darlington was coming to an end. Her father was ill and she felt guilty. For all his faults she'd always been close to him. Now he had no one. We sat together on the train to London on her journey home, and parted at Waterloo Station like in a scene from a movie, the train pulling out and me running along the platform as she looked back from the window, disappearing into the steam, perhaps forever.

It was clear more than anything else in my life that if I didn't think of something quick we would never meet again. I got a job back in Dublin, handed in my resignation and booked a flight to Madrid, landing at Barajas Airport in a thunderstorm. She was waiting with her cousin Lolo. Although we'd known each other for months in England, here in Madrid we were not allowed to be alone with each other without a chaperone.

So while she slept in the empty apartment of her cousin Carmen, who had moved to the Canaries to be with her husband, an army colonel who was based there, I stayed with her uncle on the other side of town. There was no sneaking out to be with her, either. Back then you couldn't enter a building without the approval of a *portero*. If it was after 10.30 pm then you had to stand in the street clapping your hands sharply to get the attention of a *sereno*, often a neighourhood spy.

The Seccion Feminina dictated how women should behave at work ('Conceal your physical presence. Let us be gracious and amiable little ants') and as wives ('If your husband asks you for unusual sexual practices, be obedient and don't complain. If he suggests union, agree humbly. When the culminating moment arrives, a small whimper on your part is sufficient to indicate any pleasure that might have been experienced'). Julia knew that this couldn't be her life. After I left she got another au pair job in Wimbledon but at my father's suggestion soon gave this up and moved to Dublin to live with us, working in the accounts department of the Russell Hotel. We married that summer.

On our first wedding anniversary she heard from Madrid that her father was dead. She rang Mariano and Mercedes Doporto, a couple of Republican exiles who had become our friends. He was the first director of the Irish Meterological Service; she lectured at Trinity. They went every summer to Biarritz from where they could see Spain from afar, even if they couldn't be there. Mariano had vowed never to return until Franco was dead.

Within an hour they were at our door having made the journey across town by bus. They took Julia in their arms. 'We are your parents now,' Mariano said. Mariano died before Franco and according to his will was buried in Glasnevin Cemetery in Dublin: even in death he would not countenance being in soil under a dictatorship. One of Franco's last acts before he passed into a final coma in 1975 was to sign an order for the judicial garroting of three dissident prisoners.

King Juan Carlos, put on the throne by Franco and given little chance of continuing to reign after he departed, unexpectedly became a unifying figure through the skill and apparent sincerity with which he committed Spain to free and open parliamentary politics and a complex process of liberalization and reform. Undoubtedly his most significant action was his choice of former TVE director Adolfo Suárez as prime minister in July 1976.

Suárez's policy of imposing democracy from above received overwhelming support in a referendum in which he told the nation in an historic television broadcast: 'The future is not written down yet because only the people can write it. This is why the people will have their say. The government, I heard, has prepared the instruments by means of which this say can be expressed authentically, so as to guarantee its sovereignty.'

When a new Spanish ambassador to Ireland, Joaquin Juste, invited me in the spring of 1977 to visit Spain and interview some of the people involved in the transition to democracy, there was a sense of returning on behalf of Mariano and all the Republicans who had been driven out or imprisoned or murdered or, like Julia's father, ruthlessly marginalized and not allowed to leave the country even for his daughter's marriage.

Suárez at forty-four was then Europe's youngest prime minister. He looks even younger when I see him early in March 1977 at the Palace of Moncloa outside Madrid, which recently became the new seat of government. It is just after his cabinet met to confirm a wide-ranging new amnesty for political prisoners. He's smaller than his photographs suggest, a slim olive-skinned man with a refreshingly unstuffy manner that puts people at their ease yet at the same time sustains a certain necessary reserve. '*Que joven*,' a provincial politician murmurs. '*Que guapo*' (How young, how handsome).

Suárez sums up his approach in a phrase: 'We've got to construct a real democracy without hurting anybody.' His outstanding quality, according to Carmen Diez de Rivera, is an ability to pursue a course without wavering, but always with tact. 'The first government after Franco was a disaster,' she tells me. 'They were mostly old men from the old regime. They didn't know what to do.'

Thirty-four-year-old Carmen Diez's appointment as adviser to Suárez and to his cabinet is a declaration of intent. That someone so young – and a woman, too – should reach such a position of power is all the more astonishing in a country so rooted under Franco in the tradition of machismo. It's as if Spain has suddenly skipped a generation. In public life, after decades of doddering protocol and archaic conventions, young people in their thirties and forties are increasingly in control. 'It has been … how do you say … rather shocking,' she tells me. 'But there has always been a strong feminist role on the left in Spain.'

We're sitting on a couch in her study. She wears casual flared trousers and a blouse and cardigan. Yet her informality does not seem out of place amid the Goya tapestries and period furniture and porcelain. The palace has the friendly ambience not of a museum but of a place in which people live and work.

Carmen Diez comes from an aristocratic family and worked as a teacher in Africa before studying at the Sorbonne in Paris. She met Suárez at TVE. 'I was an international editor because that was the only way I could be free to say what I thought. Everything to do with the situation within Spain was censored.'

Her politics are somewhat to the left of his. She belonged as a student to the breakaway social democrat group led by former Falangist poet Dionisio Rodrigo. She points to philosopher Ortega y Gasset, an early supporter of the Republic in the 1930s and castigator of 'the dehumanization of man' in contemporary society, as a significant influence on her thought, and she is now a director of the new liberal newspaper *El País* of which Ortega's son is chairman. She will later represent the Spanish Socialist Party (PSOE) in the European Parliament but then die tragically of cancer, aged forty-eight.

Although she plays down the significance of her position ('I am not in the government'), her closeness to socialists and communists and ability to move freely among them has been a crucial factor in facilitating the Suárez policy of governing in consultation with the opposition. The left is rapidly emerging as a dynamic force in the new Spain. No enduring democracy can be shaped without its participation. She makes no secret of her admiration for Santiago Carrillo, leader of the still illegal Communist Party, and has allowed herself to be photographed with him. 'Although very different in outlook, the two most impressive politicians in Spain today are Suárez and Carrillo,' she says.

The Socialist Party has just been legalized. Its headquarters is in a labyrinth of rooms on the second floor of a dilapidated building on the Calle Joaquin Morato. Before being admitted through a formidably thick door we have to identify ourselves over an intercom: accompanying me is Mariano Doporto's eldest son, Mariano, in case I need help translating. Inside is a hubbub of activity with predominantly young people hurrying about, arguing on telephones and typing. Looking down over them with approval is a bust of thick-bearded Pablo Iglesias, the Karl Marx of Spanish socialism.

Felipe González, already a charismatic figure in Spain, is putting the finishing touches to a speech he is giving that night to a feminist conference. 'Society here is a phallocracy,' he says. 'Women suffer a double discrimination as women and as workers. Their problems can't be divorced from the class struggle. A change in the relation between capital and labour will bring about a change in their situation.'

The Socialist Party accepts the monarchy as a medium for achieving representative democracy. 'We would only be against it if it became an impediment to this,' says Luis Yanez, a close aide of González. 'The choice in Spain is between liberty and dictatorship rather than between republic and monarchy.

The process of change is irreversible. Spain has passed the point of no return.'

To get to the third-floor office of Spain's controversial newspaper, *El País* – it's in a new printing works on the outskirts of Madrid – I have to produce a passport and go through a series of security checks. Somewhat apprehensively I step forward into a lift guarded by two soldiers with machine guns at the ready. 'I don't say people are in a panic but they are a little frightened,' says Juan Luis Cebrián, the paper's 32-year-old editor. 'But coming from Ireland, you won't have been surprised by any of that.'

All prominent figures in Spain are given this kind of protection, but Cebrián probably needs it more than most. Although only in existence ten months, the vigorously independent *El País* has already achieved a circulation of almost 200,000, making it Spain's first genuinely national newspaper. But its outspoken rejection of everything associated with Franco's regime has earned it many enemies. In particular it has incensed the ultra-right by revealing links between Blas Piñar's fascist Fuerza Nueva party and the so-called Grapo terrorists responsible for a spate of assassinations in January that nearly jeopardized the peaceful transition to democracy.

'The recent violence has all the appearance of a conspiracy against the state with the intent of provoking intervention by the army,' Cebrián says. 'Grapo has been manipulated by the ultra-right in order to stop elections taking place and provide the excuse for a coup. But although the army is Francoist, conservative and distrustful of change, it is disciplined, very loyal to the king and committed to standing by the electoral process.'

Spain wouldn't have the freedom it is now achieving without *El País* and other newspapers and magazines – in particular *Cambio 16* – that even before Franco's death were courageously creating the stimulus for democratic change. 'In the last days of the regime the press provided the only free platform to the opposition,' says Cebrián, who was the editor of the evening paper, *Informaciones*:

> There was a system of auto-censorship in force that wasn't formal censorship but wasn't freedom either. It was a system of warning, fines and prosecutions. But the emerging political groups were able to formulate and spread their ideas in print, and parties, too, in this way. Spain began to become a democracy through the newspapers. The newspapers took on the role of the parliament we didn't have.

Almost overnight, archaic social conventions and hypocritical pieties are losing acceptance. Almost anything can be and is being published. Inevitably, much of it is exploitative. Imitation *Playboy* magazines advertising 'sexy' home movies are prominent on newsstands. Strip clubs are proliferating. Even in legitimate theatre, full frontal nudity and explicit language are in vogue.

This is a dilemma for Antonio Buero Vallejo, whose plays have dominated Spanish theatre since his first success with *Story of a Stairway* in 1949. With the lifting of stage censorship almost no theme is too controversial. Subtlety is regarded as old-fashioned. 'But somehow most of the new plays lack social bite,' he says. 'They are less critical than before.' Such is the paradox of freedom: truth only seems to be valued when it is being suppressed.

Around us on the walls of his study are his drawings of friends who shared his cell during the six years he spent in Franco's jails after the Civil War. 'I was under sentence of death for eight months. But in a way I suppose that was my university, a university of life.'

The plays that established him as an internationally renowned writer – with Garry Hynes at Druid pioneering his work in Ireland – were all written under the Franco regime. 'But no thanks to the regime,' he says.

> It's true that everything had to be submitted to censors. It's true that many changes and cuts were made. It's true that many works were prohibited. Yet talking with half-words and suggestion you can turn theatre into a platform for the diffusion of freedom.
>
> It's arguable that the most critical and socially aware writing in Spain's literary history was produced during repressive periods. This happened in other countries, too. Look at what Tolstoy, Dostoevsky, Gogol, Gorky and Chekhov could achieve under tsarist censors. The genius that a writer has to develop in front of censorship has been responsible for some of literature's greatest truths.

When after twelve years' official obstruction Buero Vallejo's play *The Double Life of Dr Valmy* was finally staged in Madrid in 1976, it was mistakenly regarded as representing the new freedom of expression in Spain. It's an allegory about torture in which the victim is hardly seen at all: the emphasis is on the torturers and the hypocrisies with which they pretend to themselves and their friends that talk about injustice is an 'exaggeration' or an 'invention'. We see them degraded by their work and, through them, the political system and society that knowingly tolerates torture. 'Even after Franco all the names of the characters had to be changed so that they wouldn't sound Spanish,' he says. Under Spain's new freedom such a play might have been far more direct, but perhaps less powerful.

Most of the taboos of cinema and theatre have now been lifted. Scripts of Spanish films no longer have to be submitted in advance to the Ministry of Culture and previously prohibited themes are being frankly treated. Nudity has become almost an essential box-office ingredient.

Buero Vallejo, in contrast, got the better of the dictatorship by creating a language that used allegorical forms and relied on irony and symbolism to imply what could not be spoken.

The setting for his 1950 play, *In the Burning Darkness*, was a home for the blind. Some patients accepted being blind, others refused to conform. They wanted to see, even if it killed them. The blindness became a metaphor for other kinds of blindness in life. Perhaps the home for the blind was Spain. 'Art is a triumph over limitations,' says Buero Vallejo.

Like Buero Vallejo in theatre, Carlos Saura managed to keep making films of integrity throughout the Franco era by creating a form of seditious allegory so oblique that the censors could never prove it was there. Much of the power of his art grew out of the very restrictions within which he was obliged to work. Thus *Ana and the Wolves* might seem merely to be about a girl going to work as a governess at a remote mansion. But the demanding mother she encounters is a personification of Spain and the three middle-aged sons, with their vices and obsessions, represent the Church, the state and the army, the pillars of the dictatorship.

Similarly, both *La Prima Angelica* and *Cria Cuervos* imply the institutional violence inherent in authoritarian society, particularly the army and the Church; but this can be justified as merely the naive viewpoint of the young children through whom the action is perceived.

Saura no longer has to bother with these games, and he's greatly relieved. 'I feel liberated from the moral obligation to imply political things in my work,' he tells me. 'Now I can put all my attention into the art. I can show in a picture not the things I feel I ought to but the things that I like.'

Luis Berlanga, whose black humour led to his marginalization after an initial international triumph with the satire, *Bienvenido Mr Marshall*, in 1952 (he managed to make only three films between 1963 and 1977) urges caution. 'In every society there will always be limitations on what you can say,' he says.

> You still can't attack the monarchy or the army in Spain. Not that I want to, but I don't see why they should be untouchable things. And there are other restrictions, too, created by the capitalist nature of society. Although we have political freedom now, we can't always raise the money to make certain pictures we want to. During the Franco era we had the money, but not the freedom. Now we have the freedom but we can't get the money.

**Antonio Buero Vallejo during the Franco era.**

Pilar Miró, a former television associate of Suárez whose erotically explicit film, *The Betrothal* – in which a woman is the dominant sexual protagonist – has become a commercial success, sees the collapse of censorship as a creative challenge. 'We have had a blanket over our heads,' she says.

> We could always pretend before that we didn't think because the regime wouldn't let us. Now we have no excuses. We are sort of in the examination hall.
>
> We have to learn a new language. We have passed all our lives talking ambiguously and now we don't know how to talk in a normal way. We wrote between the lines and now we don't know how to write. We have to learn how to say *bah*.

•   •   •

If King Juan Carlos epitomized Spain's remarkable transition to freedom and democracy, Pedro Almodovar became its cultural expression. His films are a running commentary on a changing Spain filtered through an affectionately irreverent personal vision. No other contemporary director can match his sustained brilliance.

'I'm a lucky person,' he says, lounging back on the cushions of his beach couch. 'By chance I came on the scene at just the perfect time. All eyes were on Spain. There was a party. But we had to pay the price for that party. I don't reject anything, but then I survived. Not everyone did. Some died on the way.'

Spain has moved on, and so has Almodovar:

> That feeling of unfettered freedom, the feeling of creativity, a creativity that was not profit-driven, it won't happen again. Young people are much more market-driven. They feel that they have to create things that will sell. So there is not the freedom that we had in our day. Madrid is still a great city but there are now restrictions on what happens. It has become much more European with regards to how people go out and enjoy themselves. I think the *movida* marked the beginning of a new era for Spain. That democracy is now bedded down. And therefore we face the problems of a mature democracy.

He's apprehensive about the negativism of the Partido Popular (the People's Party), which was thrown out of government after the 2004 train bombings and defeated again in 2008.

> They are very much putting a break on the development of civil liberties. They are against everything. The Partido Popular used to call itself a centre-right party, but what we're now seeing is that they are an extreme-right party putting itself with the Church. They don't really accept the results of the elections. They behave like Spain is a Catholic country, but it is not. I hope Zapatero's socialists hang on, otherwise we are in bad times.

He's still planning to film *Tell Me What a Tree Looks Like*, the autobiography of a communist poet, Marcos Ana, who was imprisoned by Franco when he was seventeen and only released in 1961. After thirty-four years, during which he was tortured and twice sentenced to death and kept his sanity by writing poems ('Poetry was another weapon to fight for freedom, I don't say that my poems were good or not, only that they were necessary'), he spends his first night of freedom with a prostitute, likely to be played by Penelope Cruz, to whom he tells his story.

It's a story that confronts the painful legacy of the nation's political past, stirring dark memories. 'Ana is now eighty-nine,' Amaldovar says, 'a man completely free of hatred, a victim who does not seek revenge. For our country, after going through that awful civil war, he is a lesson in understanding.'

# eight

## Werner Herzog, Nicolas Cage, Angelina Jolie and Jon Voight

Werner Herzog filming COBRA VERDE on location in Nicaragua in 1984.

I t is early evening in late June. The window is open and the soothing smell of freshly cut grass wafts in on a breeze. The curtain is half drawn so that the television screen isn't obscured by the light of the setting sun.

Werner Herzog's haunting documentary, *Encounters at the End of the World*, about life at the South Pole above and below the ice, is showing on the Discovery Channel. It includes scary footage of scientists blasting a hole and plunging into the freezing water beneath to explore the ocean floor and collect samples. To avoid interfering with the ecosystem they disdain use of a tether line, trusting themselves to find their way back to the hole.

'I noticed that the divers in their routine were not speaking at all,' remarks Herzog. 'To me, they were like priests preparing for Mass. Those few who have experienced the world under the frozen sky often speak of it as going down to the cathedral.'

Herzog spent just seven weeks in Antarctica, filming alone with a cinematographer, curious to find out what brought people to live and work like recluses in eternal day or night. 'They are professional dreamers, they dream all the time.'

A penguin drops out of a line of waddling companions and heads off alone at a tangent across the ice into the vast emptiness. 'The rules for the humans are not to disturb or hold up the penguin,' Werner Herzog intones dryly, while his camera lingers on the penguin, by now no more than a wavering dot. 'Stand still and let him go on his way. He's heading towards certain death.'

The voice, dispassionate and ever curious, hasn't changed. We're back a quarter of a century earlier in the office building in Munich he shares with Volker Schlöndorff, who directed *The Tin Drum*. He pads noiselessly around the room, dressed casually in rubber-soled runners. He talks quietly, with the lyrical cadences of a poet.

He's set up an editing machine to show me sequences he has just brought back from the Himalayas. High on the slopes of K2, the most daunting of the peaks, he confronts mountaineer Reinhold Messner with questions no one has dared ask before.

'There's never been a climber as strong as him,' Herzog explains. 'He's conquered almost all the mountains. He's far ahead of the others.' On K2 ten years earlier Messner's brother Gunther had been swept from his side. 'We were like one,' Messner says.

He searched alone in the snow for the body until the toes were frozen off his left foot. Now he crouches in a red tent at base camp before yet another assault on the summit.

'What was it like,' Herzog asks abruptly, 'having to tell your mother that your brother had been killed?'

Messner begins to answer, then breaks down, putting a gloved hand over his face to hide his tears. The camera remains remorselessly focused on him.

'I didn't mind that I asked him such a vicious thing,' Herzog tells me. 'He knew that I would dig deep into the untouchable part of him. That sometimes I might ask things that shouldn't be asked, that there would be no mercy. And you see his reaction. I think afterwards he was glad we went too far.'

You have to be prepared to be pushed beyond the limit if you make films with Herzog, which is no more than he asks of himself. He is preoccupied with the power of the mind to triumph over physical circumstances no matter how overwhelming. Only at the extremities of experience can man discover what he's really made of.

He had no compunction while filming *Fitzcarraldo* in causing Klaus Kinski and Claudia Cardinale and other stars to endure the most atrocious conditions in uncharted regions of the Amazon, harassed by tribes that still practise cannibalism. He even pulled a gun on Kinski and ordered him to act or die. All the actors in *Heart of Glass* were hypnotized so that they could perform in a transcendental state of mind, giving voice to the irrational depths of their consciousness.

He shot the documentary *La Soufrière* on Guadaloupe just before a volcano was about to erupt, staying on with his camera crew after the entire area had been evacuated.

Among the cans of film piled on the floor behind us is new footage shot in Nicaragua, where he got caught up in an ambush while accompanying a commando unit on the Honduran frontier.

'Don't you think you're a little deranged to keep climbing mountains?' he asks Messner on K2.

'All art is deranged,' Messner replies.

This could sum up Herzog's approach to film-making. It's as if to get inside his characters he has to emulate them. Films to him are like the impossible castles of the mad King Ludwig of Bavaria's dreams.

'A film like *Fitzcarraldo* could only have been done by a Ludwig,' he admits, pleased with the comparison. 'The exuberance of fantasy and folly.'

It's no surprise that he was briefly involved with the NASA space programme in the US after going there on a scholarship to Philadelphia University.

'I worked on a documentary about non-conventional rocket propulsion systems, a rocket that would ride on a beam of light, all very much in the future. The first one wouldn't be ready before 2030 in their estimates.'

He never got beyond the pre-production stage. A security check revealed he'd broken his visa requirements. He fled to Mexico before suffering the indignity of deportation.

It was the first, if coincidental, contact with the god-defying feats his films have come to exemplify. 'The conquest of the useless,' he smiles, ironically echoing his hero Fitzcarraldo who had a boat dragged over a mountain in pursuit of his dream to bring opera to the natives.

That's what comes from growing up on a farm in Bavaria. It's the Ireland of Germany. Fantasy tends to coexist on the same level as fact. People still believe their dreams.

'It's getting lost with a civilization that through television levels everything,' he says. 'But there certainly is some sort of spirit still prevailing there.'

No matter what part of the world Herzog makes his films, he's always filming Germany. 'Even if it's in the Peruvian jungle in the sixteenth century, as with *Aguirre, Wrath of God*, it's still a very German film, or, rather, Bavarian.'

Munich prides itself on being a little Hollywood. Many of the films that seek to re-establish Germany as a force in international cinema are produced here. 'But there's one thing you should be cautious about,' Herzog warns:

Everyone speaks about the new German cinema, and I always insist that it's Bavarian cinema. You as an Irishman would understand that. You'd surely be insulted if someone called you an Englishman. We're also two very different cultures.

The images that are in my films are images that are inside people around here in the streets of Munich. I only make people acquainted with images that are somehow already deep inside them.

I'm trying to work on a grammar of new images, but nothing as sensational as completely new images that haven't been seen yet. They're really very familiar. I'm convinced these images are inner images of all of us, only that we have not articulated them. I simply put you in touch with them.

Herzog is a prophet ahead of his time, more recognized abroad than among his own people. 'I usually get the worst reviews of all here in Munich,' he shrugs.

The previous evening I witnessed this for myself at a local screening of his new feature, *Where the Green Ants Dream*, a brilliantly understated parable about aboriginals in the Australian bush defying an attempt to mine uranium on one of their sacred sites. 'I wanted to show not so much the mythology but the insistence with which the aborigines defended their religious beliefs and the dignity of their struggle for their dreams,' he says.

After the screening a woman stood up in the cinema denouncing it as a waste of her money. Other Herzog films have been similarly rejected here. *Aguirre, Wrath of God* was not considered worthy of any rating by the Wiesbaden commission that decides which films qualify for tax relief. *The Enigma of Kasper Hauser* was taken off in Munich after two weeks. When it won awards at Cannes, everyone asked why Herzog hadn't shown it in Munich. He rereleased it and it ran for twenty-nine weeks.

'There's a great insecurity among German audiences, which is perhaps understandable after the catastrophes of the two world wars. Somehow we've lost our self-confidence, particularly in cultural values.'

He can imagine a political situation developing in which he might feel compelled to leave Germany altogether. 'If I had to emigrate my first choice would be Ireland. That's because people like their poets there.'

Back in 1972 he had occasion to rent a house at Lennane harbour, Co. Mayo. 'The people asked what my profession was. They were just curious to know whether I could pay the rent. I said I was a poet and they gave me the place for half price. In Germany they'd have slammed the door in my face.'

Since then Irish references have been recurring in his films. The vision of people climbing a mountain in *Kasper Hauser* was filmed on Croagh Patrick. Skellig Michael figures prominently in *Heart of Glass*. *Fitzcarraldo* was inspired by a turn-of-the-century Irish adventurer, Brian Sweeney Fitzgerald – no one in Peru could pronounce his name – who built an opera house in the middle of the jungle.

Herzog is now planning to return to K2 to film a feature on the scale of *Fitzcarraldo*. He joined the Messner expedition to check out the logistical problems of shooting at high altitude. What he initially had in mind was a 'mountain' film in the 1930s German tradition popularized by Arnold Franck, Hans Sheinhoff and Leni Riefenstahl. But as he talked with Messner he realized that the film would be him. 'The documentary became a sort of rehearsal.'

Klaus Kinski and other actors are being packed off to a training camp in the Austrian Tyrol to get fit. 'Filming is athletes' work,' says Herzog, smiling in anticipation.

They can expect a rougher time on K2 than filming on the Amazon. 'At thirty or forty degrees below zero the camera stock can break like uncooked spaghetti and at such a high altitude the body dehydrates as in a desert. Nowhere in the Himalayas are the snow drifts more lethal, the glaciers bigger, the crevices deeper.' As Messner exclaims in the documentary, 'It's the construction site of the gods.'

Herzog whispers a translation as the film runs in the editing machine. 'I haven't got a title yet,' he says. 'You're one of the first to see it. It's still a work in progress. I have to edit it for German television. Perhaps I'll call it *The Dark Glow of the Mountain*. But that doesn't sound so good in German.'

He can't make up his mind about the ending, either. 'Because it brings me into the film and I hesitate about that.'

The sequence shows Messner arriving back from the summit and confiding to Herzog that sometimes he dreams about walking off into the snow and never looking back. 'And at the end of my life the world would end, too,' he says.

'I have that dream as well,' Herzog tells him.

'Well, we will walk together, with you behind me,' Messner laughs.

Having fallen out with Kinski, who is now dead, Herzog has since searched over the years for an actor capable of going to extremes who might take his place. He may have found him in Nicolas Cage. Cage seems to think so. Their remake of Abel Ferrara's 1992 cult thriller, *Bad Lieutenant*, now set in New Orleans instead of New York, and with Cage in the old Harvey Keitel role of a corrupt cop high on drugs to assuage his Catholic guilt, is to premiere at the 2009 Venice Film Festival.

'I wanted to find something new to do with it, not just play another New York cop,' Cage tells me. 'The first movie was very much a Judeo-Christian thing about guilt and repentance. This is more existentialist, chaos happens, there isn't always guilt, there isn't always repentance – it's a more philosophical debate.'

We're in a hotel overlooking New York's Central Park. Cage has the look of a biker in off the street. He's wearing black leather trousers and a black leather top, unzipped over a white vest. He has a lazy disarming voice, and his aqua-blue eyes are engaging. There's a clutter of thick silver rings on his long fingers. Have they some special meaning? 'Yeah, a personal significance,' he says. He doesn't elaborate.

We'd met in Athens in 2000, soon after his marriage to Patricia Arquette broke up, and again in Washington five years ago when he had just married nineteen-year-old sushi waitress Alice Kim. They now have a four-year-old son, and he has a sixteen-year-old son, Weston, from a relationship with Christina Fulton. 'I think without jinxing anything I'm feeling more content in my life right now,' he says. 'That's about as far as I'll go with that. But I'm a little more relaxed.'

His arts professor father, August Coppola, once told him, 'Tom Cruise sells perfection, you sell imperfection.'

This comes closest to explaining what to others might seem like his eccentricity. 'Eccentric is one of those really polite words for crazy, isn't it?' he laughs:

> Any actor or painter or musician has to find inspiration somewhere to make the work exciting for themselves and for the audience. So sometimes you might be perceived as being crazy in your quest to explore. I don't know if that's a conscious choice or if I am in fact definitely out of my mind. What we do is so mysterious I couldn't even begin to explain it. To talk like that sounds automatically a bit eccentric. But I'm just one human being. If you want to label me eccentric, then go for it.

You could almost read his life from his roles. 'It really depends on what my state of mind is at the time. My characters in *Adaptation* and *Matchstick Men* were very neurotic and confused people. They were forcing me to look at more uncomfortable subject matter, and that's where I was at that time.'

By contrast in *National Treasure*, a Jerry Bruckheimer blockbuster that went on to become a lucrative franchise, he plays a likeable maverick who steals the American Declaration of Independence to save it from falling into the wrong hands. 'Maybe it's a case of life imitating art. My character is a little more together. When I did it I was in a headspace where I really wanted to do something more light and playful, more like Cary Grant in *Charade* or *To Catch a Thief*.'

He seems to need some kind of authenticity to validate his performances. He had two teeth extracted to simulate shrapnel damage for his role as a Vietnam War veteran in Alan Parker's *Birdy*. He swallowed a live cockroach for *Vampire's Kiss*. I remember him showing me his fingers blistered from playing the mandolin in *Captain Corelli's Mandolin*. Director Mike Figgis worried about his sanity during his Oscar-winning portrayal of a dying alcoholic in *Leaving Las Vegas*.

'Nick has something special,' says Jon Turteltaub, who directed *National Treasure*. 'He's still a risk-taker and a rebel. Whether this comes from some creative gene he has or an anger gene I don't know, but he's certainly used it to make him who he is.'

Turteltaub should know. They were at school together at Beverly Hills High in 1980, but back then Cage was a Coppola, nephew of director Francis Ford Coppola.

'I remember being on the set of *The Godfather Part II* at Lake Tahoe and being fascinated by that world,' says Cage:

> But at the same time I felt watched and judged when I was trying to make it in Hollywood with that name. I'd encounter other actors who really felt I was only there because of my name and that I had no talent. It was always like a little pitchfork sticking in my ass telling me I'm going to have to work harder than anyone else to prove I can do this.

Cage was raised in Long Beach, inheriting a love of performance from his mother, dancer Joy Vogelsang:

> I wanted to be a film actor when I was six years old, from watching movies on television. There were people moving around inside that thing and I thought,

wow, how do they do that? How do they get inside? I'd walk to school and visualize crane shots. I remember I had a crane shot where I was getting smaller and smaller in the street and the camera was pulling up.

To avoid being bullied he'd dress up as his big brother Robert, slicking back his black hair and putting on shades and boots; a way of dressing that's never changed. 'Nick arrived at school and he felt like an outsider, I think,' recalls Turteltaub:

> He was like the only kid at the time who had muscles. Nobody had muscles, not at Beverly High and certainly not in the drama department. All the girls were like, Oooo, he's sexy. Nick doesn't remember it that way because the girls did a good job of not letting him know – girls do that – but the other guys who weren't getting dates with those girls knew. But Nick was shy. He's still shy. He's uncomfortable with himself at times.

Cage would invite Turteltaub to his house 'just to make friends, but Jon never invited me over to his house. I remember him being very popular and very socially acceptable, whereas I was awkward and withdrawn.'

They appeared together in the school production of *Oklahoma* – the drummer in the band was Lenny Kravitz – but Cage lost out to Turteltaub for the lead in *Our Town*. 'Nick understood film and film acting, and that doesn't always fit when you're doing a high-school play,' Turteltaub says. 'High-school plays were all cheery and wonderful, and not so good. And that was me. That's the kind of actor I was. But Nick quickly started having this incredible success. We were all teenagers and he was making *Fast Times at Ridgemont High* and *Valley Girl*.'

As the nephew of Francis Coppola it should have been easy for him: 'But that was the problem. I guess because I started acting professionally so young other actors of the same age didn't accept me. They said I was there because of my uncle. People at that age can be very harsh in what they say. I guess I took it to heart. I couldn't concentrate on auditions.'

*Rumble Fish* brought it all to a head. Francis Coppola treated S.E. Hinton's story of the tensions between two brothers in a teenage gang, played by Mickey Rourke and Matt Dillon, as a mirror of his own childhood relationship with his big brother, Cage's father. Nicolas was cast as one of the gang. 'In my uncle's imagination my role was very much like my father, so he had me sort of looking like him. I even had to wear his old club jacket. I was terrified but I didn't know how to say no.'

When *Rumble Fish* opened, reviewer Stanley Kaufman sneered, 'He is Coppola's nephew. Nothing else explains why this thin-voiced inadequate was given the role.' To distance himself from Coppola professionally, Cage adopted the surname of two outsiders, the composer John Cage and a comic book hero Luke Cage. 'It wasn't because I was ashamed or I didn't want to be associated with Francis. I think he's a remarkable artist. I'd work again with him at a heartbeat.'

Coppola was a little huffed. He sent him a telegram DEAR NICOLAS STOP CONGRATULATIONS STOP FRANCIS CAGE STOP and has since said, 'My thoughts on him then and now are that he is a Coppola and I wish his name was still Coppola.'

'I'm still very much a Coppola at heart,' Cage would insist, proving he wasn't trying to avoid being associated with him by playing the psycho actor in *The Cotton Club* and Kathleen's Turner's ne'er-do-well husband in the time-trip romance *Peggy Sue Got Married*.

He's clearly a Coppola in taking risks and doing the unexpected. He jumps from near-demented roles – the incompetent baby snatcher in *Raising Arizona*, the one-handed baker wooing Cher in *Moonstruck*, or Laura Dern's seducer in David Lynch's *Wild at Heart* – to being a Jerry Bruckheimer pin-up action hero in *The Rock*, *Con Air* and *Gone in Sixty Seconds*:

> It's important not to get stuck in a box. Very often if you do something that's challenging, it's going to meet with a great deal of resistance and I think those are the roles to look at, the ones that make you a bit uncomfortable. It's meant that I've done lots of flops, but I like making myself uncomfortable. It's the only way forward.
>
> My interests aren't really interests that are in keeping with many people. I like taboo subject matter. Not many people want to see a film like *Sonny*, my directorial debut, about a mother who raised her son to be a prostitute. But to me it was like, wow, this happened. I felt for those people.

When he was a child his father built him a small castle of plywood: 'I'd go in there and I could imagine I was different characters. I'd have my lunch there, out in the backyard, and pretend I was a knight or an astronaut. That was where I learned to act. I found a place where my emotions made sense. I could channel my anger and my pain through acting.'

As a father he made a similar gesture to his teenage son Weston, teaming up with him to develop a comic book, *Voodoo Child*, for Virgin Comics:

> He had the idea percolating for a while because we used to go to New Orleans together when he was growing up and it had a house reputed to be the most

haunted house in America, although I never saw anything there. We're hoping it can be turned into a movie with him playing the bad guy and me as the cop.

Comic culture has much in common with Greek mythology and I'm a great aficionado of it. When I was a kid I always wanted to be Charles Bronson or Steve McQueen … but as an actor I prefer to rip the mask off super heroes.

Of all the flawed characters Nicolas Cage has empathized with, Terence McDonagh in Herzog's *Bad Lieutenant* is the most mesmerizing. A cop with a limp and anger to go with it, high on caffeine and amphetamines, he stalks the sewers of New Orleans busting drug dealers and pocketing their stash. There's even an outrageous scene in which he pulls a gun on an old lady in a wheelchair to get her to talk, driven by the twisted urge to rescue his prostitute girlfriend, Eva Mendes.

Cage hopes to work again with Herzog. 'He's not like any other director I've worked with. He's in the middle of the whole thing, making eye contact with everyone. He has a great sense of humour and a different way of looking at things.'

Although Herzog still has an office in Munich, he and his wife Lena have for some years made Los Angeles their home. Perhaps the 'dream factory' is where he belongs. 'Most people do not even know I'm here, and this is how I like it to be.' He has lost none of his daring, as was witnessed when he managed to get himself shot on camera during an interview with the BBC. He was hit in the stomach by a random air-rifle shot, but continued filming. 'It's no big deal,' he remarked. 'It's not a significant bullet.'

One suspects that what draws Cage to him could be paradoxically a visionary spirit Herzog shares with Francis Coppola, the uncle whose shadow he has sought to escape. There are intriguing parallels between the chaotic filming of *Fitzcarraldo* and *Apocalypse Now* in that each director at the time seemed infected by the madness of their protagonists in an obsessive quest for the impossible.

'I wonder,' says Cage. 'Maybe it's time for me to change my name again.'

He's been talking with Herzog about Ludwig, the visionary Bavarian king who lived in an extraordinary mountaintop castle that bankrupted his people.

'Werner is obsessed with him, we're trying to find a way to film his life,' says Cage, who although from an Italian-American family is German on his mother's side. 'Dante on one hand, Goethe on the other. I don't know what to make of it.'

Joe Duffy uncovered **Cecelia Ahern** Peter O'Brien
**Hooray for hedonism** Christmas behind bars
Detroit Cobras **7-day TV and radio guide**

**SundayTribune** 19.12.04

# Wild at heart

Why Nicolas Cage doesn't
mind being called crazy

Nicolas Cage on the cover of the SUNDAY TRIBUNE magazine, 2004.

• • •

In order to accommodate Cage, who was tied up shooting *Captain Corelli's Mandolin* on location in the Greek islands, Jerry Bruckheimer decided to stage the June 2000 press premiere of *Gone in Sixty Seconds* nearby in Athens. Doing so meant separating newly-wed Angelina Jolie, aptly cast opposite Cage as a Ferarri-addicted punk tomboy, from Billie Bob Thornton, whose fifth wife she had become a few weeks before at the Little Church of the West in Las Vegas.

Cage is doing his best to cheer her up when we meet in their hotel near the Acropolis. 'Billie Bob is back in the States filming *Outlaws* and recording music in Nashville,' she says. 'We keep texting each other. I never really understood love. I never thought I could be somebody who was waking up in the morning just terribly upset because I miss somebody badly. It's a nightmare.'

The couple have hardly seen each other since their marriage. She got to know 44-year-old Thornton while playing his wife in *Pushing Tin*, a frenzied comedy about air traffic controllers. 'I've never been happier. I'm madly in love,' she assures me.

When she married British teen star Jonny Lee Miller four years ago – they met filming *Hackers* – she cut herself with a knife and wrote his name in blood on her shirt. They quickly broke up. She now wears a vial with Thornton's blood around her neck and his name is tattooed on her shoulder.

She seems to treat her body as an autobiography, rather like the notorious BritArt tent in which Tracy Emin lists all the people she's ever slept with. 'It's a totem pole of my life. It's a reminder of different times in my life and things that have meant something to me. I look at my arm and I see events in my life, like a warrior. They're badges of honour.'

She shows me the Latin motto, *Quod me nutrit me detruit* (That which nourishes me, destroys me) just above her bikini line. 'That's a quote that I live by,' she says.

She talks with the same confiding intensity as her father, Jon Voight, the 1970s baby-faced Oscar-winning star of *Coming Home*, *Midnight Cowboy* and *Deliverance*. A Hollywood child like Cage, she too changed her name to escape the shadow of family celebrity. 'I could make it on my own. I didn't want to ride on the back of my dad.'

Her parents divorced when she was two. She and her brother James were brought by their French-Canadian actress-mother, Marcheline Bertrand, the granddaughter of an Iroquois Indian, to live in New York and then in Los Angeles where she was jeered at Beverly Hills High – also Cage's school – because she wore secondhand clothes. 'Neither of my parents remarried. We're a family of individuals. I grew up knowing my family as individuals.'

As a small child, seeing her father in a film for the first time was a shock. 'I have a very strange image of watching *The Champ* and thinking my father had just died and crying. I think I was on his lap and he was trying to explain to me that he was right there.'

She first appeared before cameras in Hal Ashby's *Lookin' to Get Out*. 'I was only five. I have no memory of it. They were looking for a boy. They asked my brother and he said no. And then they got me to do it.'

Her father dropped out of films for several years after winning an Oscar nomination as the hardened con in *Runaway Train* in 1985, just to be around for her. 'I think he has always been a little afraid of the darker side in me,' she says. Ever rebellious, she ran away at sixteen to make her debut in *Cyborg 2*. 'When I saw it I threw up for three days. Then I went back to school.'

Film roles seem to be a kind of self-therapy. She feels like love, she's Ryan Phillippe's girlfriend in *Playing by Heart*. She needs an outlet for anger, she becomes Winona Ryder's sociopath girl friend in *Girl, Interrupted*, a performance that won her a best supporting actress Oscar. 'It's my way of tapping what's inside me,' she says. She chose *Gone in Sixty Seconds* because she wanted fun. 'I'd just got out of a mental institution with ten women in *Girl, Interrupted*. I was thrilled just to be around men and cars.'

Her father was forever telling her not to talk so freely in public:

> I think a lot of people think I try to be shocking. I don't. I say I love my brother and suddenly I'm sleeping with him. It's like I don't need to try to be shocking. I don't mind sharing every single thing because I have nothing to hide. I feel a need to make a point and to remain completely honest. If you're straightforward in Hollywood people think you must be crazy. The funny thing is that no one in the media has even scratched the surface of who I am. You're all so distracted with knives and tattoos you don't know what's really going on.

Soon after Athens and playing the title role in *Lara Croft* with her father, who had made a comeback as a villain betraying Tom Cruise in *Mission: Impossible* and plotting to undermine democracy in *Enemy of the State*, Voight appeared on the US television show, *Access Hollywood*, and claimed that she had 'serious mental problems'. He pleaded with her to seek help.

She unsurprisingly broke off with him. 'My father and I don't speak. I don't hold any anger toward him. I don't believe that somebody's family becomes their blood.'

We meet again in Cannes in 2008. She's heavily pregnant with twins, but this hasn't stopped her twice walking up the pyramid-like red-carpet stairway at the Palais des Festivals, first for the DreamWorks cartoon, *Kung Fu Panda*, in which she's the voice of a tigress, and then for Clint Eastwood's *Changeling*.

She's sitting in a high-backed wooden chair in a suite at the Carlton Hotel. She wears a flimsy shoulderless green smock and looks serene, a wild child finally domesticated. She and her partner, Brad Pitt, along with their four children – three are adopted and she gave birth to the youngest, Shiloh, by caesarean section in Namibia in 2006 – have a Florentine-style villa at Saint-Jean-Cap-Ferrat, just up the coast.

'Voicing a cartoon doesn't feel like work,' she says. 'My children were able to come and watch it while it was filmed.'

*Changeling*, based on actual events in Los Angeles in the 1920s, took much more out of her. She plays a working-class single mother who in trying to find her missing child brings down a corrupt police department. 'It was a really complicated and emotional film, and really upsetting for me. Clint just managed to help me get through it without cracking up.'

She talks of Eastwood almost as a surrogate father, perhaps missing her own:

> I just gush when you mention him. He's everything you kind of hope he would be. He's one of those people you hear so much about and think he seems so amazing, so decisive, so strong and so cool, and then you see him and he's exactly that … You just are in awe. And on top of that I've never seen a director so kind to his crew, more appreciative of every single person on the set.

Eastwood is obviously drawn to her spunkiness. 'She reminds me a lot of the actresses from the golden age of movies in the 1940s: Katharine Hepburn, Ingrid Bergman, Bette Davis, Susan Hayward, all of them,' he says. 'They were all very distinctive, and they all had a lot of presence.'

Being a tigress in *Kung Fu Panda* seems to come naturally. 'You mean my wild side, the side of me that maybe wants to fight and argue?' she laughs. 'I suppose in that sense I am a bit of a tigress, but I think every woman has got that in her. Certainly my character in *Changeling* has.'

She divorced Thornton in 2003, and had his name lasered off her skin. 'I never felt smart when I was young,' she says. 'I was a punk kid. I'd different-coloured hair. The first time I went to Washington, I spent a lot of time trying to cover my tattoos. I was always considered just a wild person, but there was a part of me that didn't feel that. I didn't feel as smart as I wanted to be.'

Setting up house with Pitt – they met playing husband and wife in the spy thriller, *Mr & Mrs Smith*, her greatest box-office hit – and having children has steadied her. She now exudes calm. 'Brad's great with houses. He really is. He's got a great eye for structure, for architecture. He chose a nice breakfast area for the children because the light is so wonderful in the morning. The most important thing for me is that all our bedrooms are very close and on the same floor.'

Being a mother didn't come easily:

> I went through a lot of my youth really thinking I was never going to be stable enough to be a parent. I always loved children, but I didn't know if I'd ever really be a good mom. I was dead set on adopting. It felt right to me, because there were children who wanted homes. I'd no maternal desire to have children. But that changes when you meet someone you love.

Soon after Cannes 2008 she gave birth to her twins, Knox Léon and Vivienne Marcheline. Earlier this year Pitt brought about a reconciliation meeting with her father, and they're back on speaking terms. 'We're in touch, but not regularly,' Voight told *US Weekly*. 'We love each other and that's the most important thing.'

Voight can't have been the easiest of fathers to get on with. Her teenage wilfulness was a reaction against his inherent caution. 'Jon agonizes his way to every decision, what his next movie should be, whether he should go out to dinner,' says Jane Fonda, recalling his Oscar-winning performance as the gentle Vietnam War paraplegic for whom she leaves her gung-ho husband, Bruce Dern, in *Coming Home*. 'He's a tortured person.'

Although he won a third Oscar nomination as the hardened con on the run in *The Runaway Train* in 1985, Voight then virtually disappeared from films until well into the 1990s. 'For years he'd turn down every role,' says close friend John Boorman, who memorably cast him in 1972 as the guilt-torn survivor of a group of kayaking weekenders terrorized by mountain rednecks in *Deliverance*. 'He's a very spiritual person. I think he went through a religious period. He took on a high moral view. He didn't want to do anything that didn't match his ethical code, which eliminated most of the things coming out of Hollywood.'

Religion is how we got talking in Cannes in 1999. 'Let me ask you a question,' Voight says. Well, why not. It must be boring having to answer questions all the time, the same ones over and over again, when promoting a film.

'Okay,' I say.

Voight bends forward, fixing me with his blue eyes.

'Do you believe in God?' he asks.

That's getting pretty personal. Particularly since it's clear Voight expects a serious answer. Not a well-it-depends-what-you-mean-by-God sort of fudge.

'Yes,' I say, sounding not at all sure, but then can anyone be genuinely sure about something so fundamental?

It seems good enough for Voight. 'I'll tell you what,' he says. 'God exists despite all the bad press.'

He's been thinking a lot about God while portraying Noah in a miniseries he filmed in Australia for NBC. 'I had all this long hair glued on to me every day,' he says. 'I felt so virile, so powerful.'

So how does he get under the skin of a man supposedly hundreds of years old?

'Well,' he says. 'You could say I've grown into the role.'

Voight was born and raised in Yonkers, the son of a golf pro. He began his acting career at Archbishop Stepinic High School (he's of Czech descent) and at Catholic university in Washington DC. Coached by the legendary Sandy Meisner at the Neighbourhood Playhouse, he made his Broadway debut at twenty-two in the long-running Rogers and Hammerstein musical, *The Sound of Music*, as the young Nazi singing 'Sixteen Going on Seventeen' to Laurie Peters, who soon became his wife.

He was spotted in Harold Pinter's *The Dwarfs* by Jennifer Salt, who suggested him to John Schlesinger for the role of Buck in *Midnight Cowboy*, which was scripted by her father, Waldo Salt. 'I love the risk of theatre,' he says. 'You just have that one take. You can so easily fall on your face. And when you get it right, there are only a few people to see it. There's something beautiful about that.'

Although *Midnight Cowboy* confirmed him as one of the leading actors of a generation that included Warren Beatty, Jack Nicholson, Al Pacino, Robert Redford and Dustin Hoffman, Voight was, even then, ambivalent about being a star. 'I wanted to be an actor. Hollywood wanted me to be a superstar.'

He turned down *Love Story* for a small supporting role as the wheeler-dealing Milo Minderbinder in *Catch 22*, then opted to play opposite Jennifer Salt, for whom he left his wife, as a middle-class student looking for a left-wing cause in the little-seen *The Revolutionary*.

Studios became wary of him. *Newsweek* dubbed him 'a notorious maverick who has made a series of box-office flops and has walked off productions and made waves on others'. *Mission: Impossible* marked the beginning of Voight's coming back into the fold. 'He suddenly switched and seemed to decide, okay, I'm going to do everything,' Boorman says. 'And he's been going from film to film ever since. When I called him to play the garda detective who becomes Martin Cahill's nemesis in *The General*, he agreed right away.'

Voight is by nature an intuitive actor, like his daughter. 'On *Deliverance*, his first response to a scene would be fantastic,' says Boorman. 'But then he'd tend to intellectualize. There was often a conflict between his intellect and his instinct. Or he felt it was too easy, that it ought to be more difficult.'

Voight may have loosened up in character roles as a villain, but he still insists on the need for deliberation. That's what he admires about the Bible. 'Every word has a purpose, every pause matters,' he says. 'It's something you appreciate as an actor, the sheer efficiency of the storytelling, it has the effortless beauty of the growing grass.'

He grabs my arm. 'Do you think Noah was a real fellow?' he asks. 'The more I look at it, the more I think the story is absolutely true. What it is saying is that what we do on this planet matters and has implications, that life on earth is beautiful and precious, that it's our responsibility to live well and behave properly towards each other.'

# SUMMER

# nine

---

Harold Pinter, William Trevor,
Sam Mendes and C.R.L. James

---

C.R.L. James in London in 1981 at the time of his eightieth birthday.

the trouble about writing on a laptop is that it is programmed to interrupt. Just now an MSN sports headline has materialized with the news that Eoin Morgan helped England to unexpected cricket victory over Sri Lanka with an unbeaten 62 in the first game of the 2009 ICC Champions Trophy. Up to his selection in England's squad, Morgan – who was born in Dublin and educated at the Catholic University School on Leeson Street – was Ireland's leading cricketer, scoring a double century against the United Arab Emirates in 2007. He signed for Middlesex and at twenty scored his maiden first-class century against the touring South Africans. A five-foot-nine left-handed middle-order batsman, his aggressive innings against the fancied Sri Lankans, following his debut against the touring West Indians during the summer, marks him out as an exciting 'English' prospect, opening up a test career that would have been denied to him if he remained an Irish player.

'How interesting,' says Harold Pinter, 'that you are – attracted – to cricket.'

It is early summer in 1994. We're in the mews adjoining his home in Holland Park, west London, which he uses as a den. He leads me up a narrow staircase to a large book-lined, L-shaped study. On the shelves familiar yellow-bound volumes of *Wisden Cricketers' Almanack* and framed copy of W.G. Grace's autograph share equal prominence with Yeats and Joyce. 'I haven't recovered from my first reading of *Ulysses*,' he says. 'I still read it. It's my bedtime book.'

He opens a bottle of chilled Chablis and scrutinizes me with dark penetrating eyes across a sturdy wooden desk on which are arranged the utensils of his trade: a yellow pad, pens, markers. Books too, including Nabokov's *Lolita* and a photograph of his wife, Lady Antonia Fraser.

He worries about the sun, which beams through the window on me like a spotlight. 'Tell me, the sun, is it too bright? Because I could put the blind down ...'

It's cricketing weather. He's chairman and former captain of the Gaieties, a wandering cricket club numbering director Sam Mendes and actors Timothy West and Jeremy Irons among its members. The first match of the season is on Sunday. 'I'm the umpire. I love the game. I play occasionally. I'm still a promising batsman. It's a secret life of mine, a private life.'

There's something of the umpire about Pinter's involvement in politics, refusing to be intimidated, insisting on fair play, calling foul while the prudent are silent. 'I was up at the American embassy again earlier this year with a delegation about Cuba' ... pause ... 'asking that the trade embargo be lifted. We had an extraordinary conversation with one of the political councillors. Very urbane' ... pause ... 'they always are.' He growls, sardonically:

> But really preposterous. No case at all. The UN – even the damn UN! – finally voted by eighty-four to three to lift the blockade, said the blockade was against international law. But the US has done damn all about it. It seems to me a goodly body of people prefer to remain in ignorance. I'm talking about people who could actually do something.

Behind him on a shelf is a pile of letters waiting to be posted. They're addressed to authoritarian regimes targeted by Amnesty International for abuses of human rights. I tell him that my teenage son Jack writes similar letters, but is it not a little bit like spitting in the wind? 'Tell him he's dead right. That it's absolutely essential to continue to crack away at all these things. I don't believe that it doesn't impinge on the consciousness of the powers-that-be.'

He's curious about someone Irish being addicted to cricket. Samuel Beckett was, of course. William Trevor even moved to a secluded house in Devon so that he could watch Viv Richards and Ian Botham playing for Somerset at nearby Taunton. Growing up in a middle-class Dublin suburb like Ballsbridge it would have been perverse of me not to be drawn to cricket. There were five cricket grounds within a short stroll of my home on Sandymount Avenue, as much a legacy of the colonial past as the postboxes with the crown repainted green or the streets with grandiose names, Prince of Wales Terrace, Churchill Terrace, Lansdowne Road and Sidney Parade.

Summer was forever associated with the smell of freshly cut grass and the whack of willow and cries of Howzat! We'd hang around the boundary chasing after balls missed by portly white-flannelled fielders. The back garden became a batting crease with three small branches from the acacia tree for stumps, and another at the bowler's end. When I was sick I'd play imaginary games in bed with a dice, pitting Leicestershire against Middlesex, the names of the real players written in a notebook where I'd tick off the runs of each six-ball over. *Wisden* was a treasure trove of statistics.

Notoriously prickly about the way the British tabloids hounded him over his divorce from actress Vivien Merchant and remarriage to Lady Antonia in 1980, Pinter rarely gives interviews. But a shared enthusiasm for cricket seems to have broken the ice. It probably helps, too, that he has a soft spot for Ireland, which he toured as an actor with the Anew McMaster company from 1951 to 1953. 'They were really extraordinary days,' he says.

Characters from his early plays were prompted by people he encountered while staying in digs in places like Kenmare, Skibbereen, Dundalk, Westport and Limerick, and later touring provincial England with Donald Wolfit.

As a young actor in rep – stage name David Baron – he'd take his girl-friends to Buñuel films. Dilys Hamlett, who later married film director Casper Wrede, best known for his adaptation of Solzhenitsyn's *One Day in the Life of Ivan Denisovich*, has recalled watching *Un Chien Andalou* with him. Pauline Flanagan, who played Portia to his Bassanio when he toured Ireland, remembers coming to London to meet his parents during a break in the season – quite an upheaval, an Irish Catholic girl being introduced to a Jewish household – and seeing films she could never have seen in censored Ireland, in particular Buñuel's *Los Olvidados*. 'My God,' he says. 'You didn't get much of that in Kilkenny.'

Cinema fed his imagination. Many of his plays are conditioned by film memories, just as his films – he's written twenty-three screenplays, nineteen of which were filmed – reflect the preoccupations of his plays. 'It would be very difficult for me to define precisely the influence of cinema in my plays,' he says. 'I feel it. And undoubtedly it's there. It tends to be a visual thing. Images insist on being written.' Lady Antonia, a historian and novelist, has remarked: 'He's got a memory like a camera, as if he's talking shots.'

**Harold Pinter in Dublin, 1997.**

He saw his first films during the war. The only child of a Jewish tailor in Hackney, he grew up in London's East End, stomping ground for Oswald Mosley's Blackshirt fascists:

> We were not well off. I was conscious of my father working extremely hard. He left home before seven and came back just before seven in the evening. I was nine when the war broke out and I was evacuated to a castle in Cornwall with twenty-six other boys from my elementary school. I saw the sea for the first time. And rhododendrons. I'd hardly seen a tree until then. Let alone sand. The experience has never left me. But I was very miserable and lonely, and I remained lonely until my teens. I kept being brought home by my mother when things got really bad. I remember coming back for the first flying bombs.
>
> The point about being a boy during the war was that everything was very precarious. You didn't quite know what the hell would happen. Bombs were falling all the time. My father was an air warden. We never went down the Tube because we had an Anderson shelter in the garden and a Morrison shelter in the house, a Morrison shelter being a big, strengthened table. So we slept under the table.

Intimacy with Strangers: A Life of Brief Encounters

Word was coming through about what was happening to the Jews and, of course, as you know, pushed aside and even denied. My father's people originally come from Portugal, where their name was da Pinta. His family and that of my mother ended up in Odessa and then made their way, without knowing each other, to England in the late nineteenth century. So we heard distant reports of people who were no longer available. They were lost.

He discovered films at the Hackney Palace. 'I think the first film image I really have is as a child of ten or eleven. I was taken by my mother to see some kind of mystery, American. It wasn't exactly a horror picture, and there was a scene' ... pause ... 'the imprint is still on my mind' ... another pause ... 'just a scene in a room, with nobody in it, an empty room, and the wind whistling outside and a dog barking. And I broke down and had to be taken from the cinema. I was petrified. And I had nightmares about that for quite a long time afterwards' ... pause ... 'this empty room.'

He saw all sorts of films after that, most with friends:

I was really brought up on English war films, some of which were pretty good: *The Way Ahead* and the documentary, *Fires Were Started*. Also American black-and-white B-thrillers. One of the greatest films I've ever seen anywhere was *The Grapes of Wrath*. I must have seen it when I was thirteen. It has always remained with me. And other films, too, like *The Ox-Bow Incident*. And then later, I was very fortunate. I stumbled upon a film society when I was fifteen or sixteen. I managed to get ten bob together and joined. I was so tall, no one questioned my age.

I saw all the French cinema, right through to Carné. The Russians, too, Eisenstein and all that crowd. It was extraordinary for a boy of that age. It was like opening a door into a totally new world. Buñuel woke me up alright. One of the great jump cuts I've ever seen is in *Un Chien Andalou*. You remember the scene with the woman and the man who is trying to get her? He's prevented by a grand piano and two dead cows and two live priests lying on the piano. He's roped to this piano. They're three storeys up in the middle of Paris. And you can see the traffic, down below. The man has almost got hold of her. And she escapes. She opens the door, walks out – and in the next shot she walks straight on to the beach. Now that was breathtaking. And that's the freedom and the mystery of cinema.

Little wonder that in a debate in school he supported a motion 'That cinema is more promising as an art form than theatre'. 'I was brought up on cinema, really. I was right into cinema years before I went to theatre, but I never dreamed at that time that I would be working in cinema.'

By Sixth Form at Hackney Downs Grammar School he had formed a group of friends, 'whom I still have. We were argumentative and energetic. We had a very close relationship.'

Pinter will hear no ill of a friend. He brandishes a cutting of an *Observer* review of a posthumous biography of Joseph Losey, for whom he wrote the screenplays, *The Servant* and *Accident*. He reads out the headline, contemptuously: 'Spilling the Beans on the Life of a Louse.' 'They're speaking about my friend,' he says. 'It's really shocking. To reduce people in this way is a disease of the age.'

He made his acting debut in a school *Macbeth*, which encouraged him later to attend the Royal Academy of Dramatic Art. He dropped out after a couple of terms, feigning a nervous breakdown. Encouraged by his English teacher, he published his first poems at nineteen, which he signed Harold Pinta. 'I used to write more or less a poem every day. They were wild, very much influenced by Dylan Thomas. But the language allowed me a great release. Although I use language very differently now, I still feel the same kind of freedom when I write' ... pause ... 'when I am able to write. When you can't write, of course, you don't feel that freedom. You feel in prison. Locked.'

Pinter lived in a succession of dingy digs and squalid basement flats in the 1950s, struggling to become a writer in between acting jobs. He'd married Vivien Merchant in 1956, having met playing Rochester to her Jane Eyre. His first play, *The Room*, written in four days for Bristol University's drama department, was performed in 1957 and attracted the attention of impresario Michael Condron who agreed to produce *The Birthday Party*. It had its West End premiere soon after the birth of his son, Daniel. Although the critics savaged *The Birthday Party*, a TV version was seen by eleven million viewers, setting up the extraordinary success of *The Caretaker* in 1960, the start of a revolution that changed the form and meaning of modern theatre.

The darkly funny, ambivalent menace of *The Caretaker*, *The Birthday Party*, *The Dumb Waiter* and *The Homecoming* probed the disturbing gaps between what people say and what they mean. When *Moonlight* was published last year, he insisted on an erratum slip being printed because a comma was used instead of a full stop in the opening line. 'A comma made absolutely no sense,' he says.

Much of Pinter's meaning is in his punctuation. 'I hear when I write. I also say the whole thing out loud to myself. A little run-through for myself.' Pauses matter to him as much if not more than words, which are deliberately

Intimacy with Strangers: A Life of Brief Encounters

banal. 'Pinter doesn't set out to confuse,' says David Leveaux, who directed *Moonlight*. 'His plays deal with confusion.'

Each play, invariably inspired by an image, is a fusion of his own experiences and the ambiguous film imagery he grew up on: the frightening claustrophobia of rooms and the menace of B-movies (both *The Birthday Party* and *The Dumb Waiter* owe much to Robert Siodmak's *The Killers*), the humiliation of the weak by the strong (*Frenzy*, Bergman's first screenplay, greatly impressed him as a teenager), and the disturbing juxtaposing and jump cuts *à la* Buñuel. Even the structure of the plays is cinematic, breaking the action into several intimate scenes between a small cast of characters (as in Carné's *Le Jour se Lève*).

But Pinter is wary of neat explanations of his work. '*The Caretaker* was an image that I saw through a half-open door of two men standing in a room,' he says. 'One was rolling a cigarette, the other was with a screwdriver. You know'… pause …

> silent and totally separate in this small room. And that was the image that triggered, if you like, the whole damn *Caretaker*. I wanted to follow it. I wanted to get in there. And live with them.
>
> But it's not always a visual image. And neither is it anything necessarily to do with something specific or concrete, or to do with my life. This is occasionally true. But I don't think the whole case can be supported through the body of my work, because a number of things have come from absolutely nowhere. I don't plan writing plays, you see, at all. They just [he snaps his fingers] click off. They spring. One moment they're not there. The next moment something is happening.

Joseph Losey, blacklisted by Hollywood during the McCarthy communist witch-hunts in the 1950s, contacted Pinter after *The Caretaker* with the idea of filming Robin Maugham's novella, *The Servant*, which dealt with the gradual domination of a master by his servant. Dropping the first-person narration, and accentuating the ambivalence of the relationship, Pinter reimagined the film in a way that made it distinctively his own. 'Losey was absolutely unflinching, he faced all the facts. We were true friends. We just sparked off each other.'

Their collaboration was to last until Losey's death in the late 1980s, during which Pinter scripted *Accident, The Go-Between* and the yet-to-be-filmed *Proust Screenplay*. In these and other films – notably *The French Lieutenant's Daughter* with Karl Reisz, *The Comfort of Strangers* with Paul Schrader, Aidan Higgins' *Langrishe, Go Down* (which he originally intended to direct himself), and *Betrayal*, based on his relationship with Joan Bakewell, which intriguingly starts at the end of a seven-year affair and ends at the beginning – he experimented with the power of cinema to play with time, blurring the distinction between past and present; experiments that fed back into his plays.

'I have the feeling that *The Go-Between* was on my mind at the time I wrote *Old Times*, which is very much to do with the past existing in the present and is full of film references evoking the 1950s. There was a mutual' … he breaks off … 'what is the word?' 'Cross-fertilization?' I suggest. He laughs. 'Cross-fertilization. Why not?'

Pinter's last real collaboration with Losey was an attempt to film Proust's *À La Recherche du Temps Perdu*. He speaks of the year he spent writing the screenplay as the happiest in his life, although backing for the film fell through. Samuel Beckett had suggested to him that he should start at the end, which he did, reducing 1.5 million words and sixteen volumes to 455 shots.

> After that Joe was terribly disappointed. We wanted to do something else together. And we couldn't get anything together. And then very late on he suddenly sent me William Trevor's *Fools of Fortune*. I remember calling Joe and telling him, 'Now listen, I think this is it. This is something I really would love to do.' Joe was absolutely delighted. So we met William Trevor. And we were all set to move. I could see Joe wasn't looking well. He seemed to have lost weight. Next thing I knew he had cancer and very shortly after he died. So, I couldn't continue, really. Pat O'Connor later did the film. I admired it very much.

Being a Jew in London was paradoxically even more dangerous after the war than before. The Labour government, believing in free speech, permitted Mosley's fascists to regroup and hold rallies. Pinter was regularly waylaid by gangs with broken bottles on his way home from the Jewish club. All that saved him was his size. 'I got into a lot of scraps. There was a lot of violence. Particularly if you were an elderly Jew around Dalston Junction. That's who they really liked doing.'

It's hard not to relate this experience of living under continual threat to recurring themes in Pinter's writing of the knock on the door, the intrusion of a menacing stranger into the safe world represented by a room and the laughter turning to terror, yet his early plays were long regarded as apolitical partly because Pinter himself denied any political intent in them.

'I had a great mistrust about the way political theatre manifested itself,' he says.

But the question of the political cast of my earlier plays is absolutely correct. I always knew that was the case. There's certainly a political structure in *The Dumb Waiter*, which is really about what happens to a man who asks too many questions. In one sense he's asking the wrong questions, but the fact that he's asking questions at all has him in deep trouble. *The Birthday Party* without any question I understand to be a political piece of work, although perhaps not directly. *The Hothouse*, which was written in 1958 but wasn't staged until 1980 and which I'm hoping to revive, couldn't be more political. It's about what takes place in what's called 'a home', a sanatorium. The staff are all brutal. Crazed, really. And you never see the patients, except when there's a revolution and the patients kill everyone in sight. The bureaucracy then covers up the whole thing, like it never happened.

Peel away Harold Pinter the writer and you find Harold Pinter the citizen. 'Yes,' he says. 'The citizen. Which I strongly feel myself to be. The citizen has responsibilities to scrutinize the society in which we live quite rigorously. I still haven't stopped doing that. And I don't intend to stop, either.'

But not as a citizen of any one country. 'I'm sometime accused of attacking the United States foreign policy illegitimately because I'm not American. I'm afraid that's not the case these days. What happens in other countries is our business. We're citizens of the world.'

Pinter might seem to be an anachronism, vehemently professing traditional socialist values at a time when socialism is no longer in fashion, deemed, in fact, to be dead. 'Well, I've never believed that,' he says.

If the terms social justice and awareness of the plight of other people still mean something, then socialism means something. The more you deride such aspirations, what you're actually doing is feeding the rich and the powerful. Look at Central America. It's in ruins, getting more and more poor the more democracy apparently prevails. Which isn't democracy at all. What it means is that the rich and the multi-nationals, the big powers, gain more power and more money. They call that democracy. I call it a load of shit.

There's something vaguely heroic about Pinter's political stance. Ranting against the tide is the instinct of a lifetime, not the posture of a rich man able to afford a conscience. When he was eighteen he twice stood trial as a conscientious objector, not because he was a pacifist but because he wasn't 'going to subscribe to the Cold War'. He was fined £30.

All the time we have been talking, something else was preying on his mind. As we part he says, 'My wife has had a dental operation today. She was under general anaesthetic. She's in bed now. I'll have to go to see her soon.'

**Harold Pinter and Ciaran Carty prepare for a public interview in Dublin, 1997.**

At the door he adds, 'What all my plays have in common is that there is a great exhilaration about getting the first sentence on paper. And I enjoy that. I still enjoy it as much as ever.'

It's now twelve years since we last talked. A massive six in the last over of a cricket match in tribute to Harold Pinter at Lord's steers the Gaieties, the team of writers and actors he once captained, to victory over a Lord's Taverners eleven that includes two former England captains, Mike Atherton and Mike Gatting.

Afterwards in the famous Long Room, Jeremy Irons and Timothy West perform a scene from *No Man's Land*, a play that was being staged at the Duke of York's Theatre in the West End when Pinter died of liver cancer, aged eighty, on 24 December 2008.

Gatting is joined by yet another England captain, Mike Brearley, in a scene from *The Caretaker*, and Pinter himself is heard in taped excerpts from an interview on *Test Match Special* with Brian Johnston.

A portrait, showing him making a forceful off-drive, hangs on the wall between portraits of Sir Donald Bradman and Sir Len Hutton. 'On the evidence of this painting,' Pinter is said to have told the painter, Joe Hill, 'I should have opened the batting for England.'

· · ·

The air conditioning is too high. The room-service instructions are in Japanese and Arabic as well as English, French and German. We could be in almost any hotel in almost any city in the world, but an anonymous room in the London Tara mid-winter in 1983 turns out to be a somewhat apt place to talk with William Trevor. 'I have no roots at all,' he tells me. 'I never know where to say I come from.'

That's because his father, employed by the Bank of Ireland in the 1920s and 1930s, had to move from town to town while working his way up from clerk to manager:

> Although I may happen to have been born in Mitchelstown, I have no roots there. The family moved to Youghal after two years. As soon as we got used to that, we were transferred to Skibbereen, then to Tipperary and to Wexford. My father always seemed to be busy settling into a new job, my mother into a new house. They forgot about sending us to school. Sometimes we'd miss a whole term. There are huge gaps in my education I'll never fill. The only thing I really regret about my childhood is never having lived long enough in any of those small towns to have developed some sense of belonging.

But he was to compensate for this in his fiction. Nearly all his characters are conditioned by where they come from. An awareness of place and time, more often than not provincial Ireland – although it may be shifted to an English setting – fills his stories, colouring everything that happens. 'All fiction is really autobiographical from start to finish,' he says, 'but it's the way it's presented that counts. You have to hide the autobiographical element. It's a complicated thing but it's not done in a complicated way. It's quite a natural development.'

Perhaps this explains why Trevor did not become a writer until he was in his thirties, and had left Ireland: he had to distance himself from the source of his material. 'Not that it was a conscious holding back,' he says. He had been a sculptor, showing his work in the Exhibition of Living Art, and the Oireachtas, winning the Unknown Political Prisoner competition in 1952, but this was partly by default.

> All I'd ever been good at in school was English. Myself and Justin Keating were always competing to be best writer at Sandford Park, but at St Columba's there was a master who didn't bother to read my essays. So I looked around for

something to be good at. Under the influence of Oisín Kelly, who taught there, I began to carve.

Sculpture ultimately became a blind alley. 'I began to realize I was tired of what I was doing. I think all the humanity that was missing out of abstract art was building up inside me.' By then his wife Jane, a Ryan originally from Tipperary, was expecting the first of their two sons. He had to earn a better living. 'What on earth could I do? All I had was a history degree from Trinity.'

It was enough to get him a job as a trainee in a London advertising agency, where there were long periods during the day when he had nothing to do. 'So I began to type out stories.' Soon they were appearing in *Transatlantic Review* and *The London Magazine*. One eventually became the novel, *The Old Boys*, which won the Hawthornden Prize in 1964.

He dropped his surname, Cox, calling himself by his Christian names, William Trevor. 'I didn't want to be the same person as the sculptor. The real me stopped being what he was doing and the other two bits went on.'

He's likened to Dickens for the range of his novels and the compassion and perception with which he evokes whole worlds of characters, while his mastery of the short-story form place him on a par with Frank O'Connor and Sean Ó Faoláin. He has lived in a secluded house in Devon since the 1960s, where he relaxes by taking his sons to watch cricket, a game he came to love at school in St Columba's:

> I often say in England that I've never really settled there, that I'm always outside society. They put it down to being Irish. But it's not being Irish. It's being a writer. You're always on the fringes.
>
> It's the same in Ireland where they say it's to do with being a Protestant. Again it's not. It's to do with being on the outside looking in, a withdrawing of yourself.

He never intended to stay so long in Devon. 'But it's hard on your family to keep moving around. You shouldn't inflict your neuroses on your children. Besides, the landscape reminds me of Ireland.'

He's a tall man with the strong hands of a sculptor, and the music of West Cork in his voice. 'Well, I go back often,' he says.

> As a child, Cork city was always the Mecca. We'd be brought there for Christmas shopping and to see Jimmy O'Dea. My father would leave us in the lavatory of the Victoria Hotel while he slipped off for a quiet one, pretending he had to get cigarettes. I've great memories of that marble place, more like a bazaar than a lavatory. But it's all gone now.

**William Trevor in the late 1980s in Cork, the Mecca of his childhood.**

He's not worried about spoiling the memories he draws on so much in his writing by going back. 'Sometimes they are sharpened. It's one thing to carry a memory around in your head. It's a different thing to go back and actually touch it.'

Some years ago he was asked to write about the first thing he remembered as a child and he went back to some of the places he hadn't seen since he was very small. 'I realized I had always been looking up at things. It was a physical thing. The angle was so different.'

This impression of seeing again his first memory – a black garden gate – inspired his story, 'Memories of Youghal', but he changed himself to a seedy, middle-aged divorced detective, snooping on a couple at a hotel on the Riviera, boring two English spinsters about his regrets for a lost childhood:

> It's a way of laughing at myself. You tend to use everything that happens to you and everywhere you've been, but changing it slightly. Whenever I write about Devon I always move it a little. It comes out as Dorset or the Cotswolds. The entire source of my information about the Cotswolds comes from my wife, who was evacuated there from London during the war. I've absorbed her memories into mine over the years.

Trevor's preoccupation with memory gives his stories a natural affinity with film, where present and past overlap. He's adapting his novel, *Elizabeth*, for BBC One. 'It's proving a mammoth task. It's set in London but there are a lot of Irish characters, and I can't cut them down. They keep taking over.'

He prefers writing for BBC Two. 'They don't make you stick to rigid lengths. You can run over or be shorter. Nobody would write a stage play to a certain length. But everything for TV has to fit into a slot. I had to write extra bits for *Teresa's Wedding* over the phone for RTÉ because it was a bit short.'

His favourite medium is radio:

> It's the same as doing a story. It can just unfold and that's that. Radio is an art form whereas television is just photographing something. With radio the imagination of the listener is connected directly with the imagination of the writer. With television there's a large amount of interpretation by everyone from the director downwards. Everything has to be set up.

Often his English characters are drawn from memories of Ireland, while his Irish characters may be triggered by people he has encountered in England. 'Think of England and Ireland as lovers,' he says. 'You only have to look at the map. It's almost as if the two islands were embracing.'

This suggestion of intimacy is reflected in the peculiar legal status of the Irish in England. They can vote. They don't require passports. They're not foreign. 'We're deemed to have a special relationship. Again, the language of a love affair.' It's an attraction of opposites:

> The English dote on the Irish in a way that's quite extraordinary. Ireland often seems to them to be everything they are not. You notice it very much watching rugby. If Ireland are playing any of the other teams the English are always up for the Irish side, even when the Birmingham bombings were a few days before.

The Irish for their part are compulsively drawn to English culture: much of what both the Irish and the English are is part of a shared experience. 'You can't really hate England and read Dickens or Jane Austen.'

His novel, *Fools of Fortune*, uses the metaphor of intermarried families, one in Dorset, the other in Cork, to explore this sense of two people inextricably bound up in each other's lives. The separate voices of two cousins, talking to each other through the memory of different but interweaving pasts, give expression to a love story of lyrical intensity yet maimed by the divisions of history.

'You start writing in the present and the past comes in whether you like it or not. A story always seems to me like a life. The present is just a vehicle that we use. The past dominates. Because that's the way we are made. We can remember.' That's been the tragedy of Northern Ireland: a people caught up in the loose ends of history or, as a character says in *Fools of Fortune*, 'destruction casts shadows that are always there'.

Trevor has managed in his fiction to confront the anguish and the violence of the North without either exploiting it or getting sucked into its politics. 'You have to stand back and take a world view of it. What you're trying to say, in fact, is that it's not just Ireland.'

One of the ways he achieves this is by turning situations around. In *Fools of Fortune* the house of a Protestant family is burned down not by Republicans but by the Black and Tans. 'I reckon that a writer doesn't honour the traditions of violence. You're not going to say that only one side would commit a particular kind of atrocity because you anticipate that tomorrow the other side will do it, the awful tit for tat business.'

Hooded terrorists rape a British soldier's widow in Belfast in 'Attracta', a short story he wrote in 1977 that is to be filmed by Kieran Hickey:

> People have complained to me saying, well actually that particular type of terrorist doesn't do rape. Well, I'm sorry, I will not accept the conventions of terrorists. By changing the roles around you are making the point that all violence is the same no matter where it happens and no matter who commits it and no matter what they call themselves.
>
> The bombing in a Bologna railway station that killed eighty people seems to me to be just the same as [the 1982] Ballykelly [bombing], except that fewer people died at Ballykelly. Violence is a conglomerate thing. Once people become extreme they're in the same pool and I pick what I want from that pool.

The moral of *Fools of Fortune* is that the violence of the English and the Irish is interchangeable. It maims everyone. Violence always does. There are no standards when it comes to killing.

Somebody once asked Trevor if he would call himself an Irish writer:

> But nobody is ever defined as an English writer, are they? There is a danger, now that Ireland is emerging from centuries of provincialism, of stressing and underlining 'Irish' as an adjective. I'm very fond of my own provincial background. But it is very stifling creatively, terribly inward-looking. We'd have to break out of that.

There's a chilling moment in Sam Mendes' 2006 Gulf War film, *Jarhead*, when a two-man sniper unit of Jake Gyllenhaal and Peter Sarsgaard, who have been waiting around in the desert hoping for some action, finally get a chance to take out a target. They have an Iraqi officer in their telescopic sights and are waiting for the order to shoot. But it doesn't come.

'I bet 90 per cent of the audience are saying, "Go ahead, shoot him!" ' Mendes tells me. 'This will give their war some meaning. But what kind of a man wants his life to be given purpose by killing someone? How do we train a man to want that kill?'

The disturbing brilliance of *Jarhead* is that it makes the audience complicit in what was sold to the world as a 'clean war' watched on primetime television like a video game, with remote-controlled bombs hitting infra-red images of convoys and installations, bereft of any apparent human consequences. 'It's a dangerous game to play,' Mendes says. 'You're teasing the audience. It's like a war-movie version of Buñuel's *That Obscure Object of Desire* where the man keeps nearly sleeping with a woman. You're thinking in exasperation, "Just fuck her!"'

Mendes was born in Reading in 1965, the son of a West Indian university lecturer and a children's author who divorced when he was five. He was looked after for several months by his architect uncle Stephen back in Trinidad. He admits that like most of his generation his only awareness of war was what he perceived through movies.

'We were not old enough to remember Vietnam. Our shared cultural memory of Vietnam is not Vietnam, it's Coppola's Vietnam, it's Kubrick's Vietnam. We think we know it, but we just know the movie version of it. The reality of war, the day-to-day relentless existence of being on the ground, is unknown to us.'

He never imagined himself making a war movie. He started to direct for the stage while reading English at Cambridge. By twenty-four he'd already achieved popular hits in the West End with Judi Dench in *The Cherry Orchard* and Paul Eddington in *London Assurance*. He ran the Donmar Warehouse from 1992, staging Brian Friel's *Translations* ('one of the great writers of the twentieth century') and directing Nicole Kidman in *The Blue Room* before reinventing the musical, *Cabaret*, which won four Tony Awards when it transferred to Broadway.

Steven Spielberg was so impressed he invited him to make his screen debut with *American Beauty*, a dissection of dysfunctional suburbia that won five Academy Awards. This led to a gangster movie, *The Road to Perdition*, and with *Revolutionary Road* to follow *Jarhead* he seems, like Oliver Stone, to be on his way to becoming a chronicler of contemporary American iconology.

He was attracted, by all the things it wasn't, to Anthony Swofford's book about his experiences as a twenty-year-old US marine deployed in Saudi Arabia and Kuwait during the Gulf War in 1990:

> It wasn't lots of explosions. It wasn't heroic. It didn't climax in a moving message about humanity. It seemed to say that this war that we were told was perfect and over in three days wasn't that at all.
>
> All those guys were out there in the desert a year, and it wasn't a clean finish, it was the highway of death, with 40,000 dead Iraqi soldiers and civilians, the burning of oil wells and the destruction of the desert.
>
> I see the desert as a metaphor for the constant yearning towards what they think is going to be the answer in the Middle East and the impossibility of ever reaching an answer. There's always one last thing. If we dispose of Saddam, it will be fine. If we just find Saddam it will be fine. If we just put him on trial it will be fine. There's the constant unravelling.
>
> Now we're in absolute disarray in Iraq with 140,000 troops trying to peace-keep, but they are troops who are trained to kill.
>
> It seems to me this was the beginning of it all. It points the way forward to now, but at the same time it makes a universal statement about why men continue to want to become soldiers and the difference between the fantasy of war and its reality.

Mendes gets a creative stimulus filming in America:

> Being European, you gain an objective distance, perhaps a clarity. You're able to step back a little. When I was eighteen I desperately wanted to do movies. People said you can't do that, nobody makes movies in England. So I gave up on that and just enjoyed being in theatre. But after the success of Nicholas Hytner with *The Madness of King George*, Hollywood began looking to English stage directors, so I found my way back into something that had been my original passion.

Even in England, despite living in a mansion in the Cotswolds during his marriage to Kate Winslet and playing cricket for Harold Pinter's Gaieties cricket club, he's always felt a bit of an outsider. His grandfather Alfred Mendes was part of a literary group in Trinidad that gathered around writer and cricketer C.L.R. James, a revolutionary Marxist admired by Trotsky and a key figure in the American black movement: they founded the literary journals *Trinidad* and *The Beacon* as outlets for their writings.

In Trinidad, Mendes is regarded as a Trinidadian. His uncle Stephen recalls that a couple of years ago Derek Walcott told someone that Alfie Mendes' grandson was doing great things in London.

'I feel like an Englishman,' says Mendes:

> But I've always sensed there's gypsy blood coursing through me. I've a Spanish name. I don't feel deep-down English. I just feel English in my tastes. I like cricket and I read newspapers. And that's what I miss when I'm away, I miss the sports pages and the cricket scores.
>
> I'd like to think the part of me that wants to go to America is from my grandfather. My immediate family are not brave in that way. They wonder why I was making a movie about American suburbia, because I'd *never* been there. But I've learned to embrace that side of myself that's a magpie, somebody who goes and finds things and possesses them through the eyes of an outsider.

•   •   •

At eighty-eight, C.R.L. James can no longer move around – the palsy that slowly set in after a car crash in Jamaica twenty years ago has finally caught up on him – but his mind is still sharp and inquiring. He talks with seductive softness, using his long, tapering fingers for emphasis. 'Your paper would like you to interview me,' he says. 'Pray why?'

He sits in an armchair in front of a TV set, a rug tucked around his long legs: he's a tall man, six-foot-three. Books are everywhere in the third-floor room in the corner house on Railton Road, a half-mile from Brixton Tube station, where a plaque has been erected commemorating the fact that he lived there.

He's been watching *Neighbours*:

> I watch all programmes, particularly the soaps. I'm not taken away by any of them. But I watch them all. I look at TV from a point of view rooted in Marxism and in reading. If you have that, it can be illuminating and strengthening. It makes it alive and real. That's the beauty of TV. There are people there. In books it's just writing.

With television he can keep up on cricket, a game he regards as having revolutionized the West Indies more than any Marxist theories: through it the

Caribbean found its sense of identity. As a teenager he opened the batting and bowling for the Maple Club in Trinidad, where he became a friend of Learie Constantine. He even played a game with the West Indies touring team when they visited Ireland in the 1930s. He reported cricket for *The Manchester Guardian* and in the 1960s wrote *Beyond the Boundary* ('arguably the best book about cricket ever written' according to cricket commentator John Arlott).

Even when he was being hounded by the FBI in the US in the 1930s, he managed to keep up with the cricket scores in *The New York Times*. His mesmeric oratory radicalized black America ('The impact of his first sentence was astonishing,' recalled film actress Constance Webb. 'He was our captive and we were a captivated audience'). His attempts to adopt a revolutionary socialist position opposed to the Communist Party caught the attention of Leon Trotsky, who summoned him in 1938 to Mexico where he was hiding out in exile in a house provided by the painter, Diego Rivera, living each day in fear of assassination by hitmen sent by Stalin.

The two men talked and argued into the evening. Trotsky regarded the black movement as a means to an end, driving a wedge for Bolshevism to revolutionize capitalist America. To James it was the other way around. 'So nothing came of our meeting.'

Now he can chuckle about his cloak-and-dagger life as an activist when he was nicknamed The Black Plato. 'Americans were scared stiff of Marxism. But they needn't have been afraid. It made no penetration in the States because although it was an intellectual force, it didn't apply to American life.'

Eventually charged with 'un-American activities' at the height of the McCarthy witch-hunts, he was incarcerated for months on Ellis Island, where he wrote a book analyzing American society in the form of a critique of Melville's *Moby-Dick*, and was then deported to Britain in 1953. 'People told me, what is going to happen to you? But it never bothered me. The black movement had radicalized Americans but the black people didn't turn to Marxism. They went along their own way.'

He found England greatly changed since he'd left fifteen years before. But there was still cricket. He began reporting county games again for *The Guardian*. Eric Williams, who'd been his pupil during his days as a teacher in Trinidad in the 1920s and was now leading the country to independence, invited him to return as editor of the party newspaper, *The Nation*. Immediately he launched a campaign to end the colonial absurdity of a West Indies touring team with Everton Weekes, Clyde Walcott and Frank Worrell being captained by the inexperienced Denis Atkinson simply because he was white. 'It isn't cricket!' James argued. Just as it wasn't cricket for the West Indies not to be self-governing. Politics and cricket became one.

The house where he grew up in the small town of Tunapuna a few miles from Port of Spain overlooked a cricket pitch. 'An umpire could have stood in the bedroom window,' he recalls. Standing on a chair at that window as a six-year-old, James could watch the Saturday matches. But he could also reach his mother's books on top of the wardrobe. 'Thus early the pattern of my life was set.'

His father's father had been a pan boiler on a sugar estate, a job held up to then by whites. His mother's father was the first non-white engineer driver on the Trinidad Government Railroad: 'My mother read everything. Everything. She read the books and I picked them up and read them, too, idolizing Thackeray, Burke and Shelley. My father was not a reader at all but rose to great heights in the teaching profession. He read one book, a book by Matthew Arnold on education.'

Although poor (with an annual salary of $40, his father 'was always desperately in debt') the family's education set them apart. By ten, James had won a nationwide scholarship to Queen's Royal College, which was modelled on the public-school system. 'When I left school I was an educated person but I had educated myself into a member of the British middle class.'

Going to England in 1931 was almost like going home. Learie Constantine had signed up as a professional with Nelson Cricket Club in the Lancashire League after touring with the West Indies in 1928. He wanted help writing his memoirs.

'Cricket was my opening to England. But it wasn't only cricket. Coloured people were making their way into the modern world and I was just one of them.'

He arrived in Nelson in the middle of the weavers' strike. Nelson had a tradition of political radicalism and was known as 'Little Moscow'. It became his university. He was speaking at meetings of the local Independent Labour Party. He gravitated to London where émigré nationalists were fomenting independence movements around the globe. 'In the 1930s in London everything was on the move. I became a Marxist because as a West Indian I had no past of my own. Mao was Chinese, Gandhi was Indian, Jomo Kenyatta was African but my past was British. Since I couldn't be a nationalist, I became an internationalist.'

With *The Black Jacobins*, a dazzling account of Toussaint L'Ouverture's slave revolt showing that historically 'black people were not always oppressed but did something', he achieved recognition as an intellectual to watch. Paul Robeson played the lead in his stage adaptation of the book at the Westminster Theatre and they became close friends. 'He had tremendous energy and drive and yet great quietness. Americans took out their fear of communism on him but although he was black he was an American black. He was always an American.'

There is a sense in which this was true, too, of James: he never completely shook off his British conditioning:

> I always realized that the main Leninist doctrine of building a small vanguard party didn't suit Britain and didn't suit America. Although I was a Marxist, I never attempted to build a Leninist party. No, no. There was a great Labour Party to which large masses of people in Britain belonged. They wouldn't have left that to join a Leninist party.

While he gave impetus to independence movements not just in the West Indies but also in Africa, the Queen's College training caused him to put principle before power. He would break with Williams rather than support the retention of the US naval base at Chaguaramas. To many he was the best prime minister the West Indies never had.

He also broke with Kwame Nkrumah as Ghana drifted towards authoritarian rule, although he would always praise Nkrumah's historic role. 'He initiated the destruction of a regime in decay, but he failed to create a new society.'

Watching television from his armchair in Brixton, he has no regrets. He realizes he will probably never see the West Indies play again: they're not due to tour England for another two years. But he saw them at their greatest. 'Today there are fine players but they are not distinctively different from the rest. Some of the older players were never fully tested. But I believe the cricketer who was most organized in every important development of the game was Garfield Sobers.'

The window of his Tunapuna childhood is now a TV screen. But the wonder and openness with which he looks out on the world has not abated. 'The culture that matters is the popular culture. TV and radio are forms of education for masses of the population in ways the masses have never been educated before. Masses express themselves through it.'

He tightens the rug around his legs. 'I'm sorry, I'm a bit tired. Let me hear from you when you get back to Ireland. We must correspond regularly.'

I wrote to him thanking him for receiving me in his home. He died a few days later on 31 May 1989 before he could reply. He was eighty-eight. The interview he gave me was his last.

# ten

Stephen Poliakoff, Jonathan Miller,
Mike Nichols and Amos Oz

Amos Oz in Galway, 1999.

i f the real-life historical events surrounding Stephen Poliakoff's suspense thriller, *Glorious 39*, had turned out differently he probably wouldn't have been here to film it.

On the surface it tells a story about a minor English aristocratic family passing a seemingly carefree summer in a sumptuous country mansion in Norfolk just before the outbreak of World War II. Whatever menace there is remains oblique and at first hardly noticed by the characters.

'The political elite of the time mingled with the aristocracy over long weekends in such homes as this, talking about appeasement,' says Poliakoff. 'We Brits wanted to do a deal with Hitler instead of standing up to him. It was an astonishing close-run thing that we didn't. If the appeasers had prevailed, Britain would have become a Vichy-like state.'

The Imperial War Museum today has a gallery of people who were on a Nazi blacklist and would have been rounded up. 'I'm Jewish on both sides, so both my parents would definitely have gone,' says Poliakoff. 'So would all sorts of people, not just communists and Jews, but people like Noël Coward, who, although extremely right-wing, was homosexual. They would have been decimated, as happened in the rest of Europe.'

It's one of the dark secrets of British history, seldom spoken about. 'I'm not sure we've ever faced up to it,' says Poliakoff, who admits he, too, failed to do so until he was in his forties – he's now fifty-seven – and his parents were dead. 'The rest of Europe, because of what happened, had to confront anti-Semitism. But we never did, although it was more and more prevalent the higher up the social scale you went.'

Nobody might guess this from his film's opening scenes. Poliakoff has a deceptive style that allows dark personal stories to emerge through lingering shots of familial happiness and a pervasive ambience of evocative music, whether in intense dramas like *The Lost Prince*, *Shooting the Past* and *Joe's Palace* – marking him out as one of the few distinctive directors still working in British television – or in his intimately observed film, *Close My Eyes*, dealing with incest, or his 1999 play, *Talk of the City*, exposing the BBC's reluctance to broadcast news of Jewish persecution in Germany before the war.

Everything in *Glorious 39* is seen from the perspective of Anne, the eldest of a senior Tory MP's three children who is just beginning to make a name as a film actress at Ealing Studios. 'She feels very secure in her world despite the gathering war clouds. Most people felt war probably wouldn't happen because it didn't happen in 1938, when Neville Chamberlain instead brought back "peace in our time".'

It's important to bear in mind how short a time had passed since the Great War. 'It's like the time between now and Mrs Thatcher,' says Poliakoff, a restless, bespectacled ball of a man with curly black hair and a beard turning white beneath his lower lip. He scatters out thoughts in a rush while still forming them:

> People didn't want to go to war again because they had fathers or brothers or uncles who died in the trenches. They persuaded themselves that Hitler was reasonable. His power was exaggerated and misrepresented. He did not have the wherewithal to flatten us from Germany. His bombers didn't have that range. And then when he did and he had the French airfields, the appeasers deluded themselves that we had no chance. Lord Halifax was within in millimetres of becoming prime minister instead of Churchill when Chamberlain fell, in which case British and European history would have been different. He was determined to do a deal with Hitler.

The suspense that drives *Glorious 39* is triggered when Anne – subtly portrayed by Romola Garai – stumbles across secret surveillance recordings in the family home that force her to face the possibility that some of the people closest to her may be involved in plotting a coup. The fact that she is adopted means that she is, in fact, an outsider without realizing it: 'It's what happened to people all over Europe who thought they were safe. Some Jews even voted for the Nazi party. Society can turn and anybody can become an outsider. The veneer of civilization can break apart. That's what happened all over Europe for Jewish people who had lived happily among their neighbours for years.'

Anne's amateur attempts to find the truth put her and anyone trying to help her in peril from intelligence agents working for Chamberlain:

> When we look at pictures of Chamberlain he looks rather absurd, the archetypal Brit with this funny droopy moustache and his umbrella, but he was one of the most dictatorial prime ministers Britain ever had. He bugged all his political opponents, boasting to his sisters, 'I know what Churchill is doing every hour of the day.' Habeas corpus was suspended and powers were introduced that could have been easily used if we'd done a deal with Hitler and become a puppet state like France. Edward VIII, with his Nazi sympathies, was sitting quite ready to become a puppet king if George VI didn't play ball.

There's something of Anne in Poliakoff, who was the only Jewish boy in his Kent prep school and remembers being a focus of attention at assembly when the Lord's Prayer was read out and he remained silent. 'But I was never physically attacked. A more subtle anti-Semitism I experienced, funnily enough, was when I was at Cambridge. There was an assumption that all Jews were incredibly rich and were in the rag trade.'

A play he wrote and directed while still a pupil at Westminster School was reviewed in *The Times* and brought him to the attention of Christopher Hampton at the Royal Court Theatre:

> There was no real writing in my family. My mum was very interested in theatre and was an actress briefly before she got married. My Russian grandmother remembered seeing Tolstoy in the street and was at the first production of *The Cherry Orchard*. The family saw the revolution from their flat in Red Square but fled to England when Stalin came to power. Her husband was a rather extraordinary man, an inventor who was one of the first people in the world to record sound on film.

Bizarrely, his grandfather came under surveillance by MI5 when he visited 10 Downing Street to help Churchill adjust his hearing aid: he was suspected of trying to bug the prime minister.

Ireland was neutral in the war, which broke out just before my second birthday on 9 September 1939. My father acquired a radio and I remember sitting with him and not understanding while he listened to news of the bombing of Coventry Cathedral. We had moved nearer to the city so that he could ride a bicycle to work as a subeditor on *The Irish Press* at Burgh Quay because there was no petrol for cars. He'd go up on the Featherbed Mountain some weekends to dig turf to keep the house warm. We ate black bread and didn't know what an orange and a banana were until after the war. The children next door lived alone with their mother, Babs, because their father, Tom Shaw, was a major in the British army. They didn't know if he'd ever come home.

One night in 1941 the house shook when the Germans bombed the North Strand area, apparently mistaking it for an English city. Not knowing what was happening, mother took us into her bed until our father came home. It had happened while he was leaving the paper. The presses were running, drowning the sound of explosions, and he wasn't aware of it until he got home. 'And you call yourself a newspaperman,' she told him.

Running through our lives was a vague sense of menace, as if something was not quite right and we children didn't know why. My mother would refer to my godmother as 'Poor Eileen' because she had married an Italian and was living with him in Milan at the start of the war: nothing more had been heard of her.

Some months after the war finally ended in 1945, Major Shaw arrived home driving a car, the first seen on our street. The father of another boy from around the corner, who had been a prisoner in Japan, had no tongue. There were photographs of soldiers standing in liberated German camps with groups of emaciated men in what seemed to be striped pyjamas. My godmother returned with her son Norberto, who was born during the war. She talked about being taunted as 'English' by her neighbours when the Allies were losing, but when the war turned in their favour the Italians jeered her because she was 'Irish'.

A new family moved in next door. As I sat in a deckchair in the back garden studying for exams a little girl peered over the wall. Her name was Anne. She had deep-brown eyes. We got talking and became friends. Her mother, Marie, asked me to babysit and would talk to me about books. It was the first time I could really be myself with a woman. Her husband, Frank Drechsler, was an engineer and they met as students at UCD. He and his brother had been smuggled out of Czechoslovakia by their parents just before the Germans invaded because they were Jews. They never saw them again. They died in the camps with most of his family.

He volunteered for the Free Czech army and after the war returned with his brother to reopen the family steel plant that had been appropriated by the Nazis. Once they got it working, the communists seized it. Frank had enough. He returned to Ireland, married Marie and became an Irish citizen. He even converted to Catholicism. He wanted to belong and he wanted his family to belong.

One day after of the fall of the Berlin Wall, which led to free elections in Czechoslovakia, I saw Frank in Merrion Street. His eyes were shining, perhaps with tears. He had just had lunch with Alexander Dubček, who had fought in the resistance against the Nazis and in 1968 introduced democratic reforms, the brief so-called 'Velvet Revolution' or 'Prague Spring', quickly suppressed by Russian tanks as a threat to communist control of Eastern Europe. Dubček, now president of the newly elected Czech-Slovak Assembly, was on an official visit to Ireland. 'I never imagined I'd live to see this day,' Drechsler said.

It was the last time we talked. Soon afterwards Dubček died in a car crash in Prague on his way to give evidence against former KGB officials. A briefcase he had with him containing documents relating to his testimony was never found. Frank died some months later of a heart attack.

• • •

The diaspora goes back to the dispersal of the Jews after the Babylonian captivity, but more generally can be applied to all migrant peoples throughout history who flee poverty or oppression, for instance the millions of Irish driven to America by the Great Famine or, for that matter, Republican refugees, including members of my wife's family, who trekked over the Pyrenees to camps in France to escape the Franco purges after the Spanish Civil War.

Jonathan Miller's parents were Jews who fled Lithuania in the 1860s and 1870s. If appeasement had prevailed in England in 1939, he, like Stephen Poliakoff, could have been in peril. Not that he's ever been concerned about historical might-have-beens. By instinct he's a rationalist who deals only with what is.

We're in the bar of Cassidy's, across the street from the Gate Theatre where he's rehearsing *As You Like It*. It's early February 2000 – the new millennium – and he's left Donna Dent and other cast members to join me. 'I love coming here,' he says. 'You always feel part of the company. It's an amiable community.'

He rubs his lower lip with his finger. It could be that he's deliberately doing this so that he can draw my attention to it. Or maybe he's only thought about it as he's doing it. Whatever the case, it enables him to argue the point that theatre is a perfectly logical place for him to pursue a career – even though by training he's a neurologist.

'How does something one intends to do differ from something one does unintentionally?' he asks me. 'Are instinctual actions actions? Is a knee-jerk an action?' Then he answers himself, as he has a habit of doing. 'I wouldn't have thought so,' he replies. 'It's something that *happens* to me.'

He rubs his lower lip again:

> On the other hand, doing as I am doing while I'm talking to you, rubbing my lower lip, is quite clearly not a knee-jerk. But it's not something I'm meaning to do, either. It's something I find myself doing while I'm talking to you. It's an action of mine in the way that a knee-jerk or a sneeze isn't. Although I didn't intend to be rubbing my lip while talking to you, when my attention is drawn to it, I would have to acknowledge it as an action of mine, a thing I was doing and I knew I was doing.

Miller has been – in a much wider sense – rubbing his lip for most of his life. Things keep happening to him without him really intending them to. Editing and presenting BBC's pioneering 1960s *Monitor* arts programme or the epic thirteen-part BBC series, *The Body in Question*, and directing plays at the National Theatre for Lawrence Olivier were just things he happened to find himself doing. 'I wasn't really interested in theatre or television when I came out of Cambridge, where I read Natural Sciences,' he says. 'I was interested in the mind, that was all. I didn't intend to go into theatre. It was a complete accident, a result of doing satirical pieces for *Beyond the Fringe*. If that hadn't happened I'd be a professor of neurology now.'

Although he can't read music, a challenge to stage *Così fan tutte* for Kent Opera in 1976 led to him becoming one of the leading directors of opera with nearly sixty productions to his credit. 'My entire life in theatre and showbiz has been the result of entirely unsolicited invitations,' he says.

Although he never consciously intended any of these sidesteps, he was happy to make them because they allowed him a wider arena to pursue his curiosity about human behaviour. He sees theatre as a wonderfully unpredictable laboratory for studying how the nervous system instigates actions. Everything he has done there has been in the nature of psychological and physiological experimentation. 'The life of the mind is the greatest pleasure there is,' he says. 'It's the only thing that interests me. There isn't anything else, really, that one can engage with, apart from one's family.'

He orders a straight Scotch. 'No ice, no water.' He lights a cigarette and coils himself into a chair, his long legs sticking out on either side. He'll be sixty-seven in July. And he's anything but hopeful about the twenty-first century.

'How could one be?' he says.

We've been through such an atrocious century. It's an unforgivable century to have lived through. We've done more harm to each other than any other century in history. I was born just when the Nazis were coming into power and when the Soviet show trials were on, and I've lived to see Kosovo and Rwanda. Human beings have killed nearly 250 million of each other in the last hundred years.

He leans across the table:

We don't seem to be able to address ourselves to the problem of our own aggressiveness and our ability to fall victim to massive ideological silliness, in the name of which we are prepared to see the world minced to pieces. If there were a God – which I don't think there is – I think he would be in the International Court of Justice in The Hague. When one is told that it's all part of a larger purpose, which is what the Russians were told by Stalin, it would have to be a bloody good purpose to make up for the things that God – if he existed – has let happen.

Although he comes from a London Jewish family, he had little sense of the world falling apart as a small child. 'I was very vaguely aware that life was threatening in some way, because we were bombed, but I didn't realize that invasion was imminent and that if it happened we would have been stuffed off to Auschwitz. I was never told about it.'

His father had been a pioneer of shell-shock studies in World War I:

Although he was too old to be called up, he joined up immediately in 1940 as a military psychiatrist working on the mental health of young recruits. Wherever he moved around the country we tended to follow him. When he was working at Northfield in Birmingham, where they did a lot of work on what is now called battle fatigue, we lived outside the city in Droitwich, so we never saw the bombing there. We overheard it, but I was never aware that my life was in danger. One just went around as a child pretending to be a Spitfire and going dat-dat-dat-dat-dat. It was a game. I think for small children even certain parts of the ghettoes were like a playground. It's astonishing what we get used to.

**Jonathan Miller at the Gate Theatre, Dublin, 2000.**

His mother – like his father, but differently – was an observer of human behaviour. She wrote novels:

> I think I probably have brought their sort of sensibility to bear in my life. It seemed quite natural for me to be in science. It was around the house. There were fundamental textbooks of biology my father had acquired as a student in Cambridge. I can remember when very young reading Darcy Thompson's *On Growth and Form*, Parker and Hassell's big two-volume textbook of zoology and Bower's textbook of botany. It just seemed a natural thing to do. And then my father gave me an old brass microscope when I was twelve and I began to see these things scurrying around the bottom of this dark tube. It seemed to me quite inevitable that I would go into that world. I became more and more interested in how the brain worked, how thought worked. I thought that if I'm going to look at thinking and brain functioning, I'd better go and see what happens when people lose bits of their brain. So I became a neurologist.
>
> People may ask what a doctor is doing in theatre. For me the connection is that just as the best way to find out about how the brain functions is to see what happens when it is damaged – in fact you don't understand anything until you see how it doesn't work – one of the best ways to take human behaviour apart is to try

and reconstitute it in pretended versions. You begin to become very sensitive to nuances, the inflections, the subtle ways in which language is used, and when you start putting it together you begin to understand what it consists of. It's a very good way of re-entering the nervous system from the other end.

But for chance, Jonathan Miller could have been Irish:

My mother's father came to Cork in the belief that he was going to New York. He was pitched off the boat at the age of twelve and didn't discover until five years later that he wasn't in America. When I knew him he was an Irishman, an upstanding Cork citizen. He was someone who came and said prayers on a Friday night over bread at supper. I didn't know what he was talking about or why he was mumbling to himself.

My family were already liberated, totally assimilated English Jews. My mother was an atheist. My father, I think, felt after the war that one owed one's people, as he said, some sort of ethnic loyalty. But I couldn't even rally to that. I've never had a smidgeon of religious belief or sentiment in my life. I've never thought of the existence of God. I haven't even entertained it as a question that ought to be answered. I really believe, as David Hume did in his essay on miracles, that if you arrange things in order of decreasing probabilities, at the bottom of the list is this cock-and-bull story that it was arranged by design.

Miller once went to Lithuania to see where he came from:

When I arrived there it was just Eastern European. I felt no affinity with it at all. I certainly don't feel at home in Israel, either. I've been there a couple of times, but not as a Jew. I regard the Levant as the fountainhead of lunacy. I once went to the Dome in Jerusalem, and walked around the Via Dolorosa and then the Wailing Wall. All I thought was that that accursed small crescent contained three of the worst delusions that human beings have inflicted on themselves, what we in psychology used to call, when we were talking about schizophrenic patients, extremely serious thought disorders. The only moment when I have any sense of affinity is when I go to New York and find myself among New York intellectuals. It isn't that I feel Jewish, but they've a way of talking and a wit and style – the sort of stuff you get from Woody Allen – that makes me feel at home.

Although his comic gifts in *Beyond the Fringe* – which he wrote with Peter Cook, Dudley Moore and Alan Bennett – would lead him into theatre, he was too busy with medicine at Cambridge to be much involved in student drama:

I was acquiring as much knowledge as I could of modern English philosophy and Wittgenstein in particular. Instead of having a religious conversion I had a great Road to Damascus moment in 1953 when I encountered a way of thinking about language that enables you to identify and discriminate between concepts and pseudo concepts. I was armed with a sophisticated tool kit for detecting bullshit and for taking apart metaphysical suggestions and all metaphysical religious concepts.

He browses around Dublin bookshops between rehearsals at the Gate:

I'm worried when I look at the bookshelves and see how little modern linguistic philosophy there is, how little logical positivism, how little modern semantics. It's really Anglo-American philosophy that I feel at home with because it uses common-sense concepts in order to take apart other concepts. I think European philosophy, the idiotic French and the gusty windbag Germans, is totally derelict.

His direction of Michael Holdern in *King Lear* in 1968 – in which he drew on his medical knowledge of the ageing process to give credibility to the character – marked the arrival of an innovative new approach to theatre:

I was interested in senility, but also in things that were deeper than senility, which is the behaviour of a father towards what he believed to be ungrateful daughters. There are all sorts of levels at which you analyze these things. I couldn't understand what I was doing in the theatre unless I had some sort of grasp of what's going to be in the head. I mean I have an intuitive eye for it. That's why before I was in the theatre I was such a good clinician. I noticed things the patients would do which gave the game away.

Does he see actors as patients, too?
'We're all patients.'
So why do people act? Why do we go to the theatre to watch plays?
Miller links it all to a child's very early acquired capacity to pretend, as he did when playing Spitfires. 'Pretending is actually built into child conduct,' he says.

A child will take a matchbox and go brum, brumm, brummm. He's not in any way disappointed by the fact the matchbox doesn't look like exactly like a car. Least of all that it's not the same size as a car. Or that making that noise is not provided by the motor. He's perfectly prepared to pretend and is entertained by pretending.
It may well be that this pretending is the bedrock of our later interest in pretending for serious. We're very interested in pretending to be other people because one of the ways of finding out what it's like to be one's self is to pretend to be someone else.

Yet even Miller, for all his rigorous scientific questioning, finds acting a mystery. 'The process by which actors arrive at being someone else is extraordinarily puzzling to me,' he admits.

I get more and more puzzled by it as I go along. I don't quite know what it is that an actor brings to the next rehearsal that's fundamentally different from the performance of the previous rehearsal. I think that a lot of the most interesting things that we come up with, whether as actor or writers, come from sources to which we don't have conscious access. It may well be that when the mind is going through a process of unconscious rehearsal – which you don't have conscious access to and are unaware of – it's doing the job more efficiently than when it's being scrutinized by consciousness. One of the reasons so much stuff is consigned to the unconscious is in order to let it get on with its job undisturbed by what consciousness is really best at, which is considering the immediate exigencies of the outside world and its contact with it.

Although Miller has written a book on Freud, he finds the non-Freudian notion of the unconscious more liberating. 'Instead of being something shameful, the unconscious that the cognitive psychologists now deal with is what I call the enabling unconscious, the unconscious without which you couldn't do what I am doing now, which is speak fluent English without looking up a dictionary.'

Or for that matter – as with his 1960s *Monitor* programmes – to subvert old standards of broadcasting. 'With *Monitor* I started doing programmes that looked at the American architect, Philip Johnson, or Andy Warhol, and of course it outraged the critics. "This is not serious art," they'd yelp. You'd reply, "Well, it will become serious art. You wait."'

Similarly with the impulse that prompted him to film Kingsley Amis' *Take a Girl Like You* in 1972. 'A terrible film,' he says. 'I'd made a very good film just before for the BBC, an *Alice in Wonderland* without the usual animal costumes. But *Take a Girl Like You* was purely commercial. I did it very badly, and I lost interest after that.'

Two adventurous years as an associate producer with Laurence Oliver at the National Theatre – directing him as Shylock in an acclaimed production of *The Merchant of Venice* – ended in acrimony when Peter Hall took over in 1975. Hall would record in his published diaries that he didn't admire Miller's 'habit of directing plays as if he were advancing a theory ... the burden of my song was that he needed to trust his instincts. Plays, because they are more human, are more complex than theses.'

Miller promptly resurfaced, directing the Mozart opera *Marriage of Figaro* and Verdi's *Rigoletto* at the ENO. He reset *Rigoletto* among the Sicilian Mafia in New York in the 1930s. 'I never intended to do an opera at all,' he says,

I knew nothing about it. I never went to it. I protested that I didn't even know how to read music. The conductor said, 'It's alright. I do.' I said, 'Well, at least I know how to move people around the stage and I know how to get them to act.' And then I discovered it was easier than I thought. I had an ear for music. I could feel what the music meant. Music is not meant to be read. It's meant to be listened to or played.

Opera was already going through radical change:

The notion of several fat people standing at the front of the stage singing in silly costumes had already gone out. By the time I got into it, singers were getting to be much better actors. They were learning to control their size and learning what to do with their hands. Although I used the music in *Rigoletto* to express what I thought Verdi was expressing, I hoped that when people came out they wouldn't quite know whether they'd seen an opera or a play. They just simply had a dramatic experience, which happened to be reinforced and given its fundamental energy by the music.

Miller has been freelancing since he quit the Old Vic in 1991 in a dispute over the cancellation of his *A Midsummer's Night Dream* for budgetary reasons. He spoke out against what he termed English theatre's 'mean-mindedness'. He vowed never to work in Britain again. 'And I hardly ever do,' he says. 'I thought I'd work better in places where people are not enviously out to get me. Critics said I was too clever by half. Well, sod them. I think being too clever by half is not clever enough.'

He still lives in the same house in Camden where he and his wife, Rachel, who is also a doctor, reared their three children. 'I'm not leaving England,' he says. 'I'm English. I come from England. My family are there.'

While rehearsing *As You Like It* at the Gate, he returns each weekend to be with his two grandchildren. 'Two little girls aged five and two and a half. They've changed my life. You start seeing things you didn't see with your children, things that are invisible with one's children because you worry about them.'

He gives a deep chuckle, rubbing his lower lip with a finger. 'I once saw a motto on a New York doctor's desk. It said, "If I'd known about grandchildren, I'd have had them first".'

Although he doesn't believe in an afterlife ('how can a person be disembodied?'), I suspect that perhaps this, for someone like Miller, might be the nearest thing to immortality: to live on in the memories of one's children and grandchildren.

· · ·

The Holocaust Museum in Jerusalem cuts right through the Mount of Remembrance. You pass along a sequence of hidden underground galleries in which the survivors and the dead tell their stories. Here in scribbled notes, grainy black-and-white family photographs and intimate personal accounts is the enormity of the death camps, death marches and death trains. You emerge finally into the light onto a cantilevered balcony with a view of the Jerusalem hills and the city itself, an eruption of hope and promise.

The original museum, replaced in 2005, sought to evoke a collective memory. Rather like a Rothko chapel, or so it seemed to me on a visit in 1989, it approached the Holocaust as a phenomenon almost beyond individual comprehension, a mass extermination of a people. Few of the faces of the victims or the places they came from had names. The new museum by contrast puts the focus on the personal, with an accumulation of detail that strips away the anonymity perpetuated by the bureaucratic Nazi practice of reducing human beings to mere numbers tattooed on arms. 'If you think about it, the number of six million Jews perishing doesn't say anything,' a museum historian told *The Washington Post*. 'It is through the individual that you can learn something.'

Among the scribbled notes in this archive of persecution are some that provided the basis for Primo Levi's *If This is a Man*, a hauntingly humane account of ten months he spent as a prisoner in the Auschwitz concentration camp in Nazi-occupied Poland in 1944, harrowing in its restraint and compassion, the work of a natural writer.

Levi had been born in Turin in 1919 to a liberal and non-religious Jewish family. Shy and frequently ill, he was bullied at school as the only Jew in his class. He matriculated a year early and enrolled at Turin University in time to avoid the Mussolini racial laws of 1938 barring Jews from higher education. He found work as a chemist under a false name and with false papers, but left his job to join the partisans when Germany invaded Italy in 1943. He was betrayed and handed over to the Germans who deported him with other Italian Jews to Auschwitz, where he was put to work at an IG Farben laboratory, but contracted scarlet fever. He was left behind when the SS evacuated the camp, forcing all who could walk on a long death march. When the Red Army liberated the camp, he was one of only twenty Italians still alive. His weakness saved him.

Although he suffered from depression in the years afterwards, it seemed that by writing about the horrors of Auschwitz Levi had found a way of living with the nightmare of his memories. He went on to publish novels and stories and in *The Periodic Table*, a collection of short essays and stories each named after a chemical element, he married his writing to his fascination with science.

On 11 April 1987 at the age of sixty-eight, he fell to his death from the landing of his third-storey flat in Turin. The coroner returned a verdict of suicide although he left no note and had been working on another selection of his more personal essays, *The Double Bend*. Whether it was suicide or not, it is hard to deny the truth of fellow Holocaust survivor Elie Wiesel who said, 'Primo Levi died at Auschwitz forty years earlier.'

The Holocaust will never be a closed book. No amount of counselling or therapy can or should erase the memory of what happened. No one is untouched by it. It lurks like a cancer in the psyche of its survivors and of their survivors, and even of those who didn't directly experience it. It will haunt humanity for as long as there is history.

Michael Igor Peschkowsky was born in Berlin in 1931. His father, a Jewish doctor, had fled there from Russia after the Revolution. A grandfather was part of the provisional Weimar government after the kaiser fell. In 1938 the family fled again to New York, changing their surname to Nichols. Michael Igor grew up to be Mike Nichols, a smart American director who makes really smart movies about really smart people. Equally adept in theatre or cinema, he has a Grammy, an Oscar, four Emmys and eight Tonys. He epitomizes the cultural freedom of the Kennedy era.

His satirical double act with writing partner Elaine May, which ran for a year on Broadway the year JFK was elected, put him high on the White House party list. He was in Arthur Krim's mansion the famous night Robert Kennedy and Marilyn Monroe met. 'They danced past me on the dance floor and I actually heard her say: "I like you, Bobby",' he recalls.

> I didn't know it was history. I was just thinking Arthur Krim has a very big house, and what will I say to Maria Callas, who I was sitting beside at dinner. LBJ was sitting on the stairs and you had to step over him when you went upstairs to the bathroom and step over him again on the way down. Those are the things that registered that night.

No director has a sharper eye for changing American attitudes than the surprisingly boyish-looking Nichols, now seventy-seven and the subject of a two-week retrospective at the Museum of Modern Art in New York in April 2009, a highbrow honour not usually conferred on popular Hollywood entertainers. His films find humour in whatever is the talking point or issue of his time. *The Graduate* wittily defined the 1960s generation gap. *Carnal Knowledge* took on the new sexual frankness. *Catch-22* found dark comedy in war. *Working Girl* was a cautionary tale for newly liberated women. His friendship with Bill Clinton didn't stop him filming *Primary Colors*, the bestselling *roman à clef* novel about a presidential candidate caught out in a sexual scandal. An aide, whose job is to cover up for him, admits ruefully: 'Our Jackie poked his pecker in a lot of sorry trash bins.'

Nichols suspects that he keeps seeing through Americans because he's not quite an American himself. 'I think it has to do with the immigrant's ear,' he tells me.

> I was seven and didn't speak any English, but I learned it with no accent in two weeks at school. For a kid, that's nothing. I guess after that I was alert to how they do things here. And then what happens is that you learn to do it just like them, but you're still listening as someone not from here. And you hear slightly different things. And you don't ever again quite trust anybody. Which is very useful for work, but it's not so great in personal life. It took me fifty years and four marriages to learn to trust enough for that.

Like his friends André Previn, Henry Kissinger and Renata Adler ('We're all immigrants from the same period: in some ways we're actually the same person'), coming as a child to America was less a flight from terror than a great adventure:

> I still remember the excitement of food that made a noise, you know, Rice Krispies and Coca Cola, and that was all very exciting. The trouble is that as time goes by and you understand what happened you begin to implode because you have no right to be here. And the six million who didn't make it weigh more and more heavily. And then you sort of break down for a while.

As Nichols did in the 1980s. 'You don't even know why you're crazy. But it's one of the things that corrupt your happiness in the sense that you didn't deserve this to begin with – and what about the others? That's very hard to get past.'

He has never been able to deal with the Holocaust in his work. 'I can't go near it, although I've tried. William Styron was my friend and we lived near each other in Connecticut and he offered me the film rights to *Sophie's Choice*.

I could imagine myself on the crane saying, "Alright, all you Jews, camera left." And I knew I couldn't do it.'

· · ·

Some Israelis who experienced the Holocaust in Europe feel a sense of shame and guilt about what is happening in the West Bank and Gaza: it's as if the Jews are doing to the Arabs what was done to the Jews. The image of camps surrounded by six-metre-high wire fences is a reproach to their dream of a Promised Land, a dream that the Arabs have now ironically appropriated. 'As long as Palestinians are homeless victims, we shall feel like strangers in our own land,' one rabbi told me in 1989 when the Intifada – the Palestinian uprising – was in its second year.

Generalizations are dangerous in Israel. There are as many different opinions as there are Israelis. But the fact that the Holocaust Jews and their descendants are now a minority in the state they created is a significant factor in Israeli politics. Israel is becoming less European in thinking and in aspirations. 'Arabs are our relatives,' one of the artists I met, Istche Mabushe, told me at the Ein Hod artist village, which overlooks the Israeli-Arab village of Paradise. 'Like relatives, we're always quarrelling.'

By contrast my driver, Itzhak Sasson, who kept a Belgian FM pistol in his open glove compartment, said, 'The Arabs can lose war after war. If we lose one, we're finished. We will survive because we have no choice. The important thing is not how we survive but that we survive.'

Writers in Israel are expected to deal with politics. Like it or not, they're seen as guardians of the truth and heirs to a tradition as seers and prophets. 'By now I've become accustomed to it,' Amos Oz says when we meet in Galway over breakfast ten years later. 'If I wrote a simple tale about a father, mother, daughter and pocket money, everyone would immediately assume that the father is the state, the mother is religion, the daughter is the younger generation and the pocket money is the inflation rate.'

He draws a line between his political writing and essays and his storytelling:

Each time I write an angry political essay telling my government what to do or where to go, I feel that I am perhaps unfaithful to my art and using my vocabulary and my ear for language in order to win over public opinion. Each time I sit down and write a story I feel guilty because people are getting killed ten or twenty miles from my home and I am writing about the sunset.

So he keeps two different pens on his desk:

They're very simple ballpoint pens, which I replace every two weeks. I write in long hand. One is for writing articles and the other for writing stories. That way I'll never forget that they're not the same thing, although I do both with a pen and paper and although I do both using language.

I have never written a novel or story in order to press home a political idea or a political message. I write because I have an urge to tell stories and I know people have an urge to listen to stories. We all know this urge. We have this endless unquenchable curiosity about the secrets of other people. We need to compare all the time. We need to see in which respect our secrets are the same and in what respect they are not. This is as old as time itself. It's older than politicians, it's older than the state and religion – the urge to know what really happens inside other people.

Amos Oz was born in Jerusalem in 1939. There is a sense in which his life parallels that of the state of Israel, which came into being in 1947: some might see him as a personification of his people. Except that he would argue that this is true of everyone in Israel. 'For fifty years Israel has had to exist in the condition of a collective Salman Rushdie,' he says.

There was a death verdict issued on the whole of Israel by Islam leaders and fundamentalist Arab politicians. We have lived in a state of existential threat.

Israel is neither a nation nor a country. It's a fiery collection of arguments. We are six million citizens, six million prime ministers, six million prophets and messiahs, everyone with his or her personal plan for redemption, everyone screams, no one ever listens. You'll never ever get two Israelis to agree with each other on anything. In fact it's difficult to get one of us to agree with his self or her self – everybody has a divided mind and soul.

Jews have migrated to Israel and settled there from 103 different ethnic backgrounds. 'Great Expectations is our middle name,' says Oz:

But the problem is that everybody has different expectations. Some people expect Israel to be some incarnation of bygone biblicality, like a setting for a Hollywood picture about the Old Testament. Others expect Israel to be a sort of dashing idealistic pioneering society. Still others want it to be a replica of an East European Jewish town of two hundred years ago. And many expect Israel to be the most Christian nation in the world, in fact the only Christian nation in the world in terms of turning the other cheek.

There was a time ten years ago when the prime minister was of Polish extraction, the Foreign Minister was Moroccan, the Minister for Defence was born in Kurdistan, the Minister for Energy was Iraqi, the Minister for Tourism was Iranian and the president of the state was an Irishman.

Yet Israel, unlike the United States, has never become a melting pot for its different people. 'We're not really melting,' says Oz. 'Instead we're a nutshell of twentieth-century humanity – idealism and fanaticism, loneliness and anger, frustration and disappointment. I sometimes can't stand it. But my condition is that I love Israel even at times when I don't like it.'

Oz was brought up speaking Hebrew, the biblical language restored not out of ideology but as the only practical common language between the many different people who settled in Israel. Everything he writes is in Hebrew: the language is his soul: 'I've never been able to stay away from Israel for longer than a year because I need to have my fingers on the pulse of the language all the time.'

Oz's parents were East European immigrants:

They spoke between them Russian and Polish so that I could not follow what they said. They read German and English for culture. They must have dreamt their dreams in Yiddish. They only taught me Hebrew. Perhaps they were afraid that if I had European languages I might be seduced and go off to Europe and catch my death.

His father's family originated in Odessa and fled to Vilnius, which was then in Poland, after the October Revolution. His father, who studied comparative literature at university, could read sixteen languages and speak eleven. In the early 1930s when anti-Semitism became unbearable, the family tried to move to the US, to Britain, to France and to Scandinavia, but failed to get visas ('They were even mad enough to apply for German citizenship'). Oz's mother grew up in Poland but went to Prague University because Polish universities would not accept Jewish students beyond a certain quota:

When her parents sensed the earth was trembling, they sent her to continue her studies in Jerusalem. But many members of the families on both sides were murdered by the Nazis.

I was reared in a home full of books in many languages, which was, as I can see now, a tiny shrine of loneliness for the forbidden and hostile land of Europe. In every bedtime story they told me I could sense that they were craving for the European winter, for the meadows, for the steeple, for everything that was Europe.

Intimacy with Strangers: A Life of Brief Encounters

His father wrote many of the leaflets that appeared in the early 1940s denouncing the British occupation of Palestine:

> I grew up a little fanatic in a very nationalistic, self-righteous atmosphere of the struggle for independence and with a huge sense of being the eternal victim of the whole world and a boy being heroically misunderstood and tragic. I threw stones at the English soldiers. The first English words I learned to pronounce apart from 'yes' or 'no' were 'British go home'.

Oz ran away from home to a kibbutz when he was fifteen, changing his surname from Klausner to Oz:

> It was very trendy for people to assume Hebrew biblical names rather than diaspora foreign names. I wanted to be born again as part of a new dynasty. My mother had died when I was twelve and I was rebelling against my father's world, which was a universe of footnotes and quotations and people gathering to argue about Spinoza and Bakunin and Dostoevsky and Plato and the purpose of life and the future of religion. I felt very stifled. I wanted to go out to the real world where people ploughed the land and carried a sub-machine gun and defended the country – a new brand of Jews mutating out of the old Jews.
>
> So I left only to discover that although people in the kibbutz were ploughing the land alright, afterwards in the evening they'd sit around arguing about Bakunin and Trotsky and the future of the world. So instead of becoming a simple tractor driver I ended up sitting in a room full of books writing even more books, which is exactly what my father wanted me to do.

He served in the army as a regular soldier for nearly three years, then as a reservist in the Six Day War in 1967 and again in the Yom Kippur War in 1973: he has two scars on his face to show for it. 'I have seen the battlefield quite a few times,' he says.

Yet as early as 1967 he endorsed the idea that Israelis and Palestinians must strike a compromise and divide the country between them:

> The Palestinian people are a nation the same as any other nation and they have no other homeland, just as the Israeli Jews have no other homeland. As we cannot unfortunately live as one happy family – because we are not one and we are not happy and we are not a family, either – we will have to live like two families. We will have to turn the country into a two-family unit, into a semi-detached home.
>
> People outside Israel feel that every conflict is essentially a misunderstanding. A little bit of group therapy, a little bit of family counselling and the trouble will go away. Get together, get to know each other and you'll see that no one has tails or horns. But in fact there is no misunderstanding between Israelis and

Palestinians. There's the tragedy of two peoples claiming one little homeland for themselves. What we need are liveable compromises. Coffee can come later.

Europeans see compromise as a dirty word, to do with appeasing, lack of moral backbone, lack of idealism, whereas in my vocabulary the word is synonymous with life. Where there is life, there is compromise. I'm in a position to talk. I've been married to the same wife for thirty-nine years. I know one or two things about compromise. There are no happy compromises.

Tragedies can be concluded in one of two manners. There is the Shakespeare way, the stage strewn with dead bodies, and justice prevails. But there is also the Chekhov way: in the end everybody frustrated, demoralized, melancholic, disappointed, but alive. My colleagues in the Israeli peace movement and myself have been working for thirty-five years trying to find a Chekhovian rather than a Shakespearean resolution for this tragedy.

Although campaigning for peace – he opposed Israel's 1982 invasion of Lebanon – he is not a pacifist. 'If the circumstances of 1967 or 1973 repeated themselves, I'd fight again, and fight like the devil. People claim that the ultimate evil is war. In my conception the ultimate evil is aggression. Sometimes it is necessary to crush aggression by force.'

Although Oz keeps politics out of his fiction, a recurring theme of his novels is fanaticism.

I deal with various manifestations of bigotry, various manifestations of cognitive blocks. But in my stories there is no political bottom line. Writing a novel is being on everybody's side at the same time. You have to identify intellectually, morally and emotionally with each of your characters. When I write a novel I try to be ageless and sexless. I don't write with my loins. I try to put myself not only in the shoes but under the skin of my various characters.

He has been particularly successful at taking on a female persona. His debut novel, *My Michael*, written when he was twenty-five, was imagined entirely from a woman's point of view. All his novels – in particular *To Know a Woman*, *Black Box* and *Don't Call it Night* – have strong female characters:

I would pay a hell of a lot if I could be a woman for at least a while and then decide freely what I want to be. I think it's kind of unjust to all of us that we don't get the chance to choose. I think it could have improved greatly the man/woman relationship if everyone had an opportunity to belong to the other sex at least temporarily.

He's never felt tempted to put politicians in his novels:

I am an author of chamber music. I am a writer of the living rooms and the kitchen and the bedroom and the nursery. I find this much more exciting than to write about the field marshals and ideologists and philosophers and politicians of this world. I think the family is the most mysterious, the most unlikely, the most paradoxical institution in the world. This is my challenge as a novelist. I want to write about the domestic world.

It's a déjà vu moment. I'm back with John McGahern in his kitchen in Leitrim, and he's arguing that a woman drinking a cup of tea is as important as the president of a country making a speech 'because both are acts under the sky'. Or maybe with that cold-fingered monk, looking up from the beautiful manuscript he is transcribing to catch the song of a blackbird.

# AUTUMN

# eleven

Michael Caine, Beyoncé, Lee Daniels,
Mariah Carey and Gabourey Sidibe

Gabourney Sidibe promoting her role in PRECIOUS, 2009.

J orge Luis Borges wrote a story, 'The Other', about an incident he experienced while sitting on a bench beside the Charles River in Boston. A man sat down beside him and began to whistle a song he recognized from his youth in Buenos Aires. They got talking and Borges realized the man was his younger self. 'Wouldn't you like to know something about my past, which is now the future that awaits you?' he enquired. The young man didn't want to know, as if terrified that they might not be dreaming and that his inevitable fate was to be the old man Borges now was.

Whether or not either or both were dreaming – blurring reality is a game Borges liked to play with fiction – the sensation of being confronted by who you once were is not just the figment of a dream: it is inherent in human experience. Who doesn't at times have intimations of Dorian Gray as the child we were lingers on forever young, trapped in an ageing body: time passes, but refuses to go away.

An obvious example is the way screen actors are doomed to grow old in the ubiquitous presence of their younger selves on screen in television reruns and DVDs. Some try to dodge being confronted by their past self by refusing to look at their old films. Michael Caine, with typical cockiness, has instead turned it to his advantage.

The title role of the spoof, *Austin Powers*, as played by Canadian comic actor Mike Myers, is a send-up of the shabbily dressed anti-James Bond spy, Harry Palmer, created by Caine in *The Ipcress File* in 1965, the same year his portrayal of a cockney womanizer in *Alfie* won him his first Oscar nomination and launched him as an iconic star of the Swinging Sixties.

Myers persuaded Caine, by then sixty-eight, to play the character's dad in the sequel, *Austin Powers in Goldmember*. 'When Mike was writing the original film, he and director Jay Roach reran *The Ipcress File* about fifty times, watching it for my mannerisms and cockney inflections of voice,' says Caine. 'The Powers character is who I was.'

Caine's father was a Billingsgate fish-market porter, his mother a char-woman. 'Whatever I am comes from the gypsies who came from Ireland to the big horse markets in south London.' Saying so, he puts his freckled hand on my even more freckled hand. 'Although I don't look it, I'm part Irish gypsy,' he laughs. 'A quarter of my father's family were Irish gypsies.'

Myers loves all that stuff because he grew up with it, but vicariously. His father came from England and was hooked on 1960s films, music and style:

So Mike was formed by all the Swinging London culture, the Peter Sellers and Alex Guinness comedies and *The Ipcress File*, *Alfie* and *The Italian Job*, all those films I made back then, which his dad loved.

His take on it all is so knowledgeable. He even wrote slang for me that was so absolutely spot on you'd have thought he lived there. Austin Powers is a nostalgia thing for him, a homage to his dead dad. So I do feel that as Harry Palmer I am the creative father of Austin Powers. Sometimes working with Mike I felt like I was his father.

That was 2001 and we've now met up again eight years later in the Magic Circle HQ in Soho, where Caine has been researching his role as a mad 84-year-old magician who befriends a little boy in an old people's home in Irish director John Crowley's bittersweet *Is Anybody There?*

'Blimey,' friends told him, 'we don't want to see you in that. You die of dementia.'

'Yeah,' Caine replied, 'but I make you laugh out loud and I make you cry your eyes out. What more do you want from an entertainer?'

Even if he never makes another film, he'll happily rest his acting reputation on *Is Anybody There?*:

John is an actor's director and he has a cinematic eye. You've got a double whammy with him. People say old people are taboo in films, but I'm seventy-six and I'm still playing leading roles. It's not like you've to retire at sixty-five because you're working in a factory and can't lift boxes any more. You can keep going as an actor as long as the money is there.

Unlike his character, Clarence, dumped by his wife and left to die alone, Caine has been married for thirty-six years to actress Shakira Baksh, a former Miss Guyana. 'I've just had my first grandson. It took me a bloody long time. I kept saying to my daughters, C'mon on, girls. Anyway, I've got one now.'

Clarence could be Alfie as an old codger. Caine borrowed the mannerisms from a lifelong friend, the society tailor Doug Hayward, who also provided the inspiration for Alfie. 'Doug died of dementia at seventy-two, so all the time I'm doing the dementia stuff, I'm thinking of him. He was my acting tool as well as my friend. It was breaking my heart as I was doing it.'

Caine keeps healthy by being his age, however young he might feel. Wintering in Miami helps. 'I watch my diet, no salt, no sugar, no dairy. I walk a lot. I have a garden, but leave the heavy work to a gardener.'

Actor Red Buttons is his guide. 'He used say old age means that when you bend down and do your shoe laces, you look around while you're down there to see if there's anything else you can do.' He chuckles. 'It's like the joke where the wife says, "Let's go upstairs and make love," and the husband replies, "I can't do both."'

Caine has just come from doing a poster of himself with a gun for the thriller, *Harry Brown*, a sort of cockney *Gran Torino*. He plays an ex-marine who takes on local 'scumbags'. It was filmed near Elephant & Castle in London, where he grew up during the war. His family's tenement flat was bombed, his home became a pre-fab hut and he left school at fifteen, the same age he lost his virginity, to work at Smithfield Meat Market. After national service with the British army in Korea and Germany he got an acting job with Horsham Rep at fifty bob a week. He took his stage name (he's Maurice Micklewhite on his birth certificate) from *The Caine Mutiny Court-Martial*, which was running in the West End in 1956.

There's a plaque to him in Elephant & Castle near a similar one to Charlie Chaplin, who also grew up there. He's sickened that nothing much has changed since he left:

It's even worse. You've drugs and stabbings. We just had alcohol. There's a whole generation of young people who have been dumped by society. They have no opportunities, no way out. Look in those flats and you realize if you cage people like animals, they will become animals. *Harry Brown* is a wake-up call. It isn't a violent film. It's a film about violence.

Two times an Oscar winner – playing Mia Farrow's unfaithful husband in Woody Allen's *Hannah and Her Sisters*, and the altruistic abortionist in *The Cider House Rules* – Caine was knighted by Queen Elizabeth in 2000. 'I only recognize myself as Sir Michael when I get letters,' he says. 'If I get a letter from someone saying Mr Caine, I let my secretary open it because I know the writer isn't up to speed. That's my only snobbery. I'll open letters addressed to Sir Michael Caine, provided they haven't got a window on the envelope.'

There's a darker side to Austin Powers, for all his *Carry On* wackiness:

It's a sort of catharsis for Mike, it seems to me. He's a very, very serious guy when he's not performing. He never laughs. If you sit down with him you'll probably wind up talking philosophy on the Kierkegaard level. Most comedians are not funny socially. I think they become comedians because they're so serious.

It's how Steve Martin was when he and Caine got to know each other playing rival Riviera con men in *Dirty Rotten Scoundrels*. 'Steve is a computer nerd. He's always on the computer. And he talks about it, which is like talking about golf.'

Woody Allen isn't much better:

I can't remember what I talk about with Woody. He usually lets you talk in case you say something funny. Then he goes to the toilet and writes it down. Even on the set as a director he rarely tells you what to do or anything. He just lets you get on with it, unless you go in the wrong direction. Like all great directors, he can put you right in two or three words. I've worked with directors who want you to go out to dinner to discuss the part for four hours and get bonged. You don't need that.

John Huston gave him his best advice when they were shooting *The Man Who Would Be King*, a Kipling adaptation in which Caine and Sean Connery play a couple of chancers back in the days of the Indian Raj:

I had a very long speech. He cut it in the middle. I hadn't fluffed or dried, or anything, I thought I was doing quite well. So I asked him why he cut it. 'You could speak faster, Michael,' – and here Caine mimics Huston's rich voice – 'he's an honest man.' And that was it. Ever since then I've been suspicious of people who speak slowly.

He credits *Blood and Wine* with changing his life. It's a tough Bob Rafelson thriller in which he and his old acting mate, Jack Nicholson, deliver a mesmerizing double act playing ruthless thieves who try to outwit each other. Caine has always been at his best paired with other actors – Laurence Olivier in *Sleuth*, Connery in *The Man Who Would Be King*, Martin in *Dirty Rotten Scoundrels*. 'I just love double acts.'

He'd more or less dropped out of films when Nicholson and Rafelson sought him out in Miami in 1995:

> I was in the doldrums. You know when you're changing over from leading man to character actor? I'd made about four really dire pictures in a row. I'd sort of retired. I wrote my autobiography. I started opening restaurants. I hadn't made a movie for over a year, which for me was a long time. They came and said, Do it. So I did.
>
> I'd known Jack since his Roger Corman days, but never worked with him. It brought me back into movies. Harvey Weinstein turned up with *Little Voice* and I was on a roll again.

He'd first met Nicholson in 1966 when success with *Alfie* – initially banned in Ireland and then released with cuts and an absurd Over-21 certificate – brought him to Hollywood to film *Gambit* with Shirley MacLaine. John Wayne took him under his wing:

> Every now and then, we used to meet and have a drink or lunch. He genuinely liked me and of course I adored him. I met him by accident in the lobby of the Beverly Hills Hotel. Many years later, Shakira was in hospital with peritonitis and John coincidentally was in the next room, dying of cancer. I was around with him at the end. We used walk up and down the corridor.

In between *Little Voice*, as a spiv who tries to cash in on Jane Horrocks' ability to mimic famous singers, and *The Quiet American* (without his clout, Phillip Noyce's powerful remake of the Graham Greene political thriller would never have reached cinemas), he also managed to fit in *Last Orders*:

> That was a chance to work with all the old acting friends I knew from London. Tom Courtenay and I go back well over forty years. Someone asked me if I ever think of my own mortality. Well, in *Last Orders* I die of cancer in the same hospital where I watched my father dying of cancer. I think that takes catharsis away.

Shooting Conor McPherson's *The Actors* with Dylan Moran brought him back to Dublin for the first time since he filmed *Educating Rita* in Trinity College in 1983. 'Boy, it's changed, hasn't it? All that prosperity. The Common Market sure was good for you.'

**Michael Caine filming Conor McPherson's THE ACTORS in Dublin, 2003.**

He and Moran are a couple of duff actors who try to swindle Irish gang-sters out of money and then try to give it back without getting their heads blown off when they're found out:

It's absolutely mad. Like *Goldmember*, only worse. It gave me a chance to play Richard III as a Gestapo officer, which is the play we're doing all the way through the film. The funniest stuff is on take three. Not because we screwed up. It just

Intimacy with Strangers: A Life of Brief Encounters

wasn't in the first take at all. Conor would add it in from what we were doing. He lets you go with the ad-libs, like Mike does. I grew up in theatre workshops with Joan Littlewood and Stanislavski, where it was all ad-libs. But I'd never done it much in movies until then.

Caine keeps copies of all his films, unbothered by so many reminders of his younger self. 'They're for my grandchildren,' he says. If he could keep just five, it would be between *Alfie*, *The Man Who Would Be King*, *Dirty Rotten Scoundrels*, *The Quiet American*, *Get Carter*, *The Italian Job*, *Blood and Wine* and *Is Anybody There?*

His role as the English butler Alfred in Christopher Nolan's lucrative *Batman* blockbusters – 'I used to be Alfie, now I'm Alfred' – leaves him free to do only films that excite his curiosity. 'If a script I want to do and absolutely must do doesn't come along, I'll retire without anyone noticing. There won't be any announcement. I'll just go like an old soldier, and fade away. That's how I see it.'

• • •

Rock music, but more specifically pop, belongs to the young. While checking proofs this morning for *Citizen Artist*, the second volume of my biography of the painter Robert Ballagh, something he told me when we were both a lot younger came to mind. He'd enjoyed brief fame in the early 1960s playing guitar with a progressive rock band, The Chessmen. But nobody outside Dublin wanted to hear their take on James Brown or rock orchestrations of the 'William Tell Overture'. More and more they had to fall back on Country and Western hits.

One night he realized he hadn't called a single tune he liked during the whole gig. He had a flash forward in which he saw himself still doing the same at sixty. He promptly sold his Fender guitar to Phil Lynott, then with a group called Skid Row, and never played again. He was twenty-one.

That same year one of the newspaper vans at the *Sunday Independent*, where I was a subeditor, managed to smuggle The Beatles out the back door of the adjoining Adelphi Cinema to escape hysterical teeny-boppers waiting out front. All I knew about the group was 'A Hard Day's Night' being strummed over and over on a guitar by Paco, a teenage Spaniard who was staying with us that summer. By the 1970s my teenage son Francis was flooding the house with The Doors and 'Light My Fire' while his younger sister Estefania swooned at the mention of David Bowie, and Antonio, younger still, was discovering

Marc Bolan and T-Rex. Jack, who was born much later, would prefer audio tapes of the satirists Lenny Bruce or Bill Hicks.

My awareness of rock or punk or heavy metal or whatever has tended to be acquired vicariously through younger ears. And thus it was again when my grand-daughter Ana, then no more than four, tipped me off about Beyoncé, so the name registered with me when it showed up in the credits for *Goldmember*. Better still, Michael Caine was eager for me to meet his exotic co-star. 'The screen eats her up,' he marvelled. 'And the thing is, you love her, don't you.'

Teen pop icons really aren't supposed to be like this. If they make a film, it's slickly packaged. No risks are taken. Everything is tailored to enhance their music franchise: safe and saccharine, nothing more. Yet here's Destiny's Child Beyoncé Knowles, the ultimate girl diva, sparring with rudely subversive Mike Myers as Foxxy Cleopatra, a funky blaxploitation undercover agent he stood up when he was cryogenically frozen while pursuing Dr Evil. After eight years without a phone call, she wants answers.

Exuding sassy attitude with her outrageous 1970s Afro hair mop, big earrings and high platform shoes, she'd put the jeepers into anyone. Not since Madonna in *Desperately Seeking Susan* has there been a more sensational cross-over by a singer.

'This is Beyoncé,' Caine says, introducing us. Whatever about leading a band which has sold more records than any other female group, away from the cameras she's a girlish twenty-year-old anxious to please. She seems eager to learn about everything. She listens. There's no sign of the arrogance or cynicism you expect to find in a music megastar. She's wearing a flimsy off-the-shoulder gingham blouse and frayed jeans. Tossing back her blonde ringlets and amplifying what she is trying to say with expressive, beautiful long-fingered hands – sometime slapping her thighs for emphasis – she seems oddly vulnerable in her enthusiasm.

'I've always been a fan of the 1970s,' she says,

> like, Stevie Wonder and Aretha Franklin are my heroes. I want to have the same influence and effect on people with my music. I want them to feel how I feel when I listen to Aretha.
>
> I've always admired the clothes my mom wore in the 1970s, too. They were crazy with all the leather and fringes, the colours and wild patterns. My fantasy was to be one of those sassy ladies. The day I was auditioning for Foxxy, I was watching Pam Grier movies continuously and listening to her so that I would get it right.

She pauses, momentarily awestruck at the thought. 'Cos I haven't lived in the 1970s. That's all I have to go on.'

She's so young that Mike Myers likes to joke that he has a hockey stick older than she is. Yet she's been on the road since her first singing group, Girl's Tyme, at the age of ten. She writes most of the songs for Destiny's Child, which signed a record deal with Columbia Records in 1996. Just after her sixteenth birthday, their first single, 'No, No, No', went number one in the US. 'It's less produced, it's more like I just went in the studio and hollered and made whatever noises I wanted, and kept the words as me,' she says.

After their second album, *The Writing's On the Wall*, went platinum, LaTavia Roberson and LeToya Luckett quit, filing a lawsuit accusing their manager, Mathew Knowles, Beyoncé's dad, of 'greed, insistence on control, self-dealing and promotion of his daughter's interests'. The quartet is now a trio, with Kelly Rowland and Michelle Williams helping Beyoncé push their sales to more than twenty-eight million records with their album *This Is the Remix*. Strutting the stage in her tinfoil hot pants and thrusting her pelvis to the beat of 'Independent Women', Beyoncé is clearly in command.

Her six months filming *Goldmember* proved so much of an escape that she claims she cried when it was over:

> I kind of forgot what it was to be a singer celebrity, because you just got used to going to work every day on the set and people not asking for autographs. It's just like you're a normal girl going to work. Some weekends I'd go and do band stuff. It was kind of a shock, everyone yelling 'Beyoncé! Beyoncé!' I realized how crazy it all was.
>
> On a set you don't have people screaming. Mike was so down to earth and cool. I'm fairly shy, and so is he. It takes me a while with people. And I think he's the same way. But we were like a family doing *Goldmember*. It was such a learning experience for me, because I didn't go to school. I always had a tutor. I didn't have a normal childhood. I've never been around people like that for so long. It just doesn't happen in my life.

Beyoncé's younger sister, sixteen-year-old Solange, performs as a support singer to Destiny's Child. They grew up church-going Methodists in a well-to-do Houston, Texas, suburb. Before becoming their manager, their father was a Xerox salesman. Their mother, Tina, had her own hair salon, where the girls used to sing for dimes. When she was five, Beyoncé burned all her mother's shoes and clothes. 'I was playing with matches. I was only a little kid.'

Mathew kept the girls practising for hours every day as he worked out their routines. Beyoncé had to keep her natural chubbiness in control by living on Lean Cuisine.

'I try not to eat carbs,' she says.

On Sundays I eat whatever I want, chocolate and cinnamon rolls and all that stuff. Every other day I try to watch anything with sugar and I run and do sit-ups. It's really hard. Watching movies, I just eat pork skins, cos that the nearest thing to tubs I can have. It hasn't been easy, cos I love to eat.

She's reconciled to being a sexual icon:

Guys are guys and guys do what guys do. But it's made it very difficult for me to meet people and get to know them. Guys get intimidated or are scared to treat you like they're only thinking about a certain thing. If I go out with a guy, people go, 'Oh, he's her boyfriend, they're doing this together, they're doing that.' So that's hard. I have to be so picky with who I ever get to know that I can't really get to know anybody. But I'm getting older. I'm starting just to say, 'Forget it, I don't care, just think what you want.'

She's not seeing anyone at present. 'I did have a boyfriend from school. But it was too hard. We were in two different worlds. There hasn't been anyone for a year and a couple of months.'

She rented a little condo while she was filming *Goldmember* in LA:

I bought all this furniture. It was my first home. But after the movie I had to move out. I put all my stuff in storage. I don't know where it is. I've stuff in my mom's house. I've stuff in Kelly's. I don't know where my home is. When I travel I don't have anything to remind me of home, I just have a camera with all my pictures in it from everywhere. So I look through that. I just have one little toilet bag. Once you travel so much for so many years, you realize you wear the same thing every day.

Her only experience of acting before *Goldmember* was an MTV update of *Carmen*:

In the beginning I was scared, I didn't know anything about anything. The first time I put on the Afro and put on the clothes and makeup and everything, I turned round and I looked like a different person, cos I was doing the whole Foxxy vibe. Once I looked like her I was okay. I didn't try to act like I knew how. I just was honest. I got through it and I learned a lot. I think it's a new chapter in my life.

Although she is about to start another movie, starring opposite Cuba Gooding Jr in *The Fighting Temptations*, acting is not going to be a priority. 'I love music too much. I'm confident in music. I'm just a beginner as an actor. But anything I start, I want to get good at.'

There's an element of acting in being a singer. 'But only a small part of it. I think acting comes in as a singer celebrity when you're tired and you have to act like you're happy. Any other time, when you're on the stage, it's really not acting. I can't describe it. It's more like whatever's in your heart comes out.'

Many of her songs celebrate a post-feminist empowerment, as in the *Charlie's Angels* soundtrack, 'Independent Women', but then there's the recurring sense of loneliness voiced in 'Show Me The Way' ('I wanna know if I could get to know you/So many things baby, I can't wait to show you/I don't know if you feel the same as I do/Give me a sign baby, show me what to do').

Maybe 'My Time Has Come' gets closest to the real Beyoncé, who missed out on childhood: 'It's okay/To be afraid/It's alright/You just take that fear/Turn it into your strength/It's called life/And that's why we're here.'

Hollywood rites of passage tales are invariably personified by child actors sucked – or pushed by ambitious or money-grabbing parents – into the professional demands of an entertainment industry that denies them their own rite of passage as children emerging to adulthood, learning, as Beyoncé says, 'to act like you're happy'. Natasha Richardson warned against the danger, herself the daughter of an acting family. But there are worse experiences than a pampered showbiz upbringing. Beyoncé is now married to the rapper Jay-Z. Although we haven't met again, she seems to have become the 'smart, sassy lady' she always aspired to be.

* * *

The film *Precious*, acclaimed at the Sundance Festival early in 2009 and given a standing ovation at Cannes, is a low-budget adaptation of *Push*, a gritty bestselling novel by the black author, Sapphire, about a sixteen-year-old illiterate HIV-positive black girl from Harlem who is abused by her mother and is pregnant a second time by her father. It is based on stories Sapphire heard as a teacher working with deprived teenagers.

Despite its American R-rating for 'child abuse including sexual assault, and pervasive language', and having an unknown, Gabourey Sidibe, who never acted before, in the title role, *Precious* recorded the highest grosses ever for a film released on limited releases – an average of $100,000 per theatre – when it opened at a few selected venues early in October 2009. Harrowing as it is, it too is a song that, defying Hollywood pressure, is being heard.

Its director, Lee Daniels, is the son of a Philadelphia cop who was shot dead when he was fifteen. Openly gay, he's the adoptive father of twin children of his brother, who is serving time. He became the first black producer of an Academy Award-winning film when *Monster's Ball* won Halle Berry an Oscar in 2002, and followed up with the Cannes award-winning *The Woodsman*, in which Kevin Bacon plays a convicted child molester:

> My mom kept saying, 'Why can't you make movies like Tyler Perry? What's *Monster's Ball*? What's *The Woodsman*? So what, you won an Oscar. Make movies my church folk can see.' So I got backing from Tyler and from Oprah Winfrey for *Precious*. Chart-topping Grammy Award-winning music friends like Lenny Kravitz and Mariah Carey helped out by appearing in supporting roles. I'm a black film-maker. I wanted to expel my demons and do a film that didn't embarrass my community. All Precious wants is to learn to read and write and take care of her baby.

This hasn't stopped some black critics denouncing *Precious* as 'full of brazenly racist clichés'. Carey, who plays a dowdy social worker who disapproves of Precious' determination to have her baby, is infuriated by the attacks. 'Lee put his whole heart and soul into this film. This was his life. It's fighting for people who are going through issues such as this. I think it explores territory many people are not brave enough or knowledgeable enough to explore.'

Carey lived in Harlem as a child, daughter of a black father originally from Venezuela and a white mother, an opera singer, Patricia Hickey, from the Bronx. Her parents split when she was three and she was reared by her mother:

> I had a difficult childhood. People still don't understand it and are confused by it. I discovered my singing voice as a little girl because it was an escape for me when things were happening in my home life.
>
> I've always felt like an outsider. A lot of it is because I'm biracial. But Barack Obama, who also had a black father and a white mother, has shattered that glass. I can actually not feel like there's something weird about being who I am, about being different, about not maybe fitting in completely with one group or the other.

Intimacy with Strangers: A Life of Brief Encounters

Gabourey Sidibe worked in a call centre. 'I was so sceptical of everything to do with the film. This so isn't my life. I didn't want to go to the audition, because I'd have to cut class at college. I was studying to be a research psychologist. But I did anyway.'

Having to weigh 360 pounds as Precious was no problem. 'I was fat to start with. I'm never going to be a size two. I'm not built that way. And goddammit, I love the way I look.'

Her real challenge was to seem downbeat and pathetic. 'A lot of the time, particularly at the beginning, Precious isn't exactly cute. That was a real physical transformation for me, rather than having to be fat. I'm normally a cute girl.'

Sidibe was born in Brooklyn but moved to Harlem when she was eight after her parents separated: her mother was a gospel singer, her father is from Senegal. 'The film is true to Harlem, but it is every neighbourhood. We're drawing attention to a subject that is taboo. There are many people losing their lives to this kind of abuse and other kinds of abuse. It's important that we turn a light on it.'

She'd been familiar with the original novel, *Push*, but never read it:

> I picked it up and put it down at high school so many times because I didn't realize what the book was about. Finally when I actually read it, it was heartbreaking. I know this girl in so many of my friends, so many of my family. I know her in myself. This girl has been neglected and ignored and she reached out for support and couldn't get it. That's what hit me. I felt bad because I've ignored this girl. But I am this girl.

Mariah Carey performed at President Obama's inaugural ball in January, and Beyoncé serenaded him with a rendering of the Etta James song, 'At Last'. At Michelle Obama's prompting, she danced with the president.

Obama has struggled to implement the changes he promised. His belief in consensus has been seen as weakness by Republicans, who, by gaining control of Congress, are able to block or mutilate his reforms of health care, taxation and Wall Street. But the historical significance of his election cannot be undone. The electorate seems to understand this, re-electing him for a second term. Beyoncé returned to sing 'The Star Spangled Banner' at his 2013 inauguration.

'For so many years, we black people have had two voices, a voice we had with ourselves and a voice we had for white people,' says Lee Daniels. 'The moment Obama became president I think all of us lost those two voices and now we have one voice. There are no more pretences, no more bullshit. We are what we are. We're in the White House.'

# twelve

Stephen Daldry, Wim Wenders, Ken Loach, Isabelle Huppert, Hans Küng, Oliver Hirschbiegel, Florian van Donnersmarck, William Boyd and Charlie Kaufman

The last conversation Harold Pinter had with his wife Antonia Fraser on the night he died was about *The Reader*, a semi-autobiographical novel by Berlin law professor Bernhard Schlink, which his playwright friend, David Hare, had adapted for the screen. 'And my last conversation with him was about it, too,' says Hare.

In one of the pivotal scenes, a deglamorized, grey-haired Kate Winslet, wearing frumpy prison clothing, stands in the dock accused of allowing 300 Jewish women to burn to death, locked in a blazing building, while she was a guard at Auschwitz.

If she had let them out, some might have escaped. She thought she was doing her job in preventing this. She asks the judge, bewildered, 'What would you have done?'

He doesn't answer. He just taps his pen on his chair.

*The Reader*, one of the first films released in Ireland in 2009, raises the issue that people cannot escape responsibility for crimes committed in their name. By doing what everyone else seems to be doing or even by being silent while they are doing it is to be complicit in what happens: each person's everyday choices may have moral and social consequences not just for themselves but for everyone.

'Societies think they operate by something they call morality, but they don't,' says the law professor played by Bruno Ganz in *The Reader*. 'They operate by something called law.' This refers to Germany in the 1960s and the trial of Kate Winslet's character, Hanna Schmitz, but its resonances today are obvious.

'Many countries, the United States being one of them, believe and act on the idea that they have a moral imperative to invade other countries and do whatever they want,' says the film's director, Stephen Daldry. 'But of course the reality is there is no moral certainty. The moral authority of the US, and indeed Britain's, has been severely diminished by the illegal war in Iraq and Guantanamo Bay and now the Israeli New Year's Day bombardment of Gaza.'

*The Reader* is about the so-called 'second generation' that grew up after Hitler, when a wall of silence descended upon Germany:

> They had to come to terms with the realization that the people they loved, their parents or their teachers or their pastors, had been involved in or were even perpetrators of the greatest crime of the twentieth century. How can such a society operate, particularly in the context of the need to rebuild after the Cold War? How can you possibly put a whole country on trial? So the so-called process of de-Nazification was for years just a veneer.

*The Reader* is told in flashback by Ralph Fiennes remembering himself in Heidelberg as a fifteen-year-old schoolboy who falls sick in the street and is helped home by Schmitz. When he recovers he goes to her flat to thank her and they start an affair in which they have sex nearly every day while he reads literature to her.

One day she disappears without trace, and he doesn't see her again until 1966 when, as a young lawyer, he discovers her true identity and her horrific secret. He spends the rest of his life battling with his ambivalent feelings for her.

'She's not a raving anti-Semite,' says Daldry:

> She's a particular woman who makes a series of small decisions that lead her to the gates of hell. She has this moral illiteracy, a disconnection between her mind and the implications of what she has done. It's important to imagine what it must have been like living under the Nazis. It's always hard to stand up when a country has moral slippage. But Germany was also a country that not only created a war but created genocide. It wasn't just the work of monsters, but of the next-door neighbour or the guy who sells bread. It was everybody.

· · ·

As chance would have it, as it invariably does, 2009 is now ending as it began, with *The Reader*. Kate Winslet has been nominated for best actress at the European Film Academy awards at Blochum in the Ruhr Valley, the industrial engine house that powered Hitler's quest for Aryan supremacy. Because of a missed connection at Heathrow I've arrived on a late flight at Düsseldorf, the birth city of the film director, Wim Wenders, who has been president of the European Film Academy since 1996, when he succeeded Ingmar Bergman.

His father was a doctor who served in the Wehrmacht. His mother was of Dutch origin and wanted to call him Wim but although he was born in August 1945 at the end of the war, the authorities rejected the name because it was not 'a proper German name'. He was given the name Wilhelm to comply, but was always known in his family as Wim.

'All I saw as a child were ruins,' he says.

> Our house was the only one left standing on the block. There were no jobs, no money, no food, everything had fallen apart. I felt very much a lack of spirituality. Maybe that's what happens after a war, people just frantically trying to rebuild. Nothing else matters.
>
> Everything was just about the future. Nobody even considered that they ever had a past, even people who had nothing to do with the Nazis, like my father. Their only aim in life was to have a place of their own again and maybe one day a car. As soon as I was old enough to have a bicycle, I'd ride off to Amsterdam on the weekends, just to get away.

American Forces Radio and Hollywood movies provided a more immediate escape. 'Rock music had an incredibly liberating effect. It was the only thing I felt secure with, that I felt had nothing to do with fascism. I couldn't trust the German culture I grew up with, neither the words, nor the images, nor the sounds.'

He became a film-maker by accident. He'd played with an 8 mm camera when he was twelve, standing at the window, just filming the street below. 'But I never thought that it could be a profession.' He studied medicine instead, even tried to become a painter, before ending up at the Munich Film School during the 1968 student riots. 'We threw out our teachers and devised our own courses.'

Wenders belonged to a new wave of German directors – along with Werner Herzog, Rainer Werner Fassbinder and Wolfgang Petersen – that emerged in the early 1970s. 'We had the privilege of creating German cinema from scratch. There was no tradition to refer to, except the tradition of America. It was like we were a generation of film-makers without a past. We made films in a complete void.'

*Summer in the City*, in which a released prisoner wanders from town to town to contact old friends, established the Wenders approach, refined into a signature with *The Goalkeeper's Fear of the Penalty*, *Alice in the Cities* and *Kings of the Road*: a sort of German-style road movie, infused with rock music, shot episodically in long takes and monochrome, featuring lonely, isolated characters forever on the move, never arriving anywhere.

He was so conditioned by American culture that inevitably after filming *The American Friend* in Hamburg (an adaptation of Patricia Highsmith's thriller with Bruno Ganz playing a reluctant hitman) he ended up in Hollywood and given the run of Zoetrope Studios by Francis Coppola, with disastrous consequences. Most of *Hammett*, his film-noir pastiche in which Dashiell Hammet gets involved in a crime that becomes the basis for his fiction, had to be dumped and reshot.

For the hauntingly elegiac *Paris, Texas*, in which Harry Dean Stanton, shell-shocked by separation from his wife, attempts to take responsibility for their young son, Wenders successfully operated outside the American studio set-up, using instead an all-European crew. 'It was a true guerrilla experience, in so far as it was shot almost clandestinely.'

Back in Germany he improvised *Wings of Desire*, an angel's eye view with Bruno Ganz as an unseen presence in the everyday lives of ordinary people in a divided Berlin, a metaphor for the cinematic experience: ever watching, never able to interfere. 'I could never have produced it on the basis of an American film where you have to define what you want to do beforehand.'

'What I love about the way Wim works, and about European filming in general, is that the film is created each day on the set,' says Ganz. 'You don't know what is going to happen and you keep yourself open. You work with persons and not with machines.'

To help Ganz feel like a killer for *The American Friend*, Wenders gave him a loaded pistol and made him walk through Hamburg with it in his raincoat pocket, 'a really scary experience'.

Dennis Hopper arrived on the set straight from Coppola's *Apocalypse Now*. 'He was stoned out of his mind,' recalls Wenders:

Bruno thinks about every gesture and every detail of his performance. He was clearly upset. One day in the middle of a scene and before the camera he suddenly punched Dennis in the nose. There was a terrific fight with both of them rolling on the floor. Years later Dennis told me that that punch saved his life. He resolved to straighten out his life, and he did.

The train journey from Düsseldorf to Essen, where I am staying, passes through Duisburg and Mülheim, cities that have grown together along with Gelsenkirchen, Bochum and Dortmund to seem like a single city with no distinguishable breaks between them. If it wasn't for the station announcements, you'd have no sense of the changing geography.

The Ruhr, with its vast resources of coal and steel, was heavily targeted by Allied bombers during World War II but bounced back to become the centre of the German economic miracle in the 1950s and 1960s. As the easy-to-reach coal layers ran out in the 1970s, the steel industry lost out to low-cost suppliers like Japan. The Ruhr switched to service industries and high technology, and reinvented itself as a culture region.

Bochum is hosting the European Academy Awards on the eve of the Ruhr becoming the 2010 European Capital of Culture. Stars will walk the red carpet in a vast converted gas-power plant, symbolizing the Ruhr's success in recycling its iconic pitheads, coal mines, blast furnaces and even breweries as universities, concert houses, theatres and museums.

**Wim Wenders hosting the 2009 European Film Awards in Bochum in the Ruhr Valley, Germany, near where he grew up.**

On the morning of the awards, 73-year-old British director Ken Loach, who is to receive a lifetime achievement honour, decides along with his regular screenwriter, Paul Laverty, formerly a civil rights lawyer in Nicaragua, to visit the neighbouring Zollverein Coal Mine, now a World Heritage Site and centre of the creative economy of the Ruhr area.

'The Ruhr miners were among the strongest supporters of the British miners in their confrontation with Margaret Thatcher in the 1980s,' says Loach, an unflinching champion of the socially marginalized throughout five decades of film-making.

His 1980 Channel 4 documentary series, *A Question of Leadership*, dealing with the suppression of trade unionism in Britain, was never shown due to political pressure, while his miners' strike film, *Which Side Are You On?*, commissioned by Melvin Bragg for *The South Bank Show*, was held back until the end of the strike.

'Melvin funked it,' Laverty claims, as we climb a 113-step stairway to the top of the Zollverein coal-washing plant to enjoy an awesome panoramic view of the Ruhr Valley. Noticing Loach being buffeted by the icy December winds, Laverty gives him his own thick woollen cap.

Off on the clouded horizon, we can see the ThyssenKrupp steel plant where much of Hitler's armaments were produced. 'Only one bomb was dropped on Zollverein during the war,' says a young attendant, whose grandfather worked here. 'All the rest fell on Krupps.'

Loach, curious as always, asks about child miners. Born in Warwickshire, the son of an electrician and nephew of a miner, he remains faithful to the working-class experience. His questioning summons up a harrowing picture of conditions that prevailed up to the 1960s. Children started in the mine at fourteen but couldn't work underground until sixteen. Their job was to sort coal with their bare hands, until the skin was scoured from them.

The minimum depth of the Zollverein mine, built by Irish engineers in the nineteenth century, was 1000 metres. With temperatures rising 3.5 degrees every hundred metres down, this meant working below was like a sauna. Men toiled eight hours, six days a week, using pneumatic pit hammers weighing twenty kilos – the equivalent to the maximum baggage weight you're allowed bring on holidays on a plane. The cumulative effect of the weight and vibration left most men with paralyzed elbows. Some 12,000 tons of coal were hoisted every day in the 1930s. Average mortality age was forty-five.

'Every second day there was a death in every mine,' the attendant informs

Loach. 'There was no university in the Ruhr until 1963 because they didn't want the workers educated.'

The sense of being in the presence of ghosts – not unlike the experience of a visit to a concentration camp – is made more surreal by the realization that the mine buildings are now used for concerts and social functions. On our way back down we encounter a party for the wedding of a prominent 69-year-old Social Democrat politician to a 26-year-old bride.

It is twenty-three years since the last shift went underground. The motto of this reinvention of the Ruhr is 'Change through culture, culture through change.'

Loach finished shooting his new film, *Route Irish*, last month. Unlike *The Wind that Shakes the Barley*, as Laverty is quick to point out, there's nothing Irish about it. The title is a term used by Americans for the highway linking Baghdad Airport with the city's International Green Zone, regarded by occupation forces as 'the most dangerous road in the world'.

Most of the film takes place in England. It's a triangular love story involving a woman and two friends who worked as private contractors in Iraq with immunity from Iraqi law under an order imposed by Paul Bremmer, the US-appointed head of the so-called Coalition Provisional Authority, to enforce the 'security' interests of a war-profiteering Haliburton-style corporation.

One of the men is killed under suspicious circumstances in an ambush, the other hears about it back in England and, unable to return to Iraq, operates out of London on the Internet, tracking down former contacts online and deciphering phone messages. As he gets closer to the truth he becomes a target himself.

'One of the ideas was to bring the war home,' says Loach. 'Since the Second World War, wars have happened in other countries with people who look foreign and don't speak our language. So we thought, let's bring it here, let's try and show what it's like to have torture and car bombs in suburban London.'

Later in the evening, dressed in a tuxedo, former Manchester footballer-turned-actor Eric Cantona, star of Loach's surreal comedy, *Looking for Eric*, takes the stage to present him with his EFA award. 'This man is a genius,' he proclaims. 'His films give us hope.'

There is a prolonged standing ovation, much to Loach's embarrassment. 'Most of us are lucky to enjoy freedom of expression,' he says. 'Many others in the world are not so free. It is important for us to give them solidarity.' Loach is not used to being so warmly received. He is arguably one of Britain's greatest living directors, but you wouldn't suspect it from the way he is regarded there.

There was the venom with which British critics led by Alexander Walker sought to prevent *Hidden Agenda*, his thriller exposing RUC and British army collusion in murder in Northern Ireland, from being screened at Cannes Film Festival in 1990. When this failed, they disrupted the ensuing press conference. In doing so they ironically helped to support Loach's central point that the British media is manipulated by elements in the secret service to stifle any proper debate of the issue of the British army's role in Northern Ireland.

*Hidden Agenda* was inspired by the cover-up surrounding the Stalker shoot-to-kill inquiry. 'What we wanted to bring out was the sheer hypocrisy of public statements,' Loach told me afterwards. 'The IRA, the UVF and the British government are in fact three gangs doing the same things to one another. What sticks in our throat is the holy approach that the British are above it all. We are clean and they are terrorists. And if you attempt to debate this you are supposed to be supporting terrorism.'

Loach came under vicious attack again in 2006 when he won the Cannes Palme d'Or for *The Wind that Shakes the Barley*, set against the backdrop of Black and Tan atrocities in Ireland during the War of Independence and the ensuing civil war. Cillian Murphy portrays a young medical student who, in much the way my father was, is drawn into the conflict as his town comes under attack and becomes leader of a flying column ambushing the British mercenaries and Royal Irish Constabulary.

Michael Gove, later to become the Tory/Lib Dem coalition government's education secretary, accused Loach in the London *Times*, a Rupert Murdoch paper, of rubbishing his own country and glamorizing the IRA, 'which used murderous violence to achieve its ends, even though the democratic path was always open to it'.

•  •  •

The awards ceremony presenter, German comedian Anke Engelke, beckons with her microphone for cameras to follow as she steps off the stage and moves among the nominees for best actress. She stops at two empty seats to introduce Kate Winslet for *The Reader* and Penelope Cruz for Pedro Almodovar's *Broken Embraces*.

'Kate and Penelope can play anyone,' she teases. 'Yes, they really can. They can play invisible women.' While a giant screen behind her lingers on a

Intimacy with Strangers: A Life of Brief Encounters

close-up of the two empty places, she chides: 'If you don't see them, that's your problem.'

Winslet's failure to show up at European cinema's big night – despite, along with Cruz, easily managing to attend both the Golden Globes and the Oscars at the beginning of the year – isn't held against her. She wins anyway, with Stephen Daldry accepting the trophy on her behalf.

Michael Haneke, a director to whom humour is as alien as a dropped consonant, repeats his *Hidden* success of 2005 by again winning best picture, best director and best screenwriter, this time for his beautifully austere black-and-white period piece *The White Ribbon*. With academic reticence, he professes himself to be 'completely bowled over' before conceding, 'Perhaps it is difficult for me to show my joy.'

No such aloofness from hitherto unknown 28-year-old French Algerian Tamar Rahim, who punches the air and shouts '*Vive le cinema!*' on receiving the best actor award for his mesmerizing performance in Jacques Audiard's explosive crime film, *A Prophet*. He plays a naive young outsider of North African origin who is sent into a corrupt prison and finds himself caught between rival Muslim and Corsican criminal gangs who regard it as their territory. To survive, he pretends to be what each of them expects him to be, only to forget who he really is. *A Prophet* mixes brutal realism with lyrical tenderness and humour. It is disturbingly and utterly memorable.

'I wanted to make a genre film where the actors would not be known but their faces by the end would have the same status as John Wayne or Gary Copper in a Western,' Audiard tells me. 'It is important for me to tell stories of people who have no history and no identity, to fabricate icons out of people we don't even know, images for people who don't have images, like the Arabs in France.'

*A Prophet* began as a screenplay given to him to direct, but he rewrote it completely, 'much as I would adapt a novel. Obviously I was going to make it something that was close to me.' It provides a chance to develop his fascination with the way people become their own invention, a theme already rehearsed in his 1994 debut, *See How They Fall*, a road movie with Mathieu Kassovitz.

'The lives we invent are the most beautiful,' says the protagonist in a later film, *A Self-Made Hero*, an ordinary man who allows himself to be mistaken for a resistance hero and in the end has to act like one. *The Beat My Heart Skipped*, winner of eight French César awards in 2005, is a remake of James Toback's 1978 film, *Fingers*, the action reset in Paris where a property racketeer tries to change his life through music. 'These people behave in very brutal ways, but the film is also about how we can make ourselves better people,' says Audiard.

Audiard is the son of a leading 1950s French screenwriter and director, Michel Audiard, whose reputation was in writing dialogue, particularly for Jean Gabin:

> I wasn't on film sets as a child. I lived in the countryside. I'd see him on weekends when all his friends would come. When you're born into this world it's quite banal. It didn't give me any desire to be a film-maker. My concern was, were they kind to me, did they bring me presents. I was protected. When I look back I thank my parents for that.
>
> My father wasn't an artist. He just went to his office and wrote. It was a generation and milieu of people before the New Wave who didn't have a veneration for the cinema. It wasn't a major form of art, it wasn't a form of art at all. They were doing it by default.

Audiard worked first in theatre and then as a screenwriter, and was forty-one before he finally broke through as a director. 'It took me years to decide I wanted to make a film. Unfortunately my father didn't live to see it. That's very sad for me. He didn't get to know my children and he didn't get to know my other children, my films.'

Like one of his characters, Audiard has in a sense reinvented himself. 'I'm not going to use myself as an example but I think it is good not to have wanted to do cinema immediately. But I've taken too long and it still takes me too long. I'd like it to have been a faster progress.'

Isabelle Huppert, who has long been as much a champion of Michael Haneke as he has been of her, celebrates with him after receiving a special award for her achievement in world cinema.

'I've never felt any inhibitions as an actress,' she tells me. She hardly needs to say this after her daring performance as a professor in the Vienna Conservatory who's into porn, in Haneke's *The Piano Teacher*, which won her the European Academy's best actress award in 2001.

Living alone with her nagging and possessive mother, she gives expression to her unlived sexuality through voyeurism. Her life is an uneasy tug of war between high culture and basic instincts. She's as impassive at a rehearsal of a Schubert piano trio in an elegant Viennese apartment as she is sniffing discarded Kleenex tissues in a porn viewing booth or prowling drive-in cinemas to spy on couples making out in their cars.

*The Piano Teacher* might seem to belong with the equally explicit *Romance*,

*Baise Moi* and *Intimacy* as part of French cinema's excursion into so-called 'sad sex', except that Haneke, of course, is Austrian and prefers to make the audience worry as much about their own responses as those of the film characters. 'He keeps a distance with the characters, and as an actor I was part of this,' says Huppert. 'I never felt like a piece of meat.'

The irony of *The Piano Teacher* is that when Huppert finally has a chance of a relationship with a man – a precocious student who is not intimidated by her coldness and sets about seducing her – she can only envisage sex with him in terms of the pornography to which she has become addicted. Businesslike as always, she presents him with a detailed list of things she wants him to do with her.

'That's the only sexual language she knows,' says Huppert:

> Even though she has never known a man before, instinctively she decides that she's going to change the rules by which men dominate women. Instead of being an object and instead of being looked at, she wants to be the one who looks and she wants to be the one who controls. She thinks that if she's treated as an object, if she's the one who's looked at and not the one who looks, she's going to lose her persona.

Huppert shrugs. 'I guess each woman wants to keep control of her life, but I hope not in the same way as she does,' she says.

> Take away her extreme side and you have something a lot of women can feel very close to, you know, this attachment to the past, this attachment to the figure of the mother. It's a very simple story everyone has been through, no? You have a mother and your mother tries to put on you her deepest desires of success – in this case success as a pianist – and then one day you have to be born again and you have to become an adult.
>
> Except that she never got the opportunity to be born again. She remains the baby she was. Because she's so scared and because she wants to keep the protection of this dreadful relationship with her mother, she doesn't want to lose control of her life. I think her only love is her mother. I think her mother fills up all her space. It's a terrible love. It's a story of an *amour fou* between a mother and a daughter.

Since first catching attention as the rebellious teenager in Bertrand Blier's *Les Valseuses* in 1974, Huppert quickly became identified with roles in which women are trapped in oppressive relationships. Always there is tension between repressed sexuality and victimized innocence, whether as the eighteen-year-old girl in *The Lacemaker* who becomes withdrawn after her first affair breaks up, or the daughter who murders her father in the real-life *Violette Nozière*. In Maurice Pialat's *Loulou* she leaves her well-off, well-meaning husband for layabout Gerard Depardieu and his loutish friends. *Madame Bovary* might almost have been written for her: no wonder Claude Chabrol cast her as a suicidal provincial wife longing for excitement, just as she personified the cast-off wife in *Les Destinées Sentimentales*.

'That is what I found quite beautiful in her character,' says Huppert. 'All women are imprisoned by their incapacity to live their desires. My characters are invariably women with the feeling of being dominated by men.'

But surely society is changing? Aren't things getting better for women? 'I think the world is largely dominated by men,' she says, crisply.

Haneke adapted *The Piano Teacher*, a largely autobiographical novel by the Austrian writer, Elfriede Jelinek, with Huppert in mind. 'I'd admired her since *The Lacemaker* twenty years ago,' he tells me. 'When I was first approached to film *The Piano Teacher*, I said yes, but only if I could work with Isabelle.'

Ask her where the urge to act comes from, and she gets defensive. 'I don't know,' she says. 'Why are you a journalist?'

She's right, of course. It's all somehow the same question. Ask Thomas Kinsella why he is a poet and he'll say it comes out of an urge to make sense of life, the same urge that prompted medieval monks to jot down lines capturing the moment of a blackbird's song. It's about finding meaning in seemingly random events that come together to make up our existence. It's about creating beauty out of chaos. It's about reaching out to the other so that we are not alone. It's about who we are.

Or to quote Robertson Davies, 'We're really beads on a string rather than single beautiful gems.' He felt compelled to continue writing right up to his death in 1995 to keep memories alive for his grandchildren, because 'it's gone if nobody passes it on'.

It's the same for Paul Auster, whose fiction is inspired by a realization that 'everyone is born out of chance'. The physicist Brian Cox, who prepped Cillian Murphy for his role as a scientist in Danny Boyle's poetic science-fiction odyssey, *Sunshine*, put the issue in a wider context in a BBC programme about the Cern atomic research centre in Geneva.

'All of us owe our existence to chance,' he said:

> It was only a freak balancing of forces within dying stars that made the creation of the crucial element, carbon – the building block of life – possible. When you study the universe you realize that life can exist only for a tiny instant of time

... that we're unique in our capacity to reflect on our own predicament. Humans are the cosmos made conscious. Life is the universe understanding itself ... The rising and the setting of the sun is the epic heartbeat that measures the passage of all time on Earth.

To the Swiss liberal theologian, Hans Küng, art is a seismograph of the human condition that represents the realities of our times. 'Philosophy comes later, only in the evening,' he smiled on a visit to Dublin in 1984.

Dressed in a conservative navy-blue suit and blue shirt and with a healthy tan, he looked considerably younger than his fifty-eight years. Asking him a question was like being in a tutorial. He'd answer comprehensively, with compelling clarity.

The frankness on the issue of papal infallibility, which caused the Vatican to withdraw his licence to teach as a Catholic theologian ('the pope talks only to those who confirm him,' he says), has been no less incisively applied to art.

'People are beginning to wonder if art is becoming increasingly function-less, meaningless, pointless as for many belief in God is futile,' he said. 'More or less anything goes. There have been so many changes in art that it's difficult to see where it's going.'

For Küng this loss of direction is a symptom of an emptiness and feeling of alienation in modern life. 'Art has to do with the question of meaning,' he said. 'If you have no meaning in human life it will also give you a crisis in the arts.' Yet even when art is symbolizing what the artist might perceive as the meaninglessness of life, it can become 'aesthetically completely meaningful'. The artist in his or her despair at the pointlessness of existence creates order out of the chaos. They transcend the visible.

'The art of the present century has brought us an unexpected transcen-dence beyond our banal, everyday one-dimensionality, surprising extensions of our experience of reality, an immense intellectual gain in the discovery and penetration of the dimensions and depth of our existence,' he argued in *Art and the Question of Meaning*.

In seeking a spiritual dimension in art, Küng is not trying to bring art back again within the autonomy of religion as it was up to the Renaissance. 'We're not looking for religious pictures. The challenge is to provoke artists to express meaning in their own language.'

For Wim Wenders, art is a search for identity. 'You could say that every painter tries to find out who he is by painting. I still like to ask that question now and then.' His 2004 film, *Land of Plenty*, shot with digital cameras in sixteen days, is a barometer of America in the aftermath of 9/11. 'I'd never been involved in any explicit political way, but the film was about a very specific situation in America, where I've lived for some time,' he says.

> It's about the climate of paranoia, and it's about the poverty that is so obvious in Los Angeles, only nobody talks about it. It's almost a taboo subject. It's not only invisible, it's unthinkable. Yet these people don't have anywhere to live, they don't have anything to eat, they have no health care, they're just dumped there. It's revolting because there's so much of everything. I made this film with quite some anger but still looking lovingly at the country.

A young missionary worker comes back from the West Bank and sees the conditions of the homeless in LA as no better than a Third World slum. Her Vietnam War-veteran uncle on the other hand sees his country and Americans through the eyes of the patriot he is. He's obsessed by the idea of Muslims as a threat and drives around spying on them:

> You feel after a while that he has a good heart and he's trying to do his best, but he was been fed the wrong interpretation of things for too long. It's only very slowly that it dawns on him that his entire image of the world may be based on lies and that maybe his country is wrong. And that for a lot of Americans is an inconceivable emotion, because God's with this country. God Bless America is no longer a wish. They say it like it's a certainty. God did bless America. They forget that God doesn't bless anything that's not filled with compassion and love.

Wenders filmed *Land of Plenty* after shooting a documentary in the Congo on the work of the medical aid group, Doctors Without Frontiers:

> I was in a town of 50,000 inhabitants that had no electricity, no money, no water, no food. All the animals had been killed. All that was left growing were mango trees. And you come back from that and you see everybody has too much and they're not even aware of the surplus of things they're surrounding themselves with. Think how different it could have been after 9/11 if instead of a war on terror we had fought to wipe out poverty at its roots.

He is not an activist. 'It's sort of a departure for me to talk about a real context, a political context,' he says. His films have always been about feelings rather than issues, what he has described as 'e-motion pictures'. Yet by reclaiming the images and language of cinema so abused and exploited as propaganda by the Nazis he made it possible for a later generation of film-makers, in particular Oliver Hirschbiegel and Florian von Donnersmarck, finally to confront Germany's past.

Oliver Hirschbiegel is the first German film-maker to ask how the German people could have supported Hitler and yet stood by while he did what he did. The significance of *Downfall*, set during the final days in the Führer's bunker below the Reich Chancellery in a Berlin surrounded by the Russians and devastated by heavy bombing, is that in confronting this question it became a box-office hit with German audiences.

There's a chilling ordinariness about the way Hitler and his inner circle are depicted going about their day-to-day routine, having their meals, washing up, pottering about. As he hastily marries his mistress Eva Braun, Hitler gives her cyanide pellets. 'I'm sorry I can't give you a better present,' he says.

After those suicides, Magda Goebbels poisons each of her children with prussic acid. 'The children are too good for what is to come,' she says, a fanatic to the end. She then goes out into the garden with her husband Joseph. They stand facing each other. He raises his pistol and shoots her, then blows his brains out.

Our witness to the last twelve days of the Third Reich is a fresh-faced 25-year-old secretary who dutifully takes dictation. She seems to be a good-natured if naive girl, awed to be in the presence of important figures, perhaps even feeling sorry for them. Through her eyes we see Hitler in all his crude banality.

This is perhaps the only way to grasp the enormity of the Nazis. It's not that they were monsters. It's that they were human and could still do the monstrous things they did. The effect is to demythologize Hitler and show him – as Bruno Ganz succeeds in doing so convincingly – as a grubby little man, full of self-pity and delusions to the end.

'The bunker not only stands for these people, the inner circle, being down there, away from the effects of their decisions, it also stands for their tunnel vision, the way they focused on a goal and pursued it ruthlessly and saw nothing else,' says Hirschbiegel.

He grew up in Hamburg in the 1960s and was taught about the Nazi era at school. His curiosity was triggered by his mother. 'She was fourteen and my father was fifteen when Hitler committed suicide,' he says.

During the war they were sent away to the countryside. They had a great time, my mother especially. She was a member of the Hitler Youth organization. So for her it meant freedom, being with other girls, helping the farmers and doing lessons at school. And Hitler was like a hero to them. They hardly noticed there was a war going on, even in the very last days. It was only when the Americans came, destroying portraits of Hitler, that it started to dawn on her. It was a terrible shock. She felt betrayed and ashamed.

The partition of Germany after the war meant that for people living in the East one tyranny was followed by another. Florian von Donnersmarck lays bare dirty secrets of communist East Germany in *The Lives of Others*, a beautifully elegiac and deeply emotional drama that won the best film and best actor awards at the 2006 European Film Awards.

It tells the story of a member of the notorious East Berlin Stasi secret police who is ordered to set up strict surveillance on the playwright lover of a celebrated actress who is involved with a high-ranking politician, but in the course of doing so he becomes disillusioned with his own life and begins covertly protecting the man he is supposed to destroy.

The idea for the film, which von Donnersmarck wrote in a cell in a Cistercian monastery near Vienna where his uncle is a monk, comes out of his childhood. Both his parents are from East Germany. Although they came over to the West before the Wall was built, they frequently returned:

> My father worked with the Catholic Church, which never accepted the division of Germany, so the Bishop of Berlin covered both East and West Berlin and was always travelling to and fro.
>
> He was a really formal and imposing figure, and my father was a bit like that too, but whenever they met to talk about how they were going to organize a Catholic old people's home or whatever, he would put on loud rock music to cover up the conversation.

From the age of eight until the Wall came down in 1989 when he was sixteen – the period during which the film takes place – von Donnersmarck was often in the East with his parents:

> I was very aware that the Stasi spied on almost everybody who did anything of importance, and I understood the conflict between communism and more democratic forms of government because I had that kind of cold war going on at home. My father was a very liberal conservative, but my mother was very active in a socialist student union which organized the 1968 student revolts in Germany.

There are plans to film a remake of *The Lives of Others* in a contemporary American setting, but following the deaths of its producers, Anthony Minghella and soon afterwards Sydney Pollock, these seem to be on hold. 'The idea is to show that what happened in East Germany is not only a matter of history, but something that is going on at the moment,' says von

Donnersmarck.'When a government is given too much power the first thing it will do is to start spying on its citizens. I don't think Americans should be focusing their protests against the Iraq war. The problem is really what they're accepting inside their own country.'

*   *   *

The European Film Awards are chosen each year by members of the European Film Academy, much the same as the Oscars. The exception is a People's Choice award, based on a poll of European filmgoers. Unsurprisingly, Danny Boyle's Oscar-winning *Slumdog Millionaire* ends the year as it started – a popular winner.

Boyle has already moved on. His success gave him the clout to do something completely different, a project he tried and failed to finance before. He's to film *127 Hours* on location in a remote canyon in the Utah desert, the true survival story of a young climber trapped underground by a fallen boulder for six days.

He's also planning a return to the stage with a London West End version of *Frankenstein*. 'It literally opens with the creature opening his eyes. He's thirty-three years old. It's his point of view.' That's not the only twist. Two actors will alternate the lead role of the creature and his creator. 'They literally create each other. Every other night they reinhabit each other.'

It's not unlike the process of an interview. The interviewer tries to inhabit the mind of the interviewed but memories of the encounter inhabit the interviewer's mind, conditioning it in unconscious ways as all experiences must. We are who we know. Without the other there is no self.

On being appointed editor of the UK edition of *Esquire*, Alex Bilmes confided to *The Guardian*, 'I'm a star-fucker and I don't mind admitting that I love hanging out with famous people.' He made his name on *GQ* interviewing Angelina Jolie, Robbie Williams and other show-business celebrities: 'Surreal is an overused word, but it's like that strange pinch-yourself moment when you think, I should not be here, I'm not good-looking enough, I'm not well dressed enough, I have no part to play other than as some kind of gawping idiot, but nevertheless I will report back this experience to the readers.'

Celebrity culture being what it is, there's no escaping the buzz or aura that surrounds an encounter with anyone in the news, no matter how gratuitously.

But writing from the periphery of the show-business world can mean that you are less likely to be seen as a threat to someone's tightly controlled market image, so needn't feel intimidated by it. In my experience, limitations other than time are seldom if ever imposed on interviews with film actors. With a writer or director or artist the question wouldn't arise, anyway. Once the talking begins it's just two people alone in a room, as Pinter would say.

If there are recurring themes running through *Intimacy with Strangers* it's partly because an interviewer brings to an interview personal preoccupations, and an interview often takes place as a result of some empathy with the subject's work. But there's more to it than that. You sense an underlying need to understand and be understood, whether purely rational with Jonathan Miller, spiritual in the manner of Hans Küng, or instinctual in the case of actors like Nicolas Cage or Isabelle Huppert.

It's what prompted Guillermo Arriaga to film *Babel*, a series of interconnecting stories exploring the distrust and fear of others who are different to us that haunts the post-9/11 world. By allowing the stories to unravel out of order, *Babel* mirrors this sense of lost people pushed to the edge of confusion and despair as they try to find someone to trust or to make some sense of what is happening.

Arriaga draws on the paradox that while digital technology is providing the means for a cyber-democracy that makes it possible for millions to connect and communicate, the prejudices that separate us are ever greater. The German media theorist, Friedrich Adolf Kittler, has similarly challenged claims that the Internet promotes human communication: 'The development of the Internet has more to do with human beings becoming a reflection of their technologies … after all, it is we who adapt to the machine. The machine does not adapt to us.'

Often the urge to reach out and connect comes out of shyness or a longing to belong, particularly among actors, yet paradoxically the nature of an artist or writer is to be an outsider.

Memory is the heartbeat of art but also its nightmare, as Primo Levi and Mike Nichols discovered. All we can do is bear witness to the particularity of the moment and hopefully transcend it, whether with wonder and awe or through humour, the natural voice of despair, a Hugh Leonard quip, a Woody Allen one-liner or a Pinter silence.

• • •

'The search for identity is a broad theme,' says Wenders. Or as William Boyd puts it, 'You try to create order in your life, but it's always a facade.'

Think back to a situation Boyd contrived in 1998. Manhattan socialites were cramming into the studio loft of artist Jeff Koons to hear David Bowie read extracts of Boyd's biography of the once-legendary but now forgotten New York artist, Nat Tate.

Apparently Tate had been for a brief while art collector Peggy Guggenheim's lover. An alcoholic and a depressive, he impulsively destroyed most of his work. Demoralized after a meeting with Georges Braque in 1959, he leapt to his death off the Staten Island Ferry. His body was never found.

None of the art lovers present realized that they were part of an elaborate hoax. The artist they were celebrating never existed. He'd been dreamed up by Boyd to spoof the lemming-like slavishness of cultural taste.

The irony is that *Nat Tate: An American Artist (1928–1960)* was subsequently serialized in *The Sunday Telegraph*. It became a literary work in its own right, as eagerly read as any of Boyd's actual novels. Even more ironically, just a few months before it appeared, Boyd published *Armadillo*, a darkly comic novel about a man with a fake identity.

Boyd admits to being somewhat confused about his own identity. Born of Scottish parents in Accra on the Gold Coast (now Ghana) in 1952, he grew up thinking of himself as a West African. 'The first half of my life was Africa. It's where my home was. I've nothing but fascinating idyllic memories of it.'

He was sent back to school in Scotland at Gordonstoun, also the school of Prince Charles:

> I always felt a bit of an outsider, which may be no bad thing for a novelist. It has always remained with me, this feeling of Britain as a place you were sent to. I think I would have been a different person if I'd been born in Fife, where my parents came from, and gone to a local school. I have no right to feel outside and not fitting it. I have all the familiar touchstones, which I didn't have in Africa. The colour of my skin made it clear that I was not a West African. But Europe was not my place either. A strange sort of deracination took place.

He didn't consciously think of himself as a writer until he found himself with time to spare at Oxford. 'I didn't come from a literary family. I must have seen a film of someone playing a writer, sipping martinis on a terrace. Maybe I instinctively realized I was unemployable.'

By twenty-nine he'd published his first novel, *A Good Man in Africa*, winning both the Whitbread and the Somerset Maugham awards: 'My theory is that everything that happens up to that moment when you consciously allow yourself to think of yourself as a writer is the raw material you plunder. You go back to that time when you weren't analyzing your experience. In my case that was Africa, which explains why it keeps popping up in my work.'

His novels are variations on the total randomness of life:

> We all like to think that life is planned and ordered but it breaks down so quickly. When you look back you realize how easily the important things could have been missed or sidestepped. What seems like a steady progression of events – went to university, got married, wrote books – could so easily have been completely different if some totally trivial event hadn't occurred.

His grandfather was wounded at Passchendaele in 1918 in World War I:

> When he recovered, he went for a medical. By holding his nose he could make his ears bleed. I think he felt he would be chancing his luck if he were to go back to the trenches. So he was invalided home. He felt he had paid his dues. But if he hadn't known the trick, we mightn't be having this conversation.

While he never met his grandfather, World War I (and in particular the Battle of the Somme, where his great-uncle was wounded) became an obsession. 'As I learned about it there was this kind of bafflement: how could it have happened, how could it have gone on so long and how did the men endure it. I wanted to reinhabit it in the imaginary way of novels.'

To confront the pointlessness of the mass carnage, the arbitrary cutting down of hundreds of thousands of young lives, Boyd reinvented himself as a film director. His debut film, *The Trench*, is every bit as shocking as Stephen Spielberg's *Saving Private Ryan*. The camera is stuck in the trenches with a group of young volunteers for the entire film. Just when you get to know them as individuals, they are ordered over the top. Every one of them is dead within a couple of minutes. End of film. 'I wanted to make fifty yards by two yards a microcosm for World War I. It's much the same idea as shooting all of Wolfgang Petersen's *Das Boot* in a submarine.'

Although Boyd spent several weeks in the Imperial War Museum researching his 1987 novel, *The New Confessions*, which in part also dealt with World War I, he has no direct experience of warfare:

> But growing up in Nigeria during the Biafra conflict in the 1960s – my father had been sent there during World War II as a doctor specializing in tropical

medicine and had stayed on – I saw at close hand a country tearing itself apart. I was never remotely near any fighting but it was frightening. There were armed soldiers everywhere.

At the age of eighteen I became very aware of how fragile our sense of order is. My father and I were driving at night. We drove through a road block of oil drums with a plank. Luckily my father heard the shouts of these half-drunk guys in baseball caps and pyjama bottoms with Kalashnikovs. It was probably the most danger I've ever been in. My father diffused it. He cracked a few jokes, very calmly. But it could all have gone hideously wrong.

It's what prompted him to write his Booker-nominated novel, *An Ice-Cream War*. 'I wanted to show that kind of completely brutal chaos. Life is chaos but even more so war. I got an understanding as a late adolescent about just how incredibly terrifying it was and how easy it was to fall apart.'

His uncertainty theory that some chance event is always liable to wreck all your plans seems to be belied by a career that has all the appearance of success: a happy marriage to Susan Anne Wilson (they've been together since they were twenty-three), homes in Chelsea and the south of France, numerous literary awards and now critical acclaim in Cannes for *The Trench*.

**William Boyd in London, 1999.**

'Yes,' he says, 'but I can think of any number of events that would utterly destroy and ruin my life. For instance, my wife's mother and my father died within a month of each other where we were both in our mid-twenties. Suddenly we lost half our parents. So one advances with due caution and proper respect for the vagaries of the human condition, and how suddenly it can go wrong.'

Advancing 'with due caution and proper respect for the vagaries of the human condition' is not in the DNA of neoliberal economists whose insistence that the state must not intervene in the 'natural mechanisms' of the market triggered the 2008 Wall Street meltdown and caused Irish banks to implode. Their ideological hubris then created widespread unemployment and poverty by pushing governments to reject the obvious Keynesian solution of austerity combined with economic stimulus.

Somewhat incongruously, my degree is in economics. During the 1932 general election my father campaigned with Sean Lemass for Fianna Fáil, making speeches from the backs of trucks after Mass. Neither of them knew much about finance, but they preached fiscal reform on the basis of what they picked up skimming through *The Economist*.

He always regretted later as an editor that he wasn't able to contradict economic experts when he suspected they were talking nonsense. So instead of English literature, on his advice I read Keynes, Adam Smith and John Stuart Mill at UCD and, to his delight, stumbled upon Joan Robinson's theory of indeterminacy, which demonstrated that all economic forecasts were qualified by an unpredictable human factor.

Or as Economic and Social Research Institute (ESRI) economist Joe Durkan admitted to Vincent Browne in a TV3 post-mortem on the collapse of the Irish economy: 'The random events that hit you are ones that no one ever predicts.' Finance, like art and the universe itself, is ruled by chance.

. . .

In 2004 *Time* magazine named the hitherto media-shy Charlie Kaufman among the world's most influential people. Hollywood A-list stars were queuing up to take roles in his films at minimum union rates. His eccentrically titled romantic comedy, *Eternal Sunshine of the Spotless Mind*, inspired by Alexander Pope's poem, 'Eloisa to Abelard', was set to win an Oscar for best original screenplay.

'It's a lot of silliness, really,' says Kaufman, apologetically. He's small and wiry, with curly black hair, like a bearded version of Woody Allen. Yet having parodied the popular obsession with celebrity in his dazzling 1999 debut film, *Being John Malkovich* – employing a comic device that enabled fans to get inside the actor's head – he is now seriously in danger of becoming a celebrity himself.

'It doesn't really affect my daily life,' he insists. 'I'm not recognizable. I'm still anonymous, which I need to be as a writer. You soon realize it isn't about anything. It's about promoting films and selling magazines. You're just part of that machine for the moment, because you're available at that moment for whatever reason.'

As with all his screenplays, *Eternal Sunshine* hinges on a fanciful concept that is never really explained. We accept it as a given, something that exists only to trigger the action, what Hitchcock called a MacGuffin. When Kate Winslet falls out of love with Jim Carrey she goes to a clinic that can remove all her memories of him. To get over his loss, he then tries the same treatment only to have second thoughts just as she's disappearing from his mind. The process of remembering in order to forget causes him to fall in love all over again.

The wonder of memory is that everyone remembers things differently. It's what gives us our individuality. The loss of memories, as with Alzheimer's disease, is the loss of self. 'We are our memories,' says Kaufman. 'They are who we are.'

French director Michel Gondry gave him the premise for *Eternal Sunshine* that we could have a sort of SMS card in our mind from which unwanted memories could be erased by a sharply focused non-surgical procedure. 'It was pretty vague, just a place to start,' says Kaufman. 'We had no characters, no story.'

So he invited his wife Denise out to dinner:

> I was trying to think of what memory really is. I think we have an illusion that it's kind of like a tape recording. We tell ourselves that we can remember things that we can't really remember. As an experiment I tape-recorded the dinner. I didn't tell her why. And the next day I asked her to write down everything that happened. I did the same. Although there were some things the same, we had very different memories of the evening. Then we listened to the tape afterwards and found that neither of us was right. In terms of specific dialogue, we didn't have a clue. And this was only the night before. So I tried to have that murky quality for the memories in the film as much as I could.

Even as I'm writing this, I'm quoting him from a tape recording I made of our meeting. Although this ensures the accuracy of what he said, everything else that happened between us, and possibly conditioned its meaning, is my memory against his. 'When I was younger and I read biographies, I assumed I was reading the truth about somebody,' he says.

> But it's all conjecture and it's all based on other people's faulty memories. I don't think that's taken into account when people are writing biographies. I don't see how anyone could possibly write a biography of my life. It's sort of that area of interaction with your wife or your kids or stuff like that that would be unknown even to yourself, let alone an outsider trying to reconstruct it years later.

That's why he brings himself into *Adaptation* – his Oscar-nominated version of Susan Orlean's *The Orchid Thief* – as a screenwriter with writer's block called Charlie Kaufman, played by Nicolas Cage, who's struggling to adapt the novel. He even gives himself a fictional twin brother, Donald, who helps him finish his own script, causing the two stories to come together with bizarre consequences.

Kaufman doesn't just deliver a screenplay. He's involved in the entire filming process. 'I work with directors like Spike Jonze on *Being John Malkovich* and *Adaptation*, and George Clooney on *Confessions of a Dangerous Mind*, who are prepared to collaborate with me beyond the writing stage, particularly in the editing and music and sound design, and all the pre-production and casting.' The Kaufman selves that inhabit his screenplays are partly their selves, too.

He was an avid reader as a child growing up in Massapequa, New York, and West Hartford, Connecticut, where his father was an engineer. 'We'd a lot of books around the house,' he says. 'I'd take them off the shelves not understanding what I was reading but wanting to be an adult. I remember carrying books into third grade, which I was trying to read, but mostly I was trying to impress my teacher, because I had an enormous crush on her. I wanted her to think I was really sophisticated.'

Did it work?

'Apparently it did,' he admits. 'She told my parents. Through her I got introduced to plays. We did school productions. I wrote a lot and read plays. I was a very shy kid and somehow this was something that allowed me to get attention. I think that kind of led me into this.'

Although he studied film at New York University, he struggled for eleven years to get an agent. 'I'd just turned thirty,' he says,

> I was working in a warehouse in Minnesota, packing books. I wanted to do what I'm doing now. But there was no other job I could get. I wondered how I was

ever going to get out of that situation. I borrowed $3000 I'd no way of repaying. I drove out to LA giving myself two months to get a writing job on TV. I was out there living in somebody's house and going through my money. I'd no car. I was getting no interviews.

Then the phone rang. He was offered a writing job on a TV show back in Minneapolis where he'd come from:

I was packed and ready to go. The night before I was leaving I was offered a sitcom job in LA. So I stayed. As it happened, the show in Minneapolis didn't go anywhere. If I'd taken that, none of this would have happened. I wouldn't have worked for seven years in television in LA. I wouldn't have sold *Being John Malkovich*. I wouldn't have got into this. So I was lucky. For a lot of people it hasn't worked out that way. I have friends who are still struggling as I did.

There are countless times I can point to where – just like other people – if I had done something else I'd be in a completely different life. If I hadn't got on a subway in a particular time on a particular day, for instance, I wouldn't have met my wife. I don't know what my life would have been, but it wouldn't have been what it is.

Kaufman's screenplays come about in much the same random way. He doesn't plan them. They just happen. 'I don't like to talk about what I'm writing because I don't know what it's going to become,' he says. 'I like it to become what it's going to become by accident. That's the part of the process of writing that I enjoy.'

This is why he tries to avoid interviews. 'I feel I'm now talking more than I used to about myself. I'm becoming bored with myself. I think I'll have to remove myself from all this.'

He'd much rather be at home with his four-year-old daughter. 'She's very dramatic,' he says,

she tells a lot of stories. She's very bossy. If we play together, she's got the scenario and she tells me what my part is and what I have to say. Her mother is a painter, so she's very good at drawing. It feels like she's somehow this weird combination of the two of us. I take her in my arms and wonder about all that is ahead of her.

I click off the tape recorder. Flying back to Dublin, I try to note down as much as I can remember of what he said. When I compare it with the transcript some days later, it seems like a different interview. Not being Charlie Kaufman, all that's left is conjecture.